FROM THE ATELIER TOVAR:
SELECTED WRITINGS

Guy Maddin

Coach House Books

Third printing, March 2004

Published with the assistance of the Canada Council for the Arts
and the Ontario Arts Council

We also acknowledge the Government of Ontario through the
Ontario Book Publishers Tax Credit program and through
the Ontario Book Initiative.

NATIONAL LIBRARY OF CANADA CATALOGUING IN PUBLICATION

Maddin, Guy
    From the Atelier Tovar: selected writings/Guy Maddin.

Includes bibliographical references.
ISBN 1-55245-131-3

    1. Motion pictures. 2. Maddin, Guy – Diaries. I. Title.

PN1995.M23 2003   791.43   C2003-904016-X

for my family and my friends

CONTENTS

THE GREAT PRETENDER

An introduction by Mark Peranson

ew artists are as underappreciated as Guy Maddin, and few underappreciated artists are in the position of being as much overexposed. But perhaps the time is right for Maddin's type of filmmaking. Nostalgia and romancing the past are currently as *de rigueur* as the glorification of kitsch, and Maddin provides all these in spades. The end of 2003 finds no fewer than three major, very different films from Guy in wide circulation: the stupendous silent movie-ballet *Dracula: Pages from a Virgin's Diary*; the peephole installation *Cowards Bend the Knee*, which mixes autobiography, Euripides' *Electra* and the Expressionist classic *The Hands of Orlac*; and the 'proper' film feature *The Saddest Music in the World*, starring Isabella Rossellini. This is an astonishing cinematic output with few equals, a cinematic equivalent to the Gretzky-led Edmonton Oilers dynasty of the late eighties. This is all that much more impressive if you're aware of the extent of Guy's innate laziness. And now you have the opportunity to share in this director's slothdom with the publication of his diaries, his assorted film writing and other curios Coach House has finagled from the vaults. And much of it is, actually, probably, close to the truth.

Guy Maddin claims to have been born on February 28, 1956, in Winnipeg, Manitoba, to a working-class family of Icelandic heritage; he resides there to this day. (In Rotterdam earlier this year, he claimed he stays in Winnipeg because he has 'a really good paper route.') He was reared above his Aunt Lil's beauty salon and at Winnipeg's hockey arena, where his father, Chas, worked as manager of the senior league's Winnipeg Maroons, winners of the 1963 Allan Cup – both recently immortalized in *Cowards Bend the Knee*. Along with glorious memories of vacations north in Gimli and scrubbing the backs of visiting unibrowed Soviet warriors, there was private tragedy: while Maddin was young, his older brother, Cameron, killed himself at the age of eighteen after his girlfriend died in a car accident; he shot himself lying on top of her grave. Tragedy lurks behind the gestating hysteria of his feature films like a child peeking out of the safety of the womb. While slacking off during his teens and early twenties, Maddin home-schooled himself, borrowing from the public library 16mm noirs, melodramas, silents and half-talkies. This autodidactic cinephilia reveals itself in, to use just one example, the Leni

Riefenstahl–meets-*Caligari* mountain movie *Careful*, in which there are moments from or allusions to directors as diverse as von Sternberg, Hitchcock, Whale, Keaton, Ophuls, Méliès, Lubitsch and Clair presented as if slapped together purposefully by Victor Frankenstein.

But while Maddin wholeheartedly embraces primitivism in his delirious cross-breeds, he despises continuity and complicates nostalgia. He juggles his numerous references, in a way, based on forgetfulness – both his audiences' and his own. After bringing up one reference, he quickly moves along, never allowing another filmmaker to cohabit his space too long, never permitting viewers to hone in on narrative. Moreover, Maddin's films are culturally toxic, and the past that he presents is one that we'd never want to live in, like the pro-incest, pro-repression Tölzbad of *Careful* or the smallpox-laden Gimli. But it's also useful to unpack 'cinephilia,' to suggest that the term is often used to describe dissimilar attitudes. The most extreme cinephilia, often practiced by members of my profession, enshrines films of the past in the museums of one's own mind, elevating them as Platonic ideals. This is physically enacted at the end of *Cowards*: after the vengeful Meta, confronted by the return of her dead father, plunges Kim Novak–style down a catwalk onto the arena's icy surface, the ruined-by-cowardice, self-deluded Guy Maddin finds himself uncannily frozen as a wax sculpture in the Maroons hall of fame. This hall of shame is one of ossified cowardice, the place where Meta's father has been hiding for the last decade, afraid of returning to the responsibilities of fatherhood – as opposed to the real Guy, whose grown-up and married daughter, Jilian, occupies a significant role in his diaries and his life – from *The Dead Father* to the good father.

Guy's cinephilia thus has much in common with the Electra complex itself. One of his ongoing projects is remaking lost films, movies that he himself has never even seen. *The Heart of the World* reimagines Abel Gance's 1931 apocalyptic science-fiction film *La Fin du monde*; other possible films in the project include Tod Browning's *London After Midnight* and F. W. Murnau's *4 Devils*. These films, as well as those which inspire his other work, have, in a way, been murdered by history and ossification, and Maddin takes revenge. But in doing so, he also admits to possessing a certain amount of guilt and shame, a result from having to resort to a type of mimicry to reanimate them. Yet he staunchly avoids literal remakes with: (a) greater rapidity of the image, a stylistic innovation thanks to digital editing that really began with *The Heart of the World* but can be traced back to *Archangel*; (b) absurdifying the narrative and an extreme complication of the plot; (c) the hyper-hyperstylization of sets and dialogue; (d) injecting autobiography, which, in Guy's case, is melodrama through and through and almost inseparable from cinematic experiences.

It might be useful to analogize Maddin's relationship to cinema's past with a gulp of mouthwash. Gargling, you feel invigorated, your breath is fresh, and sometimes, if you've chosen the right mouthwash, you've warded away the odd cavity – at any rate, you're ready to start a new day. Similarly, cinema's history has use – it's part of an ongoing narrative, one that is simultaneously linear (due to technological advances) and circular, with the reappearance of themes, faces, stories – but you've got to spit it out at the end. The more that I immerse myself in Guy's seemingly outrageous films, rewatching them over the years as means of preparing for writing essays and delivering introductions to the director, and the more that I read his writing (or, for shame, talk to him), the more intensely personal his films appear. His diaries, strewn with passages of self-doubt amid the director's amorous exploits, make it painfully clear: for Guy, filmmaking is a way of coping.

It was with great trepidation, and an attack of the shakes, that I reacted to the news that Guy was allowing his diaries to be published. But first and foremost, before he wanted to be a filmmaker, Guy wanted to be an author, and literature is as influential on his work as the cineastes earlier mentioned, including such writers as Knut Hamsun, John Ruskin, Herman Melville, Bruno Schulz and, in *Cowards*, Marcel Proust and Euripides. Published here for the first time, the anecdotal *Child Without Qualities* casts the young Guy as a Musil-like observer in the events of his past. Set squarely in the sixties, *The Child Without Qualities* is in fact one of those thinly embellished childhood fictions, written like a confessional-slash-major motion picture treatment. From *The Child Without Qualities*, written in 1992 and suffused with sadness and loss, to 2003's *Cowards*

Bend the Knee, the detached, passive observer – the Guy who lay in bed, listening to the radio late at night or spent hours as a couch potato – has become the new Maddin hero, The Man Who Loved and Left Women. This movement has been occurring naturally in his films; though the characters remain just as cowardly, they have become more active (though the murderous Maddin in *Cowards* is unconsciously impelled). Reading *The Child Without Qualities*, it's also clear why Maddin has never made a film set in his own lifetime.

In comparing *The Child Without Qualities* and the dense screenplay for *Cowards* (published in 2003), we also see the development of the mythomaniacal Maddin literary style, likewise seen in his articles on film in the *Village Voice, Film Comment, Cinema Scope* (which I edit) and other publications, reprinted herein: excessive hyperbole, often finding its punctuational equivalent in an overdose of exclamation marks; purple prose (surely influenced by frequent script collaborator George Toles); a mixing of personal mythology with actual mythology, oftentimes Greek, plentytimes Hollywood. 'How do you guys do it?' Guy once asked me, I assume rhetorically, referring to the ability of film writers to turn out relatively well-worded and entertaining analyses of motion pictures with frequency. 'Whenever I have to write something for you, it usually takes me the better part of an afternoon.' So get ready to experience the result of the blood, sweat, tears and other bodily fluids of many melodramatic afternoons.

Mark Peranson
July 10, 2003

A NOTE ON THE TEXT

This volume represents a generous – but by no means definitive – selection of the vast and varied written oeuvre of filmmaker and author Guy Maddin. Included in this is a substantial portion of the journals that the author has kept since the late nineties. These last include, naturally, Maddin's musings on topics personal, profane and provocative. Maddin did not intend these diaries to be published until, at the very least, his dotage, and they are thus presented here with the slightest of expurgation, amendment and grammatical polish. Many entries were written during Maddin's frequent coffee dates with his longtime confidant Steve Synder; during these sessions, the two would assign each other writing subjects, little prods of inspiration that would result in hastily scribbled pages of prose both nostalgic and fanciful. The diaries also contain an initially baffling constellation of names and places. Their exact relationship to Maddin gradually emerges, but a brief guide might be useful. Briefly, these figures include, most repeatedly, Maddin's late father and brother, Chas and Cameron respectively; his mother, Herdis (also known as Amma); his aunt Lil and his daughter, Jilian; comrades Ian Handford, Steve Snyder and Noam Gonick; and frequent collaborator and friend George Toles. Loni is a beachfront cottage where the author spent many a happy summer, and 800 Ellice was Maddin's childhood home.

JOURNAL ONE
(1987 – 1998)

Dream List for Dave Barber:

Greed, Erich von Stroheim
The Old Dark House (1932), Dir. James Whale w. Karloff,
  Melyvn Douglas, Charles Laughton
Dr Jekyll and Mr Hyde, (1932), Dir. Rouben Mamoulian
  w. F. March, M. Hopkins
The King of Jazz (1930), w. Paul Whiteman
Broadway Melody (1929)
Scarlet Empress, von Sternberg
Dames, Busby Berkeley
The Merry Widow (1934), Ernst Lubitsch, MGM
  Mad Love (1935), Dir. Karl Freund w. Peter Lorre
Little Match Girl, Jean Renoir
The Devil's Cleavage, George Kuchar
Fireworks, Kenneth Anger
*Any *Popeye* cartoons from the 1930s
  Pather Panchali, Dir. Satyajit Ray
  Bizarre, Bizarre [Drôle de Drame] (1937), Dir. Marcel Carné
  Blessed Event (1932), Lee Tracy; Dick Powell
  The Canary Murder Case (1929), Louise Brooks,
    William Powell
Umberto D., The Children Are Watching Us (1942),
    Vittorio De Sica
  Cleo from 5 to 7, Agnès Varda
  Day Dreams (23 min, 1928), Dir. Ivor Montagu
  A Day in the Country (1937), Jean Renoir
  Day of Wrath (1943), Carl Dreyer
The Devil Doll (1936), Dir. Tod Browning
  Fashions of 1934, Dir. William Dieterle, Bette Davis;
    William Powell
  Crime of M. Lange, Dir. Renoir
  The Greeks Had a Word for Them (1932)
  Hallelujah, I'm a Bum (1933), Al Jolson, Rogers & Hart
  Berlin, Symphony of a City
  If You Could Only Cook (1938)
  The Italian Straw Hat
  Le Jour se léve (M. Carné) Arletty; Gabin
  Laughter

16

27 November 1987

Have to move Mom out of the house – the only home our family has ever known – tomorrow morning at eight. Last night I had the first of what I presume will be many haunting dreams concerning the shop – or whatever it is I should call it now that I write about it for the first time, ironically, upon the eve of a moment after which I shall always have to refer to it in the past tense. In the dream I discover a new room in the basement, a room which has been there all along but which I have been too unobservant to notice. A nice long bowling lane of a room with an equally long storage area clumsily grafted overtop of the concrete entrance and stairway. There is a secret panel entrance but also a door, obviously located, it turns out, beside the other, always-used door, with a window in it as well, which has led into the basement area for years. Should read that Agee/Evans book to see if lengthy descriptions of home interiors are readable even in the prose of a brilliant writer before I waste any of my little spent effort on this passage.

28 December

Just tucked Jilian in after *Anne of Green Gables* at Playhouse Theatre. Watched a special 1962 *Untouchables* episode starring Barbara Stanwyck and Ed Asner as police officers helping Ness and in the process taking over the show ...

Since I last wrote in here too much has happened. I am lonely – a little – but I think it is good for me. It has been a long time since I was lonely. This period will allow me to overhaul my soul, throw together some genuine qualities and eventually dispel all loneliness with a bang.

I've even considered working for a charity. Other things to do: paint a picture of Cousin's interior in Jilian's acrylics. Hand tint that photo of Tiffany perhaps.

I slept for over two hours Xmas afternoon. My nerves completely shot. Twenty-four hours with Amma wound up tight by her organizational urges, all of us grating to each other, blasting even the dimmest recollections of the season's traditions to oblivion. Xmas Eve in a seniors' home; four p.m. dinner lasting seven minutes; all the presents ripped open in a piranha frenzy by kids who will never know the torture of waiting.

All this leaving me exceptionally irritable. Klymkiw told me a great story about his family at Xmas. He must be near the breaking point.

I had a good day with Jilian today. But I did spank her for the first time in perhaps two years. I think we understand each other more as a result ... that's a phrase. She's a very sensitive, feeling little girl who makes me very proud of her character, but I've allowed her access to my weakness, and we dislike ourselves when this access is negotiated. These are quite the phrases too. Strictness makes for happy pups. We both feel better now.

28 December 1995
Careful plays on cinema's 100th birthday, in Paris, the city of its birth. Merci, E.D. Distribution. (Just a press screening, but a projector in Paris played it all on this holy day!)

2 January 1996
One hour with hockey at Steen. My delight. One hundred more pages of *Hugo*. Tomorrow I finish that and commence another draft of *Twilight of the Ice Nymphs*. Elise watched *Long Day's Journey into Night* this afternoon. At dinner, we rewatched *All About Eve*. George has a flu for the first time in his life. He and I discussed W. Herzog and Ross McMillan as Dr. Solti. Ritchard Findlay wants Tim Roth for Glahn in *Twilight* – a horrible actor and fortunately out of our league.

3 January
Susan Minas at Alliance has suggested my name to the Cowboy Junkies for rock video work. Now I know where you go after you die. It is painful for artists in hard times, dead artists, artists no one wants, but in Canada we are put on life-support systems. No one lets us go to the grave. We walk the earth after midnight, howling. Won't someone just drive stakes through us?

5 January
Spent entire day working on *Twilight of the Ice Nymphs* script revisions, to be sent to Keith Griffiths, but not in the streamlined form I promised him; instead I sent an all-new enriched purple edition. I now have a stack of books to read in between production designing and skating (which Rob Shaver agreed was unwise

to do in −28° and 2200 windchill, a warning which suited little responsible me fine.) My book stack: Swinburne's poems; Ovid's *Metamorphoses*; Savinio's *The Lives of the Gods*; Chateaubriand's *Atala and Rene*; LaForgue's *Moral Tales*; Sachey Sitwell's *Splendours and Miseries*; and Beardsley's *Under the Hill*.

14 January, 11:55 p.m.
Glahn – (#1) Kyle McCulloch, Aden Young, Brendan Fraser?, rock star of some sort?
Solti – Maury Chaykin, Werner Herzog, (#1) Christopher Lee, John Neville, Armin Mueller-Stahl, John Colicos, Jan Rubes
Cain Ball – Jim Keller (deceased), Maury Chaykin, (#1) John Neville
Juliana – (#1) Julie Delpy, Mia Kirshner, someone from Rozema's pic
Zephyr – (#1) Alice Krige, Mitsou, Lena Olin, Sadie Frost, Katy Gardner
Amelia – (#1) Samantha Eggars, Deborah Harry, Jackie Burroughs, Diana Rigg

Please, Guy, make yourself watch *Whale Music* for the two leads. Steal set designs from Max Ophuls's *Le Plaisir*!

15 January
Dubbed *Le Plaisir*. Watched *Vertigo* and *Daughter of Horror* (1955). Browsed through Simon Schama's *Landscape and Memory*. Strongly considering showing up absent for my director-observer stint on *My Life as a Dog* – the TV series. Skate not yet fixed. There seems to be absolutely no progress since I got three producers for *Twilight of the Ice Nymphs* a month and more ago. Six weeks! Everyone can just fuck off, fuck off, fuck off! Oh boy! They sure can help, these producers. Seventy thousand dollars each and they have other jobs, paper routes for all I know! They are fucking with me. They wank with their office overhead and they fuck with me. And there hasn't been a movie made in this country yet that doesn't stink more than a dogturd! (Except *Léolo*, which stinks of excrement in unsurpassably brilliant ways.) Have another Jaguar, boys. Good night.

26 March
Have made a Gatsby list which is far too crushing a confession

even for these pages. Having turned forty recently, I may as well arbitrarily choose now as the time to assess my life: at least thirty-five years wasted, if not more. If I could pull a few productive months, or even a year, out of the remainder of my days, I think I shall shit my pants from astonishment. My Gatsby list identified the usual trouble spots, but I'm realistic about the love handles. If I can generate a handful of genuine smiles on somebody's face without ventilating my head, my list will have done its job. I want to talk about my list, but I'm afeared it probably looks the table of contents from any self-help book at Coles. At least this much is obvious: major blocks of my life-array need to be shifted, reversed, restacked, mulched. I know what needs to be done, and where; all I have to do is do it!

29 March
Just finished a phone conversation with a Kristin Lehman, actress. Seems very nice. Wouldn't it be nice if she just fit Juliana fine, then we could proceed with some ostriches, a studio and two actresses locked. At 4:30 I coffee with R. H. Thomson, distinguished star of *Avonlea*. There is a blizzard piling slush onto already six-foot-high snowbanks, and I'm wading through this shit to hobnob with Canada's TV elite. Is that where this gooseflesh has come from?

Okay, here on the very next page is the Gatsby list of what's wrong with Gatsby. All my diary false starts seem to have naked confessions similar to this. I need the whole page, I think.

Gatsby List
1. Lonely
2. Physically unfit
3. Unreliable
4. Chronically depressed
5. Spinelessly incapable of refusing to perform unpleasant favours
6. Don't read enough
7. Don't have very many real friends
8. Don't really have many fake friends
9. Never create genuine laughter or happiness in others
10. Complain about others too much

11. Never busy enough
12. Have no financial security long- or short-term
13. Write letters too infrequently
14. Am simply not living my life (to be continued)
15. Don't write diary entries regularly
16. Don't write enough
17. Crummy son, father, husband

Shaping up …
Peter Glahn: Aden Young
Zephyr: Alice Krige
Dr. Solti: R. H. Thomson; Chris Lee
Cain Ball: Tom Waits
Juliana: Kristin Lehman
Amelia: Mary Walsh

Things to Do in Response to Gatsby List
1. Work hard, be thoughtful, generate activity; loneliness should disappear.
2. Eat properly, cycle, walk.
3. Be adult about responsibilities; donate $1000 to Wpg. Film Group.
4. If I address all the other points, perhaps depression will disappear.
5. You know what to do.
6. Read more.
7 & 8. You've worn out your personal mythologies. There are other people who might be interesting who didn't happen to spend 'L'Age d'or' with you.
9 & 10. Take that hornet's nest out of your butt.
11. When you find a couch growing out of your side, take note. If paralyzed with ennui, you can always scrawl something in this therapeutic journal-thing. Use still or video camera more.
12. Perhaps it would be nice to live above month-to-month anchorite levels of subsistence. You must learn to be more thick-skinned about the film business and treat it as a source of income. Work harder to wedge other jobs into long stretches of downtime. Write for a magazine. Keep an eye open for a regular job. Pay income tax near

deadline when possible. Purchase RRSPs next year. Buy
Blue Bombers season's tickets? Ah, yes, let's buy: a fax,
a turntable, an audio-cassette recorder with jacks. Start
a savings plan if the movie goes. Ask Alan for portfolio
advice. Let's get some savings already.
13. Write and fax and phone people more. For friends and
connections.
14. GET OUT – LIVE – WORK!
15 & 16. Write more
18. Be better.

It's still March 29, my father's 78th birthday, I just realized.
Man, I still love that guy, dead nineteen years. Cameron had
been gone fourteen years when Chas bought it. How did Dad
ever get over that feeling? And all of his tears came out of
one eye.

7 April
Yesterday, drove to Gimli at eight a.m. to fetch reeds and rushes
for set dressing. Snow drifts were gigantic; whiteness everywhere made the sun oppressive. Had imperial cookies, some of
which I fed to a squirrel in our front yard at 22 Lake, where I
also planted seed in the sunny windswept Arctic diorama that
spread out around our promontory of a breakwater. Brief magic,
then back to the city, where I completed a first draft of the sets
for *Twilight of the Ice Nymphs*. I ran into Ritchard at Zines; he
had come down from the premiere of *My Life as a Dog*. He said
it was quite good; he made absolutely no qualification. I'm sorry,
even Derek Mazur, whom I now respect as a result, has stated
the qualifications inherent in the very nature of the project.
Ritchard and I will never understand each other at any level. He
is alternately respectful and jealous of the press attention I have
received, and he does not like my movies. To a lesser degree,
this may be a problem with another, infinitely smarter man, DOP
Mike Marshall. If these people, Telefilm, Alliance, etc., had
simply listened to me when I tried to explain how I took a short-
cut to my modest position in the film world, how I entered the
industry through the back door, as a novelty act without a ticket,
how I was quite clever in doing so and owed my very presence
there to peculiar trickery, then these people would not be so

quick to remove all these tricks from my bag: my Vaseline, scratches, monochromes and tableaux, all my mannered dialogues and feigned magic-lantern innocence. Now they want to make me pass muster at the front door, where I must check my bag. I now have a single free pass into a feature project, but I shall shortly be given a bum's rush when what I have to show for myself proves no better than what any gate-crashing imposter could come up with when put on the spot by so many black ties. I'm simply not good enough to play by the same rules as the established drones, so I shall fall short of them on their terms, and these are dull and loathsome talents to be shown up by. Had we discussed my strengths and my weaknesses, had we all agreed upon which we would avoid and which to face head-on, there would be an understanding sense of solidarity among my producers and me rather than an ever-renewing sense of stupidity and insensitivity all around.

Anyway, after I designed the sets, Ritchard started ordering me to include certain shots in the film – something which I by now consider insolent. He has totally betrayed the original spirit of our working agreement: that he be a totally subservient producer to my auteur. At times, I have no strength for the endless tug-of-war with this man who is either a self-serving Machiavelli or an amnesiac. He's gadget crazy, and if I don't fight this process-o-phile, the product will be as embarrassing as *The Hands of Ida* – and the end of my career. I don't have the strength at the moment. Ritchard's latest dullard hubris has me longing for the grave.

10 April

Ritchard is intractable. He will pay all six actors the same rate – $500/day. That means Alice Krige will be offered $7000. Tom Waits and R. H. Thomson will be lured with $4500 and the chance to work in the exotic locale of Winnipeg. Mary Walsh will earn $10,000, more than our three prize catches mentioned above. Aden Young, or Aidan Quinn as Ritchard calls him, will fly up from Australia to earn $10,000 in a month. After all these actors turn us down, we shall be turned down again by Pascale Bussières, Christopher Lee, and I don't know who. Why have we been talking about these people all along if there has never been any chance of signing any of them? Months ago, when

Ritchard told me the acting budget was set at $50,000, I told him to add a decimal place. He promptly lowered the budget to $44,000. I've talked to him twice since on the subject, once at great length. He says he is very persuasive, that actors will be convinced, that he will make an offer, then remain silent; that whoever talks first loses; that he learned this strategy during his days as a car salesman. It now appears that the movie will not go, or at least not on schedule, and not with the cast I want. It will be peopled with nauseating Canadians and other regular folk. How decadent.

I write these words at Zines, where I have run into my wife sitting with a book. Amma told me today that she will give me $10,000 of her inheritance – Janet and Ross getting the same. A fantastic gift – if only I could think of how to use that money to get another profession. I feel, with Jupiter's gravity, that my movie and my life are sinking together into a noxious, gaseous fuck-blah. Buck up, Gatsby! Buck up!

3 September
The picture-cut is virtually complete. I shall now travel to Toronto to discuss a 1998 job directing an opera. Should I wear black?

A semi-fine cut of *Twilight of the Ice Nymphs* awaits George in his mailbox. He will watch it tonight after his *Miss Julie* rehearsal. I pray he is as understanding as he can be. I know I dropped the ball with his script; I always did feel disembodied from this project. I don't know why. The story is very good, but I couldn't ever decide on a schema for the thing. And as I write this, my fingers still prance the Ouija board in search of one. Kyle McCulloch's voice could lock a schema in place like a bottle cap!

I have not had the energy to be angry at Ritchard for at least two weeks. How blissful this peace brought on by exhaustion is.

6 December
I got a $20,000 Manitoba Arts Council grant to make a short film called *Maldoror: Tygers*. After twenty-six days of ADR (there were twenty-six shooting days), I now have more time for fun stuff. As I write these words, I am very happy. Will this down-time first steer me back into the depression that fills these pages? I am really only sad on the days I have time to write in here ...

1 September, 1997

Steve and I toss a soft bladder around Gladstone for twenty minutes. This is my third consecutive day of catch football. I'm slowly coming back. Now I must prep for the Toronto festival: my *Devil Doll* presentation, *Twilight of the Ice Nymphs* and symposium speaking engagements. The crepe for Lauzon is being taken down; Princess Di's is going up. I think my movie is playing opposite Di's funeral – tough competition.

> *Lessons learned from shooting* The Cock Crew:
> ❖ Have a firm hierarchy in place.
> ❖ Be fully prepared (FULLY) beforehand.
> ❖ Have one administrator responsible for budgets and schedules.
> ❖ Never allow employees to moonlight. Film is full-time. Jane Tingley's grass-cutting job left her completely useless to me, even though she's a great sculptor.
> ❖ To avoid territorial squirmishes, never allow construction and props-making at same site.
> ❖ Have a foreman.
> ❖ Always have a houseboy, high tea, wine, etc.
> ❖ Have lieder sung.
> ❖ Never hire useless friends.
> ❖ Make an aesthetic checklist and run it through frequently.

4 September

Off to Toronto Film Fest tonight. Carl, Steve and I swam this afternoon. I feel great.

I shall miss my bike when I'm away. Of all things this summer that could have been, it turned out to be the time I fell in love with my bike. It's so old (sixty-seven years?) and so ugly that only old hippies pay it any mind. Blue, double-barred, double-handlebarred, saddled with a rusty jagged old metal seat that will someday sever that inner thigh artery which is never more than thirty seconds away from pouring out your life. This bike has never been oiled. As a consequence, the simple act of pedalling it is like moving a pyramid block on sand. Three years ago, a pedal poorly welded into place by my Uncle Lawrence dropped off while I was really pumping, and sent me sprawling onto the street in front of the Zoo, where I once found two pair of dentures in the dust. I cried when no one came to help me. I broke my shoulder. Now I ride this two-wheeler miles a day …

14 September
On AC 193 to Winnipeg. Fest. est mort!

Most surreal moment: Gordon Pinsent emerging from crowd at Saturday's closing party to greet me and encourage me. Arm extended: 'Guy Maddin.' My arm extended: 'Mr. Pinsent.' We speak of MTC, John Hirsch, Len Cariou; we look awkwardly about, shake hands again. Farewell and back into the crowd for the rowdyman.

Pinsent's schmoozing has worked. There must be a part for this fellow in *Nemo Electric. The Pomps of Edison. The Edison Orgy. Dad's Muscle.* What to call it!!

A salon at Laura's last night. Tara Ellis and Irish beau Andrew (a *Globe* financial page writer), David McIntosh, Nora Young, Rick and Val Gilbert, Noam Gonick and, sitting at my right with likely boredom, my beloved Jilian. Very wonderful to sit with her beneath the ripening grapes which rained down from the trellis.

On Friday, Bruce LaBruce book launch at Sneakers. Karen Freidman ('Tell Carl I should have called him, but I didn't') looking great, Gariné looking greater, little brother Torossian looking best.

I've been voted Miss Congeniality and given the Prompt Guest Award by Alliance office. Wonderful people. A twenty-minute conversation with Tony Cianciotta, a five-minute chance encounter with Claudia Lewis and a thirty-minute lunch with Charlotte Mickie survive as my most happy confabs.

Devil Doll intro went well. Three-hundred-seat sell-out. *Twilight of the Ice Nymphs* 'intro' I attempt to hypnotize the audience – goes well enough. Six-hundred-seat sell-out one day then a call for deciduous melodrama the next day in front of a three-hundred-seat sell-out. This was OK.

18 September
Steve is writing about Steve the Barber, his bald coiffurist who hates men with hair. Steve wriggles his pen, clenching his fingers into the barber's fists. He writes of the head rubs, the

backcombings, the angry hair yanks and scissor snags, the punchings, all of these dealt to the scalps of customers luckier in the follicle dept. Steve the Barber has worked at Grosvenor and Stafford for forty-seven years. It took Steve the Customer that long to find his way into that brutal sadist's chair. Steve the Writer doesn't even seem to have gotten a single hair trimmed. He has simply squared off with an older, angrier Steve, put himself under his fingers. A full-Steve from the barber. And the customer, teeth clenching and face contorting with a full-Steve of his own, could be popped like an angry grape.

19 September

Dykemaster's Daughter storyboards to go into *Border Crossings*. I must lure Roger Frappier into range for a closer look-see. To the lake! To the lake! I've been looking forward to this for months. But this weekend looks fairly sterile for companionship. I need wine, a paint box, a pain box, a book, a blanket and a chilly swim. The flesh tightens in the cold water. A housecoat, a thermos of coffee, frozen grass, a lake so cold it scalds, stubble-smoke gauzing the promontories into *Le Million* backdrops, a chilly stone retrieved from congealed off-season shore muck. My heart breaks. This is the only possible cure for post-festival letdown. Why is there a letdown when one spends the entire festival, eleven days of it, turning one's soul inside out, scraping it all of its orientation by talking about it to paid interviewers, babbling the last bit of humanity from one's bosom at parties, and rinsing off all self-worth with cataracts of alcohol. The festival guest craves the terra firma of home, and once home for refilling, finds nothing here to put in his tanks. Swimming is all I'm capable of doing. Work of any sort is an impossibility. All my friends are wonderful, but someone is missing. Someone limned out vaguely from the fragmentary contours of many others who criss-crossed my stupefied gaze over the last week.

29 September

Caelum is applying to the Manitoba Arts Council for help on his Guess Who anthology. I too am applying, in direct competition with him for the October 1 deadline: *Somalian Love Letters* will exist in six-page précis for jury appreciation. I must pull myself out of the fiscal quicksand, thickened with recent bad

☆ GET SOME FUCKING SCRIMS for ONCE!

semi-opaque b/s —L. Letters
—Lee Milton
Fleischer Bros!!!

ingenious, can leave an impression longer than a line-up for stale food, and I'm left with no choice but to over-honk my horn and veer off waving my arms with an affected haste towards a pretend destination. Never until now did I realize I was the coffee-truck-man visiting UNDERGROUND.

I'm so depressed right now — and lazy — I feel like reading — but only as avoidance of the afternoon's work I face on "Somalian Love Letters". Four hours work for $6000. I would be more repulsive to myself than ever — poor as we are — if I were to shirk this.
① The "imperial cookie" is a white disc of dough, glazed with sweet whiteness and topped, in the centre like a nipple, with a nibbly little cherry-chew. I consume these once or twice a day during periods of sensory-deprivation. Little oral-boy gets literally stuffs his face. L.O.B. must concentrate and focus his regimen to exclude pastries, pies and glazed tits. Move on. Thank you.

movies
-GO TO
Actors Revenge
-WIND
-Portrait...
-Footlight...
CARDS PROMOTIONAL MAT'L & PIECES

THE YELLOW PAPER → 29 Sept 97

FOOD & VITAMINS
CABBAGE · fish oil
PILAFS · radishes
Beans · smoked salmon
salads · tomatoes
lemons · carrots
berries · steamed veg.s
grapefruit · skim stuff
radishes · yogurt
occasional boiled egg · cast iron
PRIMO soups [WINE]
BAGELS
WHOLE WHEAT CEREALS

- READ ONE HOUR 1st in Morn
- 20/20 work-outs increase
- read or consult dictionary
- graphic novels
- watch more films in theatres
- Living Room Play.
- Rewrite & Rename Edison-Nurma
- write Minialuno!
- Web Site
- INCOME!!!
- entertain / take out
- contacts (mountains): cards, faxes, calls
- studio

- clothes
- brief case
- little water-heaters
- frames
- Bell-jar
- Mantel slip cover
- screen
- candles
- decoupage
- frames
- audiotape of TOTIV
- auto tape covers

movie notices and final creditor notices, while clanging marital tocsins of the schizoid variety drown out my cries for help. No review is entirely favourable these days – I expected this for *Twilight of the Ice Nymphs* so the quicksand should have been avoidable – but the accompanying photos of me have solved once-and-for-painfully-all just why I had the Miss Congeniality award thrust on me by the pitying Alliance publicists. Also, the stills from the movie, even in faxed newsprint form, appear to be ghastly and poorly lit. Must I do everything? Evidently I must, even though I've proven myself (even to myself) an incompetent. The 'puff pieces' have missed the point, the pans have missed the point – still sinking me like an old U-Boat on a few scores – and my face leers out like a Gwynplaine or a Jessel.

GET SOME FUCKING *SCRIMS FOR ONCE*!!

I'm so depressed right now – and lazy. I feel like reading, but only as avoidance of the afternoon's work I face on *Somalian Love Letters*. Four hours' work for $6000. I would be more repulsive than ever – poor as we are – if I were to shirk this.

John Harkness called *Twilight of the Ice Nymphs* 'the kind of really bad film that only a good filmmaker can make.' This represents the closest thing to a 'pull quote' I can get from the Toronto press this time around.

10 October

Peculiar sleeps in Paris. Must have seven naps and shits a day. My window is open with the Relais du Louvre flag sometimes flapping right into the room. Euro MTV on every waking minute. Finished Th. Metzger's *Blood and Volts* yesterday. Read the magnificent Brothers Quay script *The Mechanical Infanta* today. Within a minute spoke with a Quay (Stephen, I think) about the greatness of their piece. Expressed, also, since he would listen, my strong wish to have the Belgian Housegirl come to Olympia. Perhaps Ms. Krige would come, too? No shortage of lovely scenery in Seattle's Transcona.

Passed up trip to Maison de Victor Hugo in favour of viewing of Mitch Leisen's *Midnight* at Videotheque. Now, it's 18:40 and I must pace the streets of Paris to think of a translatable intro to *Twilight of the Ice Nymphs*. Can I recycle my attempted hypnosis of Toronto?

12 October

Wilfred's Day. Bought 1908 name-day calendar at Paris market. Should be usable for 1998. Every one of my movies played in Paris today, and I did Question and Answer for every single one. A few people saw them all, including one insane woman from a Far Side cartoon. Did a pretty good interview with Jedrek, a Pole, and his French friend, who pleased me by comparing my stuff to Jules LaForgue, whose *Moral Tales* are with me now whenever I shoot. I got to explain my *mélodrame caduc*, or deciduous melodrama, theory: the overly methodical suitor so lacks spontaneity, is so rooted to one spot, that by the time inspiration comes to him, his gesture is so inappropriately overcharged that he loudly and bark-splittingly breaks apart and all dignity falls like leaves, stripping him to public nakedness, whatever. Caduc! Hugged and kissed Manu and Fabrice. Wakeup at 5:45 a.m. Breakfast vaguely planned with Lucius Barre. Goodnight.

13 October
Iberia flight 4425 to Barcelona. Need Spanish/English dictionary.

Perhaps my *Dead Father* negative is at the John Turner Archive in Ottawa? And perhaps Patrick Crowe can get me thousands of $ for the junk I keep in Steve's attic. I need money very badly. Can get it by:

❖ selling archives
❖ getting movie going
❖ writing diary for someone else's film
❖ getting job (reg)
❖ getting job (directing TV and/or rock video)

Mused today about turning Neemo the son of Edison into Neemo the daughter. Much is gained and lost. I'm so at sea with narrative. My head swims, and George would kill me for even thinking about the script changes that pass, like taboo thoughts, into my consideration. Make a list.

14 October
Most wonderful little noises in the world are the ones made, mostly without change in nineteen years, by Jilian as she sleeps – which she did in my hotel room in Sitges last night.

We strolled the Mediterranean beaches for a couple of hours before bed – wonderful moon and surf – before an incipient cold gave a weird tincture to my dreams: I had to sneak one of my mother's young lovers out of Aunt Lil's bathroom, where he had post-coitally showered, and past Lil in her favourite chair, and also past Gramma – who had conveniently retired to her bedroom. (Amma decided to keep Gramma busy there by taking her knitting in to do at her mother's bedside.) But the naked paramour emerged, all damp and clean, not from Lil's bathroom, but from the basement, up the very stairs that killed Gramma. He walked through the kitchen right at Lil – it dawned on me I could introduce him to Lil as a friend of Janet's husband – but he made a sudden left and, toothpick in mouth above steamed and soapy neck, departed through Lil's back door, just as Lil herself did on her fatal ambulance ride to Grace Hospital.

15 October
The wallet photo of 'Chas at Saltaire' is propped up in a little sand boat rendered by Jilian on the beach in the Mediterranean salt air. Dad could never have thought, while posing some fifty years ago with British Columbian tree saw and cigarette, that this very pose would be repeated by him (exactly, down to the length of the smoke and the degree of breezy freshness buffeting his young glass eye) on a beach in Sitges, Spain, twenty years after his death. Jil, who never met Dad, sleeps next to him in the sunny sand. The same waves that carried Homer, Ovid and Jason roll up with the same music they've always played. I lie in the shade of an ancient cave.

16 October
11:10 p.m. Sitting on our balcony overlooking the sea. The moon is not out yet, but a single bat circles above our courtyard, passes in front of the huge white wall of the hotel making himself nature-show visible, then sweeps, squeaking slightly I think, past my face. Jil pointed out this bat to me. I've always wanted to see one properly. We keep our door open nights here for vampires. As fathers will, I show off for my daughter by attempting to jam the bat's sonar with a loud fart, which echoes throughout the courtyard, off the pool, off all the balconies – my own sonar. A partially concealed female head in a room across the way pivots in puzzlement or disgust.

18 October
Martin Sheen looks out at the moonlit Mediterranean from his balcony just one bat sweep away – his profile as unmistakable as his voice. A drunken, crickety, pulchritudinous night. Sitges! Vene! Vale!

22 October (4:15 a.m.)
Ian has earned my undying love by nailing backs, or fourth sides, to various archways and flats which comprise the unpainted walls of my sets. He's done this in the same sloppy way that my father built fences, but the effect is amazing: everything takes on weight, the third dimension of things is real, the cheese quotient for the decors has been reduced to zero. I'm thrilled.

On Monday morning, I walked down to the seaside for the last time, very grey, hazy but warm. Opened up an *Interview* magazine I grabbed from the deserted lobby and while standing in the sand, found a photo of a topless Uma Thurman sitting on an identical beach. Then I jumped into the warm, churned water, surfed on two or three waves, walked back to the hotel and flew home to Winnipeg, arriving twenty-two hours later to an ice-encrusted city. Beautiful, leaf-naked and tiresomely slippery – fifteen-car crash on St. James Bridge, and muscles never before used strained horribly simply by walking on such a thinly-glazed surface. Defecated a week's worth of *carne*, went swimming – six-month pass purchased – watched *Ambersons*, ate Goldeye, tuned in the first inning of World Series, then went to sleep in deep depression at 7:30 p.m. after a typical exchange of childish sulking fits with my wife.

24 October

Teva and Holly meet me at Seattle airport. They have three boughs of lilies, very reproductive things, for me and the Quays. Already I forget what happened after: dinner with tons of wine before *Twilight of the Ice Nymphs* screening. The evening goes on in raging cataracts (again) of Chardonnay until, time flowing well past 10:00 a.m. GMT, the Quays having watched my doc and my feature, everyone, Noam and Aubrey, Gariné, Timothy, Stephen, Holly, Teva and others either pair off or don't pair off in at least half the possible permutations. At least one monstrously unnatural act is performed. Next morning, many throbbing hangovers accompany us on a search for the horny and rotten salmon, said to be still running by Steamboat Island. We stare into the murky pools of water at the languid, bruised and flaccid fish – or are those our reflections? We reek of roe.

A seminar with REM video director Bangs, Quays, Noam and me. Packed, attentive, keen, American (!), college students. Noam teaches me the meaning of ephebephilia! Godzilla. Hormones and hangovers.

27 October

Scarecrow Video in Seattle, where I see a Japanese VHS of *Archangel*, which I autograph for the store. Always feels like a sad joke on myself to autograph such things. George and I once found an autographed collection of poems by Irving Layton in the ten-cent bin at the bookmart. We left it there.

Each of Holly and Heather has an older brother with Tourette's. Noam pronounces to a packed dining room that he can't stand heterosexual porn because it's full of women having sex. Cynthia Plaster Caster sits next to Stephen two seats down. Aubrey wears hairpins to present a birthday gift coiffure to the public – his hair is a series of blonde curling ribbons. Benjamenta or Noam removed all the pins and his hair unfolded into ancient Greek horns, like eagle tufts, to go with his eagle's beak and ephebishly ivory skin – a perfect Pan!

Every girl in Olympia has a pierced navel. Oh Sarah. Year of Sarahs. Two girlies say they will do anything to work with me. A Tokyo emigré named Kent gives me Timothy Brock soundtrack CDs (*Caligari* and *Faust*; the latter I trade with Stephen for Brock's *Sunrise*). The Quays, it turns out, have no

French distribution. Must phone (fax) E.D. Sarah walked out halfway through *Archangel* and never came back; was never seen again. The Quay movies are better and better each time out. Kahla the Dansk Croat makes cool art, paper-tissue lamps in 3D bear shapes, looks great/is funny.

When I get off this plane, I am to be kinder to Elise. We are to 'do things for one another.' I'm tired, and I'm sure she's resentful of the housework this agreement has compelled her to do just prior to my return. Should be a loving and wonderful reunion.

Teva gives the Quays *Judging Dairy Cows*, a photo-filled book featuring close-ups of cow rear ends, with tails held in nine and three o'clock positions by cropped-off farmers. Timothy finds a fantastic armless adolescent girl doll at Teva's. With Quay movements, he swings the legs back and forth, activating a swivelling of the head. Stephen suggests a tracking shot past the vista through both armpit holes. Timothy looks down the loose panties, smells the 'leg mould' growing on the upper thighs. Stephen lays the doll down on her back to close its one working eye. I'm eager to smell this white mould, to be part of a Quay epiphany: this is Schwab's and they've just discovered their next star. This one to be lent out to Koninck Studios by Teva, the twenty-one-year-old Selznick of Olympia, for the doll's talent has already been valued highly by this keen judge of the latent power in unlikely knick-knacks. Noam is present at the epiphany. The doll is to be shipped soon to England – the Quays commence writing her first scenario tomorrow.

21 November

Elise pretended to be my sister for about forty-five minutes worth of theatre sports. Script adaptation for the screen continues with a lot of disorientation on my part. Remember the three-way conflict rules from *Sweet Smell of Success*.

Robert Enright book launch, the excellent *Peregrinations*. *Dykemaster's Daughter* excerpted in *Border Crossings*. I don't have many extra words in me today. The WP has left my eyes filmy, my ears ringing, my thinking sleepy; add to this the postal strike, the fact that I slept in, and a curious lack of phone calls, and I've had what seems like my own personal Good Friday. Everyone else is bustling around in their usual excited Friday hormone haze, a horny day-long rush hour, but everything in my personal sphere seems recently sermonized, tranquil, closed and stupid.

28 November

Sold *Gimli Hospital* to Bravo for $5000. Possibly teaching two courses at U of M for $8500. E.D. wiring me $3000. Possible articles to sell to *Border Crossings* and *Take One*. I'm broke but accumulating enough artificial light at the end of the tunnel to feel occasionally giddy. Tonight I shall watch a Velcrow Ripper movie, then formulate a pitch to the WFG for a salon/workshop.

On top of Carl's Fyxx confession that he tried sleeping one drunken night at the age of twenty-three with his own twenty-seven-year-old sister while her husband, his brother-in-law, slept upstairs ('She bought a case of beer and invited me back to her place so I thought: all right,' puts two thumbs up), Steve sits here in the same Fyxx and tells me that at eighteen he went to his first whorehouse – the Samoa Club in Idaho Falls – as an expedient virginity-chaser and tribute to Stephen Daedalus in 'the only readable part of *Portrait of the Artist as a Young Man*.' Ten bucks did the trick and an instantaneous conclusion upon first contact made the whole thing painless if not slightly humiliating. The Samoa Club had tall windows with palm-tree silhouettes. Other and subsequent whorehouses in Idaho Falls included the Gem Rooms (across the street), the Hub and the New Grand Hotel. Room with a bed and a bathroom – from the latter emerged the whore in some black-lace easy-on-and-off thing. After loading herself up with lubricant in a haunchy corner, the veteran tutor would grab at Steve for a quick sore inspection, make him useful amid all sorts of Don Martin sound effects, then shove him into the field of play. A cowboy town with plenty of illegal gambling and whoring to keep the spurs jingling, these Idaho Falls transactions of Steve's must have been spongy, swampy, soaked-cake occasions for paralyzed little Steve. Whorehouse right next door to a café where teen Steve learned to drink coffee – two vices learned but twenty feet apart. Infamy!!

4 December
Steve and I at Great Canadian Bagel. Two bagels and mug of coffee: $2.24! Quiet. Non-smoking means no women come here. Have swum twenty days in a row now. (30/30 today). My 'weight training' is every second day now; thirty minutes of high rep/low weight stuff. 500 reps of 300 lb leg press. 150 reps of all arm work. Really scrawny routines, but I'm getting fitter I swear.

6 December
Twenty-five-day streak at Sargent Park. Ninety minutes today with Steve, the last forty-five minutes in the pool made effortless by my surging strength and thirty synchronized swimmers plying and plashing near this old crocodile. If I can make it till Fri morning, the day I leave for the Genies, I shall have done thirty-one consecutive swimming days.

Steve and I just made a pact, shaking on it, to lose nine pounds by March 6, three months from today, to be achieved by walking more and exacting more fat-content vigilance from ourselves, each other. That will take Steve down from 170 to 161, me down to 166 from 175. With muscle-toning and all that jazz, we shall be dudish drones brimming with health; we shall knock china off shelves with cumbersome and throbbing priapi, carried before us like difficult fire logs.

In July of 1995, some three weeks before my wedding, I accepted an invitation to the Chicago Underground Film Festival for the sole reason that it would give me a chance to meet their guest of honour, Kenneth Anger. Upon arrival, I met a charming festival assistant with the Truffaut-ish name of Nicole Berger, whose job it was to make sure the festival guests got booked into their hotels and made all their appointments. Soon, we were both skipping out of our obligations together, I missing a symposium or two, she abandoning her post at the taxi stands and cocktail parties. We went out for late-night snacks when she should have been debriefing projectionists. I think she had decided she hated her job long before I arrived, so I won't flatter myself that I had any influence over her behaviour.

On my third night there, we took in a tap-dance festival that left us both vibrating with awe. Then, afterwards, at exactly eleven p.m., while strolling in front of the Hilton after a summer thundershower, we were suddenly kidnapped by a very talkative and skinny young man by the name of Dogg, who implied through a menacing power of suggestion and no gun, that we should accompany him to the nearest automated teller so that he could help himself to my daily maximum withdrawal. As Nicole, Dogg and I strayed further away from the bright lights of the Hilton, the streets became absolutely dark, densely entangled with low branches and unmowed grass. I couldn't believe that the pleasant feeling I'd had just moments before had been detoured into the panicky dread I felt while we tried to grope our way to a bank machine in the dark. Nicole and Dogg were arguing about her alleged racism. I stayed out of it. I tried to wish myself out of this place. Was this sudden reversal of fortune a swift and simple punishment for all the pleasure I had just been craving?

My card wouldn't work in the bank machine, neither would my MasterCard. So Dogg decided he would keep us until the computer lines got untangled. Besides, he was definitely hot after beautiful Nicole by now. Passing street corner after street corner, where he waved at a variety of what he claimed were his boys positioned at their neighbourhood posts, Dogg took us to his bar, some half-mile's walk later, where he bade two gun-packing cronies join us and watch over us as he went about brief business among his gang friends in the dark and clamorous place. He quickly returned and all five of us sat at a table. He told me to order beer with my credit card, which I did. My plastic was now up and running, but Dogg paid that no mind. He was clearly bent on possessing Nicole, either by charm or by force.

Nicole put on a spectacular display of keeping Dogg interested in the art of seduction just long enough to forestall his more violent impulses, then just as our captor moved in for his reward, she would cool off and unflirt with him, pushing him back verbally, demanding some sort of respectful space for herself. Which eventually frustrated and angered the ardent brute until he was on the verge of summoning a spree of violence against her, and me too I guess. (He said he would have us 'popped.') At just this most dangerous moment, she would turn on a dime and reintroduce playfulness and flirtation into her tones, rekindling the hopes of Dogg's inner gent. One moment she would cup the man's face in her hands and admire it, the next she was dressing him down for his impertinence. In this fashion, back and forth, Nicole kept her menacer at bay for a couple of hours while we all five of us (the two henchmen never said much) kept up the drinking and small talk. We spoke of Winnipeg, Nicole's hometown of LA, and even Minneapolis, a town I know well and Dogg's birthplace. I kept buying rounds. To an observer we two prisoners might have looked only slightly out of place in that club, uncomfortably undemographic but hardly kidnapped. Clearly, Nicole was to be raped, but she and I sparkled out conversation, even laughing loudly at some of Dogg's jokes. (Some were even funny.) The whole evening wore on so slowly it became easy to forget the circumstances. It felt like Dogg was trying to sell us insurance. I forgot to be terrified and grew bored. I longed to return to my room at the Congress for sleep.

Then, in a change of strategy, or just to be sadistic, Dogg ordered me to join him outside. In the blackness of an alley I was to pee for him into a puddle. I couldn't do it in spite of all the beer I'd bought and drunk. Dogg taunted me for being afraid, said he would 'pop' me if I was afraid. Of course I was afraid, and bored and detached and feeling like the script need a better pace, but who can pee on demand anyway? Finally, I dribbled out some urine into a rain puddle in the darkness at my feet and we two menfolk returned to our table. Now it was Nicole's turn to be taken outside. Dogg took her away and I never saw him again. He left me with his boys under the understanding that I was to go nowhere. Poor Nicole had no choice but to go with him.

I spent two more hours with those impassive sidekicks, buying enough beer for their already drug-addled heads finally to render one of them unconscious. He crashed to the floor with a pitcher of ice spilt about his great belly. His gun spilt out, too, onto the floor beside him. No one touched him or his gun. The Tarantino moment for me to grab the gun and get on out just wasn't in me. The gun owner just snoozed on upon the butt-strewn floor for the rest of the night. His comrade kept up a heavy-lidded consciousness; we talked about our kids, each of us had a daughter. He seemed nice, but he had his orders to do me great violence if I attempted to leave.

Finally, at four a.m., just as the bar lights flashed in closing, I asked permission to use the john. As I strolled away from the table, a numbed and indecisive sleepwalker, Nicole appeared at the front door of the bar, waving me urgently to her side. Without looking back I ran at her and into the open door of a taxicab. She dived in and the cab sped off. The cabbie had saved her from the probably unarmed Dogg, just when she'd run out of stalling tactics and he'd thrown her to a sidewalk some two hours of strolling away. Nicole somehow remembered the location of the club and got the heroic hack to drive there, where he was able to scoop me up as well. We had no money to pay the driver, but he took us to my hotel, the Congress, which was also where Dogg claimed to be staying in a heavily guarded room on the second floor, my floor.

Nicole's aplomb was impressive, her heroism toward me absolutely charismatic. I can't even ask myself if I would have been able to do the same thing for her. I was too busy trying to get closer to her myself. Soon, she found herself in the company of another dogged man. We napped together on my bed, too tired to sleep. She kept completely clothed and insisted that she sleep with her head at my feet, and vice versa. Was this supposed to discourage charged thoughts? I couldn't believe I was lying right next to a recently rescued girl and was trying my damnedest, just like the unlucky Dogg had for four hours, to charm her into submission.

We never reported the incident to the cops. I don't know if Dogg really had a room at the Congress. I just wore a dissembling baseball cap crammed low over my face for the remainder of my stay. While having drinks with Kenneth Anger I was able to pique his interest in my kidnap story for exactly one minute before a loud bar band frightened him away to his room. I drank too much and felt sick, even nodded off a little in a restaurant washroom before Nicole rescued me once more. Next day she went back to LA without even saying goodbye, disgusted, I assume, with the anticlimactic nature of my character.

Can music ever be overlooked, as the madeleine it is, in anything written on nostalgia? I suppose the Robert Walser POV allows for lacunae galore. Anyway, if only I had this kidnapping to do over again, I would not end up crunching empty air in Astaire 'A Fine Romance' fin-flapping embraces.

George peculiarly warned me that students would zone out of my syllabus if it were not at least two thirds contemporary film. I think I must zone them in only to movies of beloved-by-me status or fizzle trying. To fail to reel either them or myself into *Ferris Bueller* would be demoralizing. It must be *L'Age d'or*! Possible movies: *Woman's Face, Vampyr, Napoleon/J'Accuse, They Won't Believe Me, Devil Doll, The Wind, Random Harvest, Possessed, Gun Crazy, Curse of the Cat People, Snake Pit, Sweet Smell of Success, Fearless* (that's new!), *Dr. Jekyll and Mr. Hyde, Humoresque, Letter from an Unknown Woman, Days of Heaven* (*Quick and the Dead, Red River, Johnny Guitar, Forty Guns*), *Written on the Wind, Blonde Venus or Dishonored*, Berkeley, *Luna, Scarlet Street, Svengali, Forbidden Games, Hawaii* (almost contemporary), *Zero for Conduct, Night and the City, Ivan II, Little Match Girl, Bill and Coo, Horror of Dracula*, Quays, *Trouble in Paradise*, DeMille's *Cleopatra, Cyrano de Bergerac, The Obsession of Billy Botski, Mabuse*.

10 December

Things I want: Paul Hammond's book on *L'Age d'or* from the BFI, the Taschen book on photography for Jilian's Xmas. *Dr. Mabuse* from Red River.

Did I mention I found Aunt Lil's diaries last week? Little jottings about card games played, shower gifts bought, records purchased, that fill two little volumes. I was very sickened about their whereabouts.

Made payments of $350 to attorney, $580 to phone company, $300 to Gastown Labs, and $900 to MasterCard (and all of a sudden $109 to Videon) by way of chipping away at debts.

I now owe:

$3000 to Ritchard Findlay
$3000 to Gastown
$2985 to Mastercard
$800 to cellular MTS
$700 to Bon Voyage Travel
$15,000 to Canada Council
Untold thousands to Revenue Canada

I should have coming in possibly:
$8500 for two U of M classes
$2000 for appearance fees
$5000 for Bravo sale of *Gimli*
$2000 for Jonah Stone rock video

Patient Canada Council can wait a long time. Bon Voyage can wait a little. So can the cell phone shitbags and Findlay.

15 December
Exec class post-Genie flight back from Toronto/Gariné II. Met with Reg Harkema (gave him an *Odilon Redon* he requested) and Don McKellar (who saved a doomed Ronald Coleman mustache just so I could see it and approve of it, which I honestly and truly did). Don and I had an hour chat over coffee about *Edison and Neemo*. I couldn't completely discredit what he said:

❖ script much too long, too talky
❖ possibly combine Faraday and Neemo (to make Neemo more active, give him more trouble with E.), therefore less Keaton (impossible to do anyway), more conflict
❖ to make Neemo's film more about his business with his dad and his difficulty with women (he felt Zella needs to be someone)
❖ to keep the battle scenes at the end, but to make them come out of the racism and sexism scorched into Neemo by E.
❖ don't squander the 'shocked' and 'electrocuting' qualities of N.! They are underused at present
❖ to frame the story more (but subtly) as a Neemo POV so we feel the titanic effect of E. more, so the story is more focused, a through-line, etc.
❖ shorten talk early on and everywhere; shorten more to 90 min.
❖ to make Neemo present right away, at the boxing match/ at the Persian's visit?, to make us see E. through N.
❖ this all could make for a boy's adventure story, lending a style, an excuse for mischief (racism and sexism), an excuse for the melée at the end.

- a thought: N. embracing more Indian women, killing or hurting them during his 'sexual practice' period before fucking Toni.
- keep Grandpa
- he agreed about a Baum spirit and had just read Kleist's 'The Betrayal in Santo Domingo.'
- he likes the title

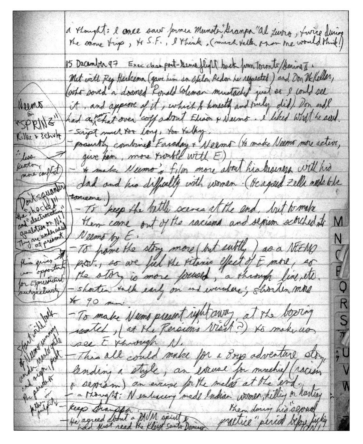

I don't know what to make of anyone's suggestions anymore. No one person can understand exactly where George is coming from with his script; no one knows him as I do so no one can see the wonders in scenes which are so blithely deemed dismissible.

And yet I myself am having trouble ascribing to some of the scenes any substance that matters visually to me. I want holes punched in the dialogue, lyrical scenes with pantomime, more inventions, more electricity as a hurtful affliction (hurtful to others). This might allow me some room to invent the visuals. Simply: maybe the story should be about how Neemo, as an invention of his father, is as hurtful to others as his father is, then, as he matures and learns a little humanity, a little something outside the realm of capitalism, he becomes less hurtful. Scarred, but human. Maybe, but maybe I'm just screwing everything up in my inept desperation to find the handle.

17 December

Welcome Noamie back to Winnipeg with a drive-by hug on King Street. Tumultuous autumn for this great pinko fag! Ritchard Findlay found me in the Underground, where I was keeping vigil over pretty Sarah (whom I must phone) and demanded a full explanation of my 'betrayal' – why have I gone over to the other producers, the Boneyards? Since confrontation is work, and I feel I've done enough for Ritchard, I gave him soft-soap till he stopped asking for the real goods. I have no idea if he bought any of my crap about a year's long sadness, requiring a completely new cast of characters in my life, but he paused in his whining long enough for me to make an escape. I still got a $20 parking ticket. Ritchard's bald blinkiness already breaks my heart; I have no need to pay guilt premiums from beneath my windshield wipers.

29 December

Henry Jarvis Handford, first second-generation drone, born by Caesarean to Liz Jarvis at St. B 4:30 p.m., 9 lb. 8 oz. Auburn hair. High temp. IV as precaution. Let's videotape this drone. Helen Harvie and Jil Maddin distaff drone offspring previous.

New Year's Day, 1998

Picked up Herdis at airport (from Ross's) and went to St. Boniface for first time since June 25, 1977 (one Saturday before death of Nabokov), to make thirty-five-minute video (very obnoxious of me) featuring Henry Jarvis Handford – or Jarford, as I nominated the little three-day-old to be. A beautiful

Caesarean baby. Liz and I crewed his shoot, Liz climbing, rent abs and all, onto a stool to get me some foot candles. Steve, Donna and Melissa showed up. Ian took us down after an hour for pie (cherry). His brother Jim left this message after being informed of Henry's birth: 'Hello ... This is Jim ... Handford ... Ian's brother. You phoned about your baby. It is 7:26.' Beep!

6 January
Twilight of the Ice Nymphs plays this weekend at the film fest founded by the recently late Sonny Bono (skiis, trees) in Palm Springs, where the old mayor's trees will be hung with crepe. Ms. Krige may attend. Lovely chat with her just now.

18 January
Jake Moore, who will be my placard-carrying babe in my boxing-ring video on 27th Jan., suggested last night that little Sarah be a co-babe in the ring, revealing in the meat of her suggestion that Sarah is in love some rock 'n' roll musician, probably not forty-two years old. I am a little crushed, but not completely deterred, for I didn't get to be forty-two through impatience.

When Ian Handford was eleven, a tipsy six-foot fourteen-year-old Shirley Snidal dragged cute little Handford into the bushes and kissed him silly for a couple of hours. At that point a special Snidal 'woman-brand' was put upon his brain. As a teen he hung with sixty-year-old Carmen Snidal (Mrs. to the Dr.) and fifty-year-old Aunt Peggy. One night during hide 'n' seek he passed a few hushed, charged hours cowering in a tool-shed with the highball-tinkling aunt. Oh, the summers he passed sneaking into Mrs. Snidal's room to wear her bathing suits and into Shirley's room to read her diary – proclaiming 'I love all Snidal women!' I believe even cousin Liz Snidal once joined Ian in the bathroom while he bathed and where she smoked on the toilet, pooping – Ian smoking in the tub to cut the smell. Did this really happen? Steam. Another hide 'n' seek hormone herd-up beneath the stars at Loni ends with Emu beating the bushes for more Snidals. The Man Who Loved All Snidal Women.

26 January

Recent pull quotes:

Noam brings a Snoop Doggy Dogg resembloid back to his hotel room in Twin Cities for some cruising sex. How old was this fellow, Noam? 'I don't know. When you're dealing with a guy that black and that downtown, small talk is really low on the list of priorities.'

Director Ross McMillan's Saturday night speech to the cast of his play just before they go onstage. 'Sorry I'm late and a little bit messed up. Someone just forced me to snort a lot of coke at gunpoint.'

George: 'Seems like a waste of a gun.'

28 January

Shoot video today. Must buy Vaseline as charm at Shopper's Drug Mart on way to Les Rendezvous.

Had a warm dream recently about Aunt Lil, who came home to 802, jingling the shop-door chimes on her way in and announcing in a way that was as loving as she was, but with more sporting candour than she had: 'I'm home, my love.' Then she hugged me in the shop hallway. Kim Novak as Judy couldn't have said this line better; in fact, I think it was Kim who said it. I'm thinking now of when Lil hugged me farewell from her bed at 802. Much frank meaning in her look, much exhausted distraction in mine, having just stepped off a frazzling roller-coaster ride with Dody. Sex is a stupid little jab of the needle, an anaesthetic that becomes, quickly, less and less effective with each application. But how it has worked to local effects when my grandmother, my father and my aunt all died. One could almost surmise that sex kills loved ones, but this is no more true than a notion that anaesthetic cuts open the chest.

1 February

At Second Cup after filmmaking class. Had students storyboard Charles Simic's poem 'Postage Stamp with Pyramid.' Must teach *A Woman's Face* on Wed.

15 February

Last Tuesday I went to a fashion show at Betelstadur. Perhaps my earliest memory is of my mother modelling in a fashion show.

My mother who was beautiful to my young eye, even though I was born in her fortieth year. So this memory has her in her early or even mid-forties. She decided I would model with her, on some sunny afternoon at the dawn of recollection, in the rec hall at the Lutheran Church on Victor – a DORCUS function (DORCUS must be an acronym for something). I can't believe my mother actually went to church quite often when I was young, finding less reason to go after a cruel eulogy delivered upon the sins of dead son Cameron – at least this eulogy being the stated reason for her churchy truancy, but in fact her attendance did not trail off until half a dozen years later. But of course I'm confusing church functions, between a Wednesday night or such and actual Sunday church services, which I don't think my mother ever went to, either before or after Cameron slid into the vague Lutheran version of hell.

This early fashion show was very crowded, my mother full of performance intensity, the kind she showed when one of her children readied itself for competition at the stadium. There was much daubing of my face with the maternally spittled Kleenex, much concern over my 'cowlick' – a word married forever by such occasions to wet Kleenex – a little bleached peacock's tail of blonde bristles which splayed across one topmost corner of my forehead. And which, perhaps because of much wishing on my part, has now fallen out completely, by far the most salient bald spot on my patchy coif.

I think the attention I received from the audience, however polite, scared me into reclusiveness for years. And the whole incident – a little boy with face glazed by saliva doggedly following the vogueings of his mother – was somehow completely forgotten until Tuesday's announcement by Herdis that she would once again, this time seven sizes larger and about forty years older, be strutting the catwalk again. This earliest memory popped into spit-licking freshness, and superstition – a fear of symmetry – took over. Would this first memory of Amma make this new modelling foray my last memory of her, by means of some symmetrical law of cruel fate? Would the daubed removal of the last bits of my caul sit forever as a bookend episode to my mother's last touches – toes lightly grazing runway as she tips calcified Achilles over teakettle into an open grave at the end of her mannequin's stroll? Would the fashion show, to put it

simply, kill my mother? I've made a study of what kills fathers
– new lawn mowers, new televisions, a clean bill of health – but
suddenly I developed a layman's hunch on what could spell
Amma's end.

I arrived at the fashion show in high emotion, wearing all
my nerves on the outside, a gallon of tears behind each eye and
brimming over. The show took place in the Betelstadur multi-
purpose room. Portable chairs traced out an imaginary runway.
Widows of various states of 'here-ness' filled these chairs. Racks
of clothing closed off the back end of the room, offering privacy
to the gaggle of octogenarian models who fussed energetically –
to judge by the bobbing together of so much hairsprayed helmet
visible in back. I spotted my mother's unique species of meticulous 'do – a neat and comforting rococo nest of platinum mater-
nity – among other drab models of fendered and fibreglassed
stylings. Eighty-nine-year-old Uncle Ron and I sat at the end
of the imagined gangplank – the feared open grave gaped at our
feet in spite of my knowledge that the whole room was carpeted
every inch in brand new broadloom. I suppose this seniors'
home will forever punish me with its newness. I had always so
much feared the squalid decrepitude of old folks' homes like the
old Betel in Gimli, and was so comforted by my response to the
newness of my mother's new home these last ten years that I
suppose it is this newness that will let go something like a wrecking ball and destroy me when it chooses to.

Well, the show started, and prose fails me. The entire piece
lasted precisely one hour. I was assailed, delighted and ruined
by humours from all points of the compass; as the minute hand
went round so did all feelings. There was dignity, senility,
warmth, dewlaps, laughs, delirium, loss, widowhood, flirtations,
cackles. Old women feeling fabric, old women feeling for dead
children, old women wandering off-track. When my mother
appeared, I thought I heard myself sob out loud. When I told
her I would like to come to the show she beamed, like Dickie
Moore in *Blonde Venus* – 'That would be so nice!' – and so she
was proud to see me there, one of two males, the only person
under eighty in the room. And I was proud of her, for looking
so poised, for selecting such beautiful clothing for herself and I
guess for her being proud of me, and tears sloshed around inside
the orbs of my eyes because of self-pity (the fleet passage of time,

etc.) and because of self-pride, too, for detecting the dangers involved in this symmetry thing. (Steve Burke had told me I was treading into dangerous emotional territory here; I likened it to a hot curling iron up the ass and he protested, 'But that heals!') One model wore a skirt, unfortunately, for elephantitis of the ankles gave her galoshes of flesh to wear for the rest of her life. She seemed terribly sheepish in this unflattering state, her face drawn in behind its glasses beneath a nicotine-washed perm and trim. Still another stopped halfway to lift her blouse and have her elasticized waistband extended by an arm's length to demonstrate how comfortable the slacks she displayed would be after a huge meal. Or, by sinister implication, after mysterious bloatings unique to the aged, or maybe worse still, after tubes and bags had been appended to one's digestive system and one needed a practical if not discreet hiding place in the clothing of the broken-down.

But always there was dignity, even if there was a clenched fist of veins coming out of a new sporty top where a head should be. I love my mother and I think I can actually feel it in the present. I've always mourned my inability to feel appropriately in the present, needing dreams to love later – on the installment plan. But as I sat with Uncle Ron, I felt a hot and tear-gushing love for him, he who sat beside me suavely flirting with each model, only spoiling it when he repeated his Maurice lines without variance to each of the eight models. I loved him too, simply and silently.

By the end I was dizzy with queerness, and eager to get out. Like all children of elderlies, I was bored too. Through the strangest ringer, yet bored.

9 April

At Facets, I purchased *Possessed*, *Seven Chances*, Dreyer's *Joan*, and, for the fourth time, *Imitation of Life*. In NY, I purchased *Dishonored*, *Betty Boop Vol.1* and DeMille's *Whispering Chorus*; in Boston, Sabrina bought *The Cheat*, while I nabbed Lon Chaney's *Shadows* and I can't remember.

David Schwartz was a wonderful host at NY's AMMI. Mike Rubin was an ultra-enthusiastic conversationalist at a first-time director's fest sponsored by MOMA and *Interview* magazine. I had my picture taken with Gariné, a wonderful idea until it shows up in that magazine's back pages. A man scheduled to do a phoner with me from Kansas City called forty-five minutes late today and I refused to answer. Another triumph for passive aggression!!! Why didn't I buttonhole J. Hoberman about the relative merits of *Exotica* and *The Crossing Guard*? Because he seemed to be doing fine without too much film talk. Speaking of too much, I invoked the contagions of early thirties Nazism at least five times while complaining to Hoberman about *Titanic*; will he have any choice but to conclude I'm an anti-Semite today? Gariné improves your stock, but renders it unstable on the market, simply by standing next to you. Now that I'm her official boyfriend, could there be a weird, or not-so-weird, stock-plummeting glut effect? I don't want to be in anyone's portfolio who would have me as an asset.

13 April

Touring with *Twilight of the Ice Nymphs* has become unbearable: to most, the movie is simply not very interesting. It may not be 'pretentious' but it is 'tedious.' 'Your new movie is not funny, yet your other movies are funny. Could you explain?' My own *Stardust Memories*. Just one more trip – to Missouri – in support of this abomination, and I will have learned enough lessons from the lash for now I think. No, no and no more festivals, please no more, just turn them down, places like New Zealand and Australia, just turn them down. I've nothing to say about the picture, and I'm giving really bad interviews precisely at the time Alliance can get plenty of them for me. What a squandered opportunity.

I came in during a technical delay of the La Chaux au Fonds screening *Ice Nymphs* on Saturday, so I sat through the last half with a riled and bored throng of Swiss zombies. I grew so sad I thought I could never go onstage for Q&A. Olivier's diffidence somehow 'principled' me out there, but only one question: 'What does it all mean?' Followed by a personal first: a girl stood up and hurled something at me – some sort of foil ball. Swiss anger or Swiss irony? Either way the gesture was about as funny as the movie, and aptly opaque. I felt like apologizing to everyone. How could Olivier and Anais make this movie the central jewel of their festival, their Outerspace 2300 Festival, without having seen it, knowing it to be unsubtitled? Ah, what sopping soggy cold wet slushy sadness as I slogged through the town's strange zoo, where half the animals are on the wrong side of the fences, and finally to my Moreau Hotel, where only after ten minutes of ringing did slow Seraphino admit me through the front door. Absinthe.

16 April
Came back on Monday night without having written and story-boarded the Rasputina video. I did, however, cull many micro-scripted and constipated details from a few pages of lateral thinking spent in Schulz's *Spring*. Exhausted, frustrated, annoyed with myself and with Swiss Germans, I drove my mom home after she met me at the airport. My temper with her inexcusable. Jilian had arrived back in Victoria safely, Amma told me, and now wanted to live with me in Wpg. Got to my apartment needing to phone Melora and Jilian promptly. Elise was in my home, and, unobservant of my listening ability – always – promptly told me about a dream she had, a twenty-minute description in Teflon prose and no punctuation. Doesn't anyone realize dreams have to be recounted like news stories, complete with headlines? Elise sulked when I told her I had work to do

that night, work that would mean my economic salvation. Shamelessly she begged for twenty minutes of conversation. I countered (why was I countering anything?) with the point that the video had to be dealt with promptly, and that I had been very worried about Jil, with whom I hadn't spoken in weeks; she'd been in Mexico sending me troubled dreams. Caving in from exhaustion, I watched, with pleasure as always, some video with Elise, Betty Boop stuff. Jil, it turns out, had 'the time of her life' in Mexico – a mansion, two hundred margaritas, scuba diving. Elise spends the night. Jil leaves an excited message about getting a job with her first application. She also found her very first apartment with Elissa: quite a happy day! I wish I could save her message on a cassette somehow. I must work on this technology! She was so happy! Not coming to live with me, but so happy I had to be happy. Her coming here always seemed like confused reportage by Amma.

17 April

I forgot to phone Frank Gorshin at his home when *Twilight of the Ice Nymphs* played NY. Now I'm sure he's hurt and angry. I would never have guessed, back in 1966, thirty-two years ago, when I first saw that amazing, wild, perfect Riddler on TV's *Batman*, that someday he would be pissed off at me. Or sulking or hurt in a way more typical of vintage Herdis than Riddler. What a sweet old crust he is! What a little fuck-up I am.

23 April

This journal has devolved from its original purpose as a bound collection of 'miniatures' to a log book of flatulent boasts. Just as a tonier moral order shall soon rule my life, so, soon, shall this book be as toney. But for the record, Mundwiler punched in on Tuesday night for some spirited visiting, followed by an unshared viewing of *Gun Crazy* – not much comfort there, I'm afraid. But Carla's fun, and she sent me, via the waitress, a lipstick kiss upon a napkin at Bar Italia in front of George. George and I spoke of attitudinal approach to First Nations warriors in *Edison and Neemo*. I want Harmony Korine to play Neemo.

24 April

They buried Dr. Snidal (Dear Dr.) today, a service at the university hospital, in the same theatre where he debuted as the Dead Father. The Snidals are a giant family; they have epic sprawl in my mythology. The Orris family too. (I dreamt last night of an overly tall Lloyd Orris.) There are other important families – the Handfords, the Isaacs – but this dead and perpetually dying patriarch Dr. Snidal is big in every way, a 6' 7" tall mantis, a part-time martinet with a booming laugh sent out in a constant broadcast across Lake Winnipeg. *His* chair in the porch. *His* approval the only one sought during croquet. Let's, without the arrogance of self-reflex, raise our yogourt spoons in readiness for the tasty delectation of our future memories. Bring the Dr. and bring him on again. The songs of Dr. will be sung as long as I can sing, and a lot longer if I can help it. Bzzz bzzz bzzzz. System!!! Flip it!! Flip the system! Crap!!! The Super bee!!! Onions and telephone both thrown in the swamp. Volleyball. Football. The Wolverine Eddie Chudd. The unlocked back door. The MD plates. NIAGARA. Bobby, Peggy. SAM. (Mmm, another purring purring digression!) To Dr. To Dr. To Dr. I love you. I'll be seeing you! Of course, I didn't even go to his funeral.

Started swimming a few days ago. Tues, Thurs and today, Friday – for just twenty minutes each time, and rode my bike to the pool today. (My six-month pass expired on April 22; I shall get another today.) Man, am I tired. I have much to regain in conditioning, and no cute Sarah as a vague fitness target. Not really anyway. I can't go to the Underground for soup and a bagel every day for a second consecutive summer. When did I sign up for this foreign legion of forty-somethings who travel the world with paperbacks and sit in cafes where cute barristas work? Pathetic muteness! But better to be mute! Sometimes I look up and see nothing but colleagues, men my age, all arrayed with novels and notepads around the central view. Sometimes we log long fruitless hours in trial-and-error attempts to fathom the work schedules of the loveliest. Shouldn't these schedules just be posted on the Internet? It would save everyone a lot of time. I'm sorry!! But can I stay away?

14 May

Steve asks me to write about an early crush. So, her name was Wendy Crewson, and she appeared at the Gimli Yacht Club in 1971 when she and I were fifteen. She was very nubile and flirty, with a wide face and bass-like lips, and eyes on either side of her head. The prettiest fish-faced girl in the world, and two virgins, Jamie Handford and I, fell madly in love with her. Paul Searle, who liked his position as the only sexual male in our group, dismissed Wendy and our madness for her, dismissed her as a fish-face – which she was and which was precisely the essence of her perfection. When she made eye contact with me, rolling either one eye or the other in my direction from a profiled side of her almost gilled head, my ears issued a shrill scream. Jamie's usual Tourettey *eeps* and *urps* disintegrated into stuttery fragments of themselves. She had little leather anklets which broke my heart. Jamie and I logged twenty-hour vigils at the Yacht Club waiting for her to show. One night, all of us kneeling in Snidal's veranda for a tumescent game of 'Swear Dare Double Dare Promise or Forget,' Wendy kissed Jamie on a dare. In that great polarization of ardour that happens when circuits break, I felt my immense loves for Jamie and Wendy trade places. Then trade back, then spin wildly like a hotly oiled electric motor, until I found myself coiled in their love for each other, and being completely left out of this science experiment, with nowhere to spend this love. Which promptly blew out a painful hole in my chest. Jamie meanwhile spun out of control, eyes rolling in his face; one felt the back of his head unscrew and fall off like a hubcap. Words sang out of a suddenly loquacious mouth. He was reliving the death of his little brother, right there in the veranda. Jamie dragged out little Brucie's tricycle, crumpled it beneath a red pickup truck, spread Brucie like tubes of oil paint down the Academy Road which lay at our feet, scattered his brother's brains and bones and blood in a wet and incredible horror show conducted amid teenagers silent save for the sound of breasts and zits growing. Wendy wept maternally and buried her face into the neck of Jamie's now-rigid, totemic body. His story flowed out like blood. His parents materialized in the wreckage, grieving, hating and vengeful. All the component parts of his memory lay before the voodoo raconteur, never to be put back properly again. Jamie had won the day. But it came at perhaps too great a cost. He could never be repaired from that day, and Wendy left forever that night, to the city, then to another city, then just gone. I was left to pick up the pieces of my best friend, dump them back into his head any old way. We lay about in great trembling sighs for the rest of the summer. Twenty-six years later, Wendy showed up acting opposite Harrison Ford in *Air Force One*, playing the American First Lady.

16 May

The end of the riotous week of lilacs in Winnipeg. The air is thick with their almost rotten-sweet drunkenness (metaphors be mixed!). I'm at Bar-I. Having left a warm but impotent message for Gariné about her wonders, I strolled through the fermenting floral corridor of McMillan, past Steve's, where I saw the furry white sphere of Carli the Cat, sitting at her tree-branch window flap. I called her, and with a cat-jolt of recognition she came to me, and I dared my former pet with only my pointing finger lest I rouse a lot of loose hair from the affectionate but stupid animal. Then I turned suddenly away, not even saying goodbye because Carli would perceive a farewell as a summons and follow me. I turned to look and her attention had already wandered inward; she had the same aspect as Mike Gottli does now after his accident, perhaps thinking of much, or perhaps steeped in a sweet amnesia.

20 May

Noam just phoned to say his long-standing crush on Jonah may be over; he's spent a lot of time with the brilliant twenty-one-year-old, receiving glimpses and flashes of the little space above his lower back where, apparently, much hair grows. Not very ephebe is the concern.

On Saturday I got a boner while talking film theory with Steve Burke; this because, during the discussion, Carla disrobed Fleur on my living room floor and started necking with her. Much Jack Daniels splashing in the corner of the room. When invited to join the hardwood fray, I stoically demur, but the four of us promise to follow up with a 'Fish and Kiss' dinner and dance with Jackie Gleason later in the week. Steve assured me that in polite society boners are permissible when conversing with a pal if two naked girls are necking in proximity.

22 May

I've been having monumental problems with laziness lately. I've taken at least a month off now since my second-term work binge; I've read virtually nothing, ignored my daybook, rarely daydreamt of my film projects. I find myself unable to execute phone calls that a child could make; perhaps I should get a child to do some of the stuff that's backlogged on me. Things to do today: Fax Cinema Nova in Brussels with a paean to occasion its death; fax Gariné; phone John Powers; score a Caelum *Black as Death* ticket for Carl; change my plane ticket for Gariné/Hamilton visit; work out at two p.m.; buy some clothes for UK or at least scrape mud from shoes. I feel like going to bed, and it's only 9:30 a.m. At this point I feel like all the women in my life are a waste of time: Carla, Elise and Gariné are dead ends. Even sweet poetry-spouting Teva is ultimately impossible to find a place for, unless I want to stay in touch with the younger generation. Warren Beatty with Sinbad on *Vibe* discussing his favourite rap artists, legitimizing them as the new sixties Russian protest poets. Never has anyone been so white and wrinkly before, never has Beatty been less charming. And Sinbad went down too; never has he sounded more empty and stupid. When will my eighties end? I feel cemented into them like river shoes.

25 May

On Air Canada to Montreal, then on to London, where I shall hide from people, buy new shoes, browse for books and, perhaps, swim every day (?). The plane gave me a peek of a spectacular forest fire north of Thunder Bay before steering directly over the source of megatons of smoke, leaving us all craning our necks to see underneath the plane.

Steve Snyder brought his bike to the Pan Am Pool yesterday. (I've been doing twenty minutes of weights and twenty minutes of swimming every day for the last two weeks, eating wisely and cycling a bit as well in a last-ditch attempt to be fit just once in my life. I want results by summer's end.) Defying the saw, Steve has actually forgotten how to ride his bicycle. He's always between gears, pedalling in thin air, with a very loose seat/suppository swivelling its way up his ass. His bike riding was so frail, and so slow, I could barely travel as slowly as he and still keep upright on my own bike. Still he fell behind my meandering wobbles by a hundred yards again and again, continually making curious traffic decisions. I think a joint bike ride always occasions philosophy clashes – and bitter arguments. Nemesis George marvels that after fifteen years of weight lifting and a year of swimming, Steve still manages to find muscles that he's never used, and is therefore incapable of using them. I guess I prefer chasing people rather than leading people to goals. I'm extremely competitive.

Went to Caelum's first feature on Friday. *Black as Death, Sweet as Love. Something as Something.* I'll learn the title eventually. Great look and atmosphere and some wonderful little scenes. A performance- and character-driven movie tastefully acted much of the time, with the egregiously bitchy Allery Lavitt surprisingly bland. Who would have guessed? A few scenes were willfully about nothing and could have been about a little more, and some of the comedy tried a little once the movie promised that it would not try at all. But very encouraging. Caelum has a sweet and gentle tone as unique as his own speaking voice. If only he can avoid the anomie of all Winnipeg artists.

Mailed Gariné a little present via two-day Express Post: a tape of *Slow-Assed Dirges II* and an ancient nun statuette which I quite love and which I hated to part with. Investing precious gifts in cul-de-sac relationships is an unwise but common occurrence in my personal history.

I am really looking forward to this trip to London all of a sudden. It reminds me of my trip to NY in '81. It's virtually pointless. Just a treat. And I shall get shoes. In '81 I had white beaded penny loafers three sizes too small from Greenwich Village – very faggy! I'm just going to walk the streets of a hubbubbling city absorbing the zeitgeist. I shall shop for paperbacks as I did at Gotham Books in '81 (you still find NYC '81 inscribed in many of my favourite reads), and perhaps I'll go see a show, just as I told myself I saw Killing Joke in New York. I will go see *Lolita* for some reason; this will not match my Paris viewing of the restored *Vertigo*. The old trip and this new one are on either sides of a big summer, and I'm spending my last dime to go. One more trip I hope to make soon: a frequent-flyer trip to Victoria to visit Jilian. Away from all the women, and very, very (in a cowardly way) HAPPY!!!

Where do I like to shop? Where have my favourite places been? I started my first love affair with a store in 1962, a hobby store in Polo Park where Aurora Monster models were sold. Ross bought me a *Creature from the Black Lagoon* from there. The model-kit boxes were stacked up high, with a tiny version of the lid illustration visible on the box ends. That was the first model. I think Ross probably made it for me. As he did the second one, the Mummy. The Werewolf was probably the third. Then I was making them on my own. Any place that carried these were CHARGED with (what I didn't know was UNIVERSAL) power. Gooch's on Sherbrooke. Rudy's on Ellice and Sherbrooke. Eaton's Annex downtown. I bought models of Frankenstein (First Prize Novelty Division at the Bay's Paddlewheel model-making contest, Dracula, Bride of Frankenstein, The Invisible Man, Hunchback of Notre Dame, King Kong (spent my one and only allowance on this before my mother cancelled the planned $5-a-week stipend in anger over my inability to save the first fin for more than five minutes. All other models were purchased with $$ filched from the change dish in the kitchen; I must have had a collection worth a suspicious $100 or so – a lot for a kid with no apparent income), The Guillotine (which worked), Godzilla, an oversized Frankenstein Monster (which Father Bauer pretended to be scared of when he slept in my bedroom), and, finally, just before the Age of Crispy, in one of my last model-making euphorias, the Saturn V Rocket with command and lunar modules, and, I believe, the second and third stages.

But I speak of places to shop, and there was one hobby shop on Portage and Langside that I could walk to barefoot and there purchase endless cheap but large plastic figurines of aliens and soldiers which made my head swim with their orangeness and greenness or newness or rubberyness. All these stores practiced a segregation away from the model cars, ships and airplanes, and put into a separate aisle-ghetto of their own all the monster or novelty models that I preferred. This kept me away from all the dour builders of serious things, kids with patience for rigging, sails, balsa wood and kite string. Merk's Drug Store at Banning and Ellice supplied *Famous Monsters of Filmland*, *Creepy* and *Eerie* magazines. During the Age of Crispy I shopped at Muir's for the *Sporting News*; at Baldy Northcott's for coloured baseball gloves and bats, and the Bay, where I knew Cam had bought his gun – perhaps even from Ed Ulmer, the Bomber punter who worked in sporting goods. In the eighties I bought records and books. Records on Wheels on North Portage for many imports, but mostly at Roman Panchychsyn's Impulse Records on Lilac. I had been buying my Lou Reed and Mott the Hoople records at Autumn Stone and some other big store on Kennedy north of Portage in the seventies. Also in the seventies was Stereo Swap Shop on Gertrude and Osborne – the closest this shy boy ever got to trendy Osborne Village during those scary years.

When I started buying books in the eighties, Mary Scorer on Osborne was the best, but I purchased many pocket books at the Polo Park Children's Hospital Book Mart – bags and bags at a time, from 10¢ to 65¢ max. Even though I worked at a Le Chateau in 1982, I think I was still too scared to go clothes shopping in one. I liked the U of M bookstores and U of W's made me pleasantly indignant during coffee-break jaunts from my WCPI archives job, so poor was its selection. A bookstore for an entire campus in a room the size of a kitchen. It still exists this way. Pathetic. Wonderful. I liked shopping at the Book and Record Place on Albert, but the proprietor, an old chain-smoking and hacking Lionel Barrymore type, never priced anything and so I never bought. I bought most of the George Ade I love so dearly, and all the S. Sitwell, at High Brow Books, first on St. Mary's then on Notre Dame, run by a blobby chess nut named Les Mundwiler (or Big Mouth in German), father of my Carla.

Now, in 1998, I shop for books mostly at the Grant Park McNally Robinson mega-store and Café au Livre. Elise even worked there. I found a great second-hand bookstore in Milwaukee. In Toronto I still go to HMV, Sam's and Tower for videos and CDs, but with decreasing enthusiasm. The World's Biggest Bookstore on Edward Street once thrilled me with its volume and now bores me. When I lived in the Annex in Toronto I must have gone every day to Book City on Bloor West – a boring store – and another on Bathurst near Dupont that specialized in Pre-Raphaelite lit (!) – I bought *Under the Hill* there! For 78s, Minneapolis was the source of all my trouble. Lee's and some other place, the only exclusively 78 rpm store in N. America, got a lot of my money. Bought a couple of gramophones there, too. I browsed once for an hour in this forgotten Twin Cities store while Catherine Stenger recovered from one of Steve's 'holistic stretches,' or pile-drivers, in a nearby park in 1988. Broadway Books, near the Club Morocco, produced a few prized purchases. I must have browsed past something called *The Triumph of Death* by Gabriele D'Annunzio for seven years at Red River Book Store, before finally buying it, being smote by it, then finally buying everything by this wonderful life-and-ethos changing author. I bought some Robert Walser short stories in Reykjavik. Now, I don't even like to shop.

30 May
Met the Quays and their mechanic Ian at Gordon's Wine Bar up from Embankment in Soho. Great bar. They spring for wine, quite a bit, and I dumped £15 on cheese and paté. Then Stephen went to Fist in Pockets, Ian went to his cottage, and Timothy took me to his club. Then, on to Laura DeCasta's Soho Club (where in February I dropped hundreds of dollars and just fucked myself over with gallons of wine. Much dignity

squandered.) Last night, I just left my MasterCard behind the bar – the waitress would not give it back – as I lowered brain and body into alcohol and red ink, ending by fiddling away under the table again. A pretty girl offered to leave with me on a sobering stroll for coffee, but she ditched me or died in the loo and I set off alone, totally forgetting my credit card, which kept on buying rounds without me, until I was miles away – and drunker than ever. I bought a hot dog and a kilogram of cookies, which I tossed all over the streets one by one, motivated by the frustration of loneliness and an irrational need to see how far and in how many different directions I could throw cookies. When I stepped stupidly right into the path of a throttling double-decker bus, seeing red two-storeyed God for a half a second, I jumped back out of the way, took a deep breath with a leery smile and threw away the rest of the cookies as a tribute to my luck. I walked and walked without knowing where I was, and for the first time in my life, found myself phoning up hookers – their numbers being posted in all the payphones on the way home, or wherever I was going. It seems even the hookers go to bed early, or one needs to know a special phoning code, or they were all working. But I was spared an unnecessary and lurid episode and passed out quite deeply in my eventually found room just as the dumb London birds started chirping – five a.m. – my sleep haunted by my lost credit card. Somebody give this guy a large film grant.

I did meet the editor of *Sight and Sound*, nice guy, and Mika Kaurismaki's producer, who's also worked with Michael Winterbottom. Oh my God, *Reap the Wild Wind* is on TV, with C.B.'s fantastic introduction!! I'm very hungover and must fetch my card, my laundry and my composure in the next five hours before my talk tonight at the Lux.

24 June

Steve says I should write something about family dinners. Too big a subject, but a couple of aspects are easily noted. Did I mention my mother's pride in the symmetry of the dinner table? Chas sat antsily at the head with a couple of overcooked medallions of beef – the only food he would eat. Opposite, at the other end, sat eldest son and most gifted progeny Ross. On either side of Ross and Chas were two: Janet and Herdis, Cameron and Guy. The perfectly symmetrical table easy for a child to set and a glory to a mother's eye. When Cameron excused himself from all earthly dinner tables, the cavity left in the family was most apparent at suppertime. We ate with a great deal of imbalance; the table feeling too weighted to one side, tippy as a canoe. Unwittingly conducting ourselves in a painful parody of a religious dinner, with its empty expectant chair, we forgot to leave a door ajar to allow the ghost to sup with us. Only by hauling Aunt Lil, but not Gramma, from downstairs were we able to go back to a full table. But this left our most aged matriarch below, to grope blindly with her pioneer fare all by herself. And she had a habit of singing of her loneliness in epic sagas, which spiralled up the heating vent straight into our dining area. Eventually, our family chose to eat at staggered times, and never together, and in this way an unstable compound was broken into stable elements. Each eating from a casserole dish, but one at a time, in a dinner spread out over hours, my impatient father washing the dishes after each of us left a plate on the table. Five different sinkfuls of soapy water, and a higher increment of blood pressure for each staggered place setting soiled. Dad frothed and raged more than his sink bubbled and steamed. At least in this fashion, Lil and Gramma could join in the cafeteria-style procession of Icelanders that ate in quiet privacy, confusion and hostility each night.

Jilian should receive a little gift tomorrow: H. Bosch paperback, Billie Holiday cassette, Loud and Gloomy Mittle Europeans cassette (Korngold, Mahler, Sibelius, Strauss). I'm making her Bernard Hermann tapes as I write this.

Sammy went two games and nine ABs against Cleveland without a HR, then promptly hit #31 against Detroit. (22 in 25 games.) He ties Rudy York for most HRs in any month with 18. (Det. Aug. '37).

Dave Van Horne is in his thirtieth season as an Expos announcer. He's always looked fifty-five years old. Did he really start at age twenty-six? Is he eighty-five years old now? What's going on?

Mark McGwire hit #34 tonight. Ricky Henderson, who turns forty later this year, leads the majors with thirty steals. Randy Myers, a terrible pitcher, just got his league-leading twenty-first save – his ERA well-above 4.0. Correction: Troy Percival has twenty-three saves.

George and I are going to do a 'ruthless pass' through Draft #1 of his *Edison and Neemo* on Friday, something we should have done ten months ago, except George firmly feels his script is completely finished. He warned me tonight, when I told him I'd like to shorten the script by ten minutes (it's running at just under two hours), that this would be very difficult. If only George could be as ruthless with his own stuff as he is with all the films he watches so critically. He becomes testy on the subject of this script, and I have to keep reminding myself what a dear friend he is. But he also feels *Twilight of the Ice Nymphs* was a perfect script and that I cut too much out of that. It may well have been near perfect, but it was beyond my abilities to get its potential out of it. And I'm not interested in tackling something beyond my abilities or I will have my second straight unqualified failure. And I'll be the unemployed and unemployable one. I think I'm driving him crazy with my constant insensitive remarks about *Ice Nymphs*, about which he is very proud. I keep forgetting that when I insult my own work I'm insulting him as well.

28 June

I think I had the Westinghouse Playhouse 90 Extravaganza Dead Father Dream 21st Anniversary Special last night. Everything was reduced to Japanese simplicity. Chas had not died. Chas had expressed his ultimate disgust with us by going to live with another family. I knew he was gravely ill or maybe even dead by now – I had not seen him for some time. I needed to see him desperately, at least once before he died, to nurse him back to health, to prove to him my worth, to convince him to stay with us for the little time he had left, to express to him my love. (Chas is a fifties TV father gone missing. A future obituary photo printing itself in the air.) I summarized all these feelings simply and with circuit-breaking passion: 'Alright! Enough! Twenty-one years of this is enough! Where is my father? Let's get him back here. Just let me know where he is so I can start working on his tortured breast, so I can divert whatever love he has for others back into our home. If he has already died with his love misdirected I won't bear it for a second!' By this time, I'm wailing inwardly, with absolute impotence. Tears are filling my skull to bursting, there are so many tears in my head the plates in my head bone are trembling – a teardrop away from exploding with grief. Dad, all alone in the spotlight, within a shroud of cigarette smoke, turns his face away in boredom. Playhouse 90 was used up entirely by my sob-wracked voice-over, leaving no room for Ernie Kovacs, Imogene Coca, William Bendix, Judy Garland, Steve Allen or Oscar Levant. All of these left in the green room while a detached B&W head of Chas floated ghostily in front of dark Kinescope curtains. Strike up Jack Parr's band, let Walter Winchell name the guest stars for next show while the end credits run. Let them run forever on the show that never ends.

JOURNALISM

DEATH IN WINNIPEG

errill and Wayne Osmond slump down depressed in their red-sequin-appliqué jumbo-spandex lobster suits while buoyant brother Donny touches his toes for no other reason than to thrust out the saddle-cut rear of his gaudy pantaloons, and in so doing, inflames an already sorry sibling situation. More later.

Winnipeg, November 2000. All is enveloped in a sad atmosphere. My city is plunged in the perpetual night of its notorious winter, lugubriously ice-encrusted, bedecked with crystalline stalactites and crosscut by great white ways of snow banks, all arrayed behind an intricate scrimshaw of frost. The city is a bleak and wind-buffeted Luna Park carved from a glacier – an Expo of melancholy. Here, we throng no midways, cavort in no pavilions. Winter pedestrians are less common than wild dogs.

Winnipeg is a Siberia, a skagway, a vast plain of ice. Its only hill is a mountain of garbage – fifty years' worth of civilian refuse – which in the winter children use for toboggan sliding. But sledding can be dangerous, for from this hill the permafrost pushes up odd items buried by our ancestors; I was once impaled there by the very same stag antlers my father had thrown out two decades earlier.

It is onto this drear landscape that ABC has descended to shoot *Inside the Osmonds*, its sweeps-week biopic (airing February 5), which follows the soaring and crashing fortunes of America's favorite Christian rockers from 1970, the moment they cut the Andy Williams umbilical cord and went on to record twenty-three gold records, through to the early 1980s, when the family was pushed to the verge of bankruptcy beneath a darkling cloud of suspected unhipness.

Why come to such an Arctic outpost to shoot a script set almost entirely in California? Probably has something to do with the tax credits we Canadians use to steal film work from Americans. But also, I'm told, because of the near-Branson-like proliferation of theaters here in Winnipeg, many of them deserted and available as dirt-cheap locations. Or perhaps because we have living here the 'secret shag man,' who has been hoarding rug for half a lifetime and could carpet all the high-ways in Canada with that deep-piled floor covering needed in daunting profusion by the Osmonds' art department.

Whatever the reason, I'm thrilled ABC is here. As a filmmaker myself, I have my own mission of mischief. Having been given permission to hang around the set by Richard Fischoff, one of the show's preternaturally gracious producers, I intend to conceal a Super-8 camera on my person and shoot my own subversive version of the script. While ABC's camera rolls, so will mine. Simple. I get a $200 version of a five-million-dollar movie. My secret filmography is bulging with projects exactly like this.

I'm also thrilled most of the shooting will be done within five blocks of my home, meaning I can still have lunch with Mother every day.

On the first day of shooting, I visit Winnipeg's International Inn, which is today doubling as a Las Vegas nightclub where the legendary Osmond prodigies hone their act for a smattering of bored drunks. As I stretch in indolent repose at one side of the set munching a strawberry, I notice how remarkably the actors resemble the Osmond Brothers as I remember them. Being the same age as Donny, I remember them well, especially those fluorescent Chiclet teeth all loaded with Osmond DNA.

The fine young artificial brothers, looking warm and cozy beneath period-perfect wigs, are power-chording unplugged guitars and lip-synching to 'Crazy Horses,' one of the Osmonds' zestiest sorties into Mormon rock. These early-seventies proto-mullets are so natural I'm no longer self-conscious about my own new toupee, which I'm debuting on this occasion. Clad in buttery-soft, fringed white kid leather with matching macramé belts and white platform boots, the five counterfeit siblings retrace to perfection the famously wild and white choreography unleashed on a semiotics-ignorant public almost thirty years ago. These osmonoid performers are really caught up in the song's feral rhythms, rudely beating on brazen vessels, bellowing like stags, and harmonizing like horny barbers: 'What a show, there they go, smokin' up the sky-y-y-y-y – yeah!!! Crazy horses, all got riders, and they're you and I-I-I-I-I-I – I!!!' When the number is over, I forget myself and – this is inexcusable for a supposed filmmaker – applaud wildly, actually ruining the take, because the cameras are still running, and the sparse audience in the scene is supposed to be apathetic. Sheepishly, I promise to stopper my fervour. Fortunately, the next take is the keeper.

I'm astonished to find myself a fan of this music. I decide that this song wasn't ready back in 1973, but it's exactly the right vintage now!

After this scene I'm feeling not quite canny – perhaps a winter flu is coming on – so I wend my way to the washroom to shiver awhile astride a urinal in hope of restoring my comfort and vigour. Suddenly, a beaded leather bullwhip lashes my backside and wraps itself around my midriff. No, it's not a whip after all, but just the long leather bugle-beaded fringe from the vest of one of the young Osmond clones – Donny, it turns out – who has run in with fringes flying and now stands beside me, racked with shivers of his own.

I've never been struck so suddenly by an actor's appearance before. I can't help noticing the baby cloudlets that hang illumined in his eyes. His facial tint is ivory white against the ebon darkness of his clustering locks. He is a masterpiece from nature's own hand. Not yet thirteen years old! His name is Thomas Dekker. What parts he could play for me! (And I don't even know what he looks like without his wig!)

At lunchtime I can feel my cold coming on for sure and, not wanting to infect Mother, I stay at the location and show Thomas my camera – just the Super-8 – and assure him I use real 35mm ones for my official movies. Thomas is from LA and ripe and ready for a career. His credits include leads in *Village of the Damned* and *Star Trek: Generations*, series regular on *Honey, I Shrunk the Kids* and the voice of Fievel in *An American Tail III* and *IV*. Thomas is very clever, too. By the end of lunch he's pitched an intriguing script idea to me – the story of an underground therapist who cures an elderly man of his decaying memory by transplanting into his head the fresh brains of kidnapped children.

Over the next few days, I'm happy to fall into the pleasing monotony of the set, to bask in the mild soft tungsten glow while Thomas works himself hard. 'One Bad Apple.' 'Goin' Home.' This little would-be Donny and the other mock Osmonds must mime out at least eighteen songs in the picture, a fact which keeps workday O-pee-chee sweet in spite of the very long hours.

I've made it about halfway through the shoot and I keep forgetting to use my Super-8. Oh well. Today Thomas must practice his choreography for 'Yo-Yo,' his favourite Osmond song. 'Yo-Yo' is pop music perfected, with a lyric that gathers up the threads of many human destinies in the warp of a single idea. When Thomas sings it, the words actually seem to rise from his mouth and burst like bubbles.

There are so many great people working on this movie! I get a chance to speak with Veronica Cartwright, who plays Olive Osmond, mother of the famous brood. Veronica was also going on thirteen when she was acting in *The Birds*. She says Hitchcock even brought a cake on set the day of her birthday. I also chat up Bruce McGill, the man playing clan patriarch George Osmond. Fresh from his stints in *The Insider* and *Bagger Vance*, McGill agrees with me that Thomas has a great future. *The Osmond Story* is very melodramatic. I like it when George Osmond, the father of some seven superstars, makes his son Merrill (Ryan Kirkpatrick) relinquish his theme colour (purple) to Donny. Merrill is stuck with wearing black for the rest of his career.

Few people today realize how carefully the Osmonds dressed. Not only did Pa George assign each a distinct colour – red, blue, yellow, green – but to each son also prescribed a unique talismanic belt buckle. Jimmy kept his pants up with a brass monkey; Wayne used a little steel airplane; Alan, an eagle. As Donny, Thomas gets to wear a special heart-shaped buckle – strange coincidence, since I too wear one of these. In fact, he wears the same metal valentine I got on a belt from Mother many birthdays ago! No matter where we first meet, Thomas and I start each morning by aiming our teeny 'hearts' at each other – a private ritual that gladdens the hour of ungodly call-times.

Never have I been on such a happy set as this. I haven't heard a single complaint from cast or crew in the two weeks I've been here. This afternoon, during 'Sweet and Innocent,' the camera tracks between the legs of all the brothers, through a colour-coded corridor of human thighs, until it halts in razor-sharp focus upon the craziest little horse of them all – purple Donny, who kicks up his heels and sends many a loose sequin through the rent air! At home in the wee a.m. I fracture Mother's fragile drowse with a sneezing fit brought on by inhaled sequins. Even my insomnias are dazzling these days!

A peculiar revelation today. The part of Donny is played by not one but two actors; not just Thomas, who plays Donny up to the time of 'Puppy Love,' but also by a perfectly nice boy named Patrick Levis, who plays Donny from age fourteen on.

Thomas seems not the least bothered by this switcheroo. I guess he's known about the other Donny all along. Still, I keep an eye on him to make sure he's all right, to spot upon his good-natured face the first indication of this secret injury to his spirit. At lunch my vigilance pays off. One minute Thomas and I are happily double-dipping figs in our hummus, the next he suddenly excuses himself to pretend he's fetching his Discman from his trailer. Dissembled in that winning smile he has parlayed into so many roles, Thomas dons a huge parka and plunges into the brutal night winds. Greatly concerned for my charge, I dash out after the boy, catch him in midstride, and, with both our coiffures flapping, I demand that he confess his grief at having his part cut in two. But, strangely, at this moment grief comes to me instead. Tightly wound up with overprotectiveness, I'm surprised to find tears springing to my eyes – tears that roll down my cheeks in the raging wind as I hug Thomas consolingly. Wigward the saltwater falls, down into the blast-beruffled plume.

Shooting will be finished soon and all the actors will be going back to their distant homes. Tomorrow is the last and biggest day. The sham Osmonds get to meet the real Osmonds, onstage at Winnipeg's Walker Theatre, in the picture's climactic scene. If I know anything about movies, I know Thomas belongs in this scene, but the director has put the older Donny in instead. To Thomas's credit, he gives not the slightest indication of disappointment, but I know he must be devastated. Ever the pro, Thomas intends to show up tomorrow and watch this final scene anyway.

To cheer him up, I ask Thomas if I may sit with him. As with all young actors, his sensitive instrument must be carefully guarded from clumsy outsiders. As a director always happy to discuss the craft of acting, I can use my profession as a pretext to ride shotgun next to little Thomas without his suspecting I sit there as a concerned friend, as one who would fall on grenades for him. In whatever emotional chaos that transpires, I can offer invaluable comforts to a troubled breast. Tomorrow!

O-Day at the Walker Theatre. I'm not even the director and I'm dizzy with fear. Since late last night, real Osmonds have been flying in from all parts of Utah, one by one: Virl, Merrill, Wayne, Jay, et al. – the first Osmond reunion in seventeen years! The Winnipeg that awaits them this morning is locked in a cruel dome of permafrost – forty degrees below, and twice as cold with windchill! We Winnipeggers pride ourselves on moments like this. Compulsively, we muse about the impact our perfrigid town will have on the unsuspecting who visit us. How will the newly arrived celebrities cope with being here? Will they be frightened when their nose hairs are twisted out by the invisible pincers that stab into one's nostrils at temperatures this low? What will Donny make of that first biting mouthful of air outside the airport when the cold rips into his lungs like a swallowed scissor? Will he wonder why his eyelids have frozen shut as he gropes toward his limo? And what will happen to the real parents, George and Olive, now elderly? Will the cold simply kill them? Will they be borne home in coffins, in the chilled cargo hold of the same plane that brought them here as warm and loving parents? Marie, the most reluctant to confirm her appearance in the picture, and her famously deaf missionary brother Tom are the last to touch down on our airport's frost-heaved runway. Will the real Marie regret most of all her decision to come all this way to face the real Donny, with whom she is rumoured to be fighting?

Since six this morning, the theatre has been packed with hundreds of extras, fifteen-year-old girls garbed in the frayed flares and ill-fitting miniskirts that were so specifically 1973. All their hair is as straight as Marcia Brady's, or as feral as Chaka Khan's. All their shirts are plaid or denim or both. All corduroys are narrow wale. Eyebrows are plucked and repencilled in thin and arching cursives. The cumulative effect is eerie. It's a velour goldmine! It *is* 1973!

The seaside sounds that rise from chattering hordes of girls haven't changed since my youth. Suddenly, a redolent simoom of *adolescent girl* wafts up and over me. I suffer a brief flashback: as a well-groomed and courteous high-schooler I was completely invisible to all these cool prom-night smoochers; now, in a queer form of time travel, I'm re-experiencing this invisibility, but as a very confident adult in a Prada overcoat. This time, I'm just as glad to be a nonentity to these girls, these girls who look just a little bit raunchy with their chubby legs squeezed into rank white pantyhose and Naugahyde hot pants ready to burst! I'm pleased as a seal to sit out of camera's range with a solicitous eyebrow cocked toward uncynical Thomas.

Now, I hear a rumour: all Osmonds, as resourceful in middle age as they were precocious in youth, have arrived safely at our location. No frostbite, no gangrene. I'm told they're tucked warmly away backstage.

Never have I felt so much excitement on a set in Winnipeg. My head burns, and little crisping shivers run across my clammy skin. We all know this last shot is the money one. The blocking is actually to be very simple: the fake Osmonds will stand six abreast upon the stage, mouthing out 'He Ain't Heavy, He's My Brother.' Halfway through the song, the real Osmonds will stride onstage to replace their doppelgängers and finish the number. Three cameras will cover them with every possible lens length. Then, in a matter of minutes (if they get it in one take), all bona fide Osmonds will be picture-wrapped and freed to bomb outta here, straight back to temperate Utah. The end. I'll take Thomas out for fries and a shake – our own little wrap party – and we'll put our heads together over how we're going to shoot his script.

Now the houselights go down and the First A.D. gets all the cameras rolling. I let Thomas hold my Super-8, tell him to go ahead and squeeze off a few shots.

Action! The extras start their teenybopper shrieking as directed. The imitation Osmonds go into their imitation singing. Suddenly, the lights go on behind a scrim at the rear of the stage to reveal a phalanx of grey-haired old men – it's the real Osmonds! Alan, Merrill, Wayne, Jay. Not-so-old Jimmy and Marie are there as well. The scrim rises, the fake Osmonds discreetly disperse, and these genuine articles make toward their rightful place at the front of the stage, goldfishing all the while to their own thirty-year-old recording.

At this awful moment, some sadistic god swings a huge wrecking ball at me from behind that scrim. That we all must age I've always suspected, but never has this fact been taught more dreadfully. So quickly did time hiccup ahead thirty years and thrust at me these actual Osmonds – Osmonds left bent and trembling by decades of mixed fortunes. Thin-thatched and achy, they brandish their white and wizened faces like so many death masks, their old Osmond grins the only things unchanged from moments before. Survivors of heart disease, brain tumour, multiple sclerosis, wrecked marriage and tithings – the terrors of the manifold earth – these Osmonds no longer dance, but hobble, creak and drag themselves forward. They are unstoppable, like a tsunami of Time growing in fearsome height as they approach me.

Worst of all, these harmonists of the apocalypse are suffused with an intense love of performing – so clearly are they enjoying themselves in spite of their sudden aging – and an awesome love of each other, love for the skeletal ghost members of their cherished family, and a still unalloyed love for the old music which they joyously feign to perform. Somehow, it is all this enduring Osmond love that foreshortens my own life, frightfully so.

Unable to brake their momentum, the teenaged girls continue to shriek lustily at their suddenly aged idols, dizzy old semitransparent men who confusedly look about to find themselves reunited in Winnipeg, the last outpost. I stand gaping at my kindred spirits, the old, the infirm. I hear only the polar wind whistling outside. It whispers a death sentence in my ear. It sounds like 'Puppy Love.'

In the aftermath of this one shot, Osmonds real and ersatz mingle about on the stage awhile, hugging, kissing, reminiscing. Elderly George and Olive totter out to be together with all their offspring at once, perhaps for the last time. I find myself studying the slow progress old George makes from son to son, stopping to pose for pictures, to extend a trembling and veiny hand to a young actor, before shuffling offstage where darkness and silence merge.

I'm left to ponder the inscrutable auguries of George's footsteps, and the cryptic meaning of petrified bubble gum strewn across the decades like bird entrails. I wonder what undignified choreographies my own footsteps will trace upon the years left to me.

In the sky above frozen Winnipeg, with gum stuck to their hooves, and lashed into frenzies by colourfully beaded whips, the crazy horses rumble out of town, carrying Thomas with them.

FACE VALUE: ON *MINORITY REPORT*

Just give me the legal dream team that pushed through all constitutional obstacles to install Pre-Crime, then get me the real John Ashcroft, and all together we just might be able to forestall the baseball strike that threatens this fall's World Series. Remembering that the tragic death of a child is the source of all motivation in the picture, I kept waiting for Spielberg to deliver closure with an emotional knockout punch – as he did in A.I.'s last act. Spielberg promised as much in interviews, but when the moment comes for hyper-seer Agatha to describe to grief-benumbed parents the supernatural filial love that lives on in their son radiantly after death, frisking somewhere in the unlived regions of the dead child's life, you know the director wants a powerhouse meltdown from Tom Cruise's anguished Anderton, and Vanilla Tom just doesn't come across.

Cruise has famously smothered all his demons with the help of Scientology, and the resultant control he projects makes implausible his sorties into areas where his characters lack control. There is never a gesture, a word, an involuntary action that might reveal his real face, the inner face that might reflect even dimly remembered terrors or humiliations from a less serene time. I look in vain at this face for evidence of a weakness, a decadence, a criminal subsoil, anything mysterious. Cruise's processed charm is so devoid of affecting connections that it's distancing. This is why tabloids pick on him as an implausible lover or husband. He's the stuff beards are made of. Remember, Cruise was closet-vintage Rosie O'Donnell's favourite dreamboat. This Teflon perfection is also why he's actually scintillant in, and the perfect correlative to, the *Mission: Impossible* stories, whose plots unscroll with the zeal of someone else's dogma – massively convoluted, but too tidy, and difficult to relate to. Drained of any lurking shadow, Tom's franchise face bathes in a lucrative nimbus of inner armistice that reflects nothing back but its own flawlessness. Correction: near flawlessness; at forty he's now wearing braces to fix up his twisted chicklets.

Think of real faces! Those of Peter Lorre, Steve Buscemi or William H. Macy, all capable of suffering intelligently. Of

Anthony Quinn – at any age! – capable of great suffering, unintelligently!! Richard Widmark or Rock Hudson!! I like to think of any of these people in the Anderton role, and especially Macy in that fabulous jet-pack chase scene Spielberg cooked up. And let's for a second consider that great mug belonging to the guy who gets frightened to death in the back alley in *Mulholland Drive*. The deep-dish face of this anonymous quaking actor conveys an oil tanker full of dread in every second of his brief appearance, as Cruise could never have done. May kindly God intervene – for this month only, just for a change – and slap this amiable chump onto the cover of every magazine in the world.

BULLY FOR BOLLYWOOD'S MUSICAL MELODRAMAS!

Western white folk are ashamed and disparaging of melodrama, superior to it. Here, soap operas are derided as simp fodder, watched guiltily, or worse, enjoyed ironically. We don't even know what melodrama is, other than it's an invasion on good taste, an easily detected enemy. We think we don't need a Senator McCarthy to rout it out, and we think we can expunge it ourselves, but I've got news for you. Melodrama is everywhere. And it's not ever going away.

In our lives, melodrama is hyperbolized, it's the narrative of our dreams with all the nocturnal terrors and desires given the respect they deserve. It's the chaos of the everyday ordered into an obedient cast of characters we can understand – that rival at the office is elevated into an amnesiac double-agent, a distrusted step-parent becomes a boy-ripper, the simplest insecurities are inflated into immense conspiracies or life-threatening predicaments. These magnifications happen in our nightmares and our movies again and again, not because of lapses in taste, but because they are the TRUTH. Melodrama makes our true feelings easier to recognize. Much like the philosophical dictum declaring that everything more or less tastes like chicken, all good stories contain at least traces of melodrama. It's the cow brains that make the hot dog taste good, and we're gobbling it down without even realizing it.

Somehow, Hollywood has always disguised its melodramatic structures behind what passes for 'realistic' speech patterns, trendy filmmaking tropes and an anal perfection of continuity. Now Bollywood singing and dancing has swum into our mainstream. And we love it! We LOVE it!! I certainly love it. These Indian musicals are positively tumescent with infectious alien conventions. The most oft-cited trait of Bollywood pictures is their 'over-the-top' plots – their melodrama! We love their melodrama! We're as delighted by it as visitors to the monkey-house are by the antics they see in the cage. We laugh at the ease with which characters slip into song, chuckle at the burst-dove passions that unite couples eternally and consign them to tragic ends. We note almost anthropologically how the actors aren't even allowed to kiss onscreen (my eyes melt at the wet sari shot), and spit up great whoops of glee at the characters' hysteria, jealous brooding and oaths of vengeance – gestures imported from a remote, perfumed land. I often feel a pleasurable frisson of colonial condescension bristling through the audience, and myself, during these frenetic three-hour family saga melees.

Bollywood film language evokes for us Westerners more innocent times – the days when our corny ancestors believed in such unrealistic stories, told with a charming technical naïveté. Oh, the zoom!! (Only Bollywood fully exploits the zoom shot to grab and isolate a suddenly wounded pair of eyes, an alert and devious ear or a grimace of grief!!) And the soundtrack never fails to underscore the biggest emotions with the biggest of musical surges!! The euphoria!! The smouldering!! The energy!! The villains!! The shameless exploitation of beauty!! We're even astounded into Margaret Meade-ish admiration of the dancing – dancing turned inside out, miraculously so!!

Admit it, the pleasure you feel watching these pictures is a vicarious one. Through these phantasmagorias we get to enjoy the enviable experience of Indians who regularly ingest melodrama in doses large enough to kill the average educated North American. We get to see what it's like when a soul bursting with emotion literalizes itself in song or dance. We get the cathartic resolutions that Chekhov, on the other end of the melodramatic spectrum, withholds. We get to see our frustrations, fears and hatreds – still recognizable, but contorted to fit into super-beautiful characters careening through the craziest of plots. Sounds like a dream to me!!

Raised on Hollywood pictures, you crave melodrama without knowing it. You live it, you sleep and dream it, and you unwittingly watch it at your cineplexes already. Only you can't recognize it until it's imported.

Now that Toronto filmmaker Deepa Mehta has made *Bollywood/Hollywood* (2002), a departure from her usual textured, multilayered dramas like *Fire* (1996), there's a unique chance to compare on a moment-by-moment basis the melodramatic conventions of the world's two filmic superpowers.

Mehta's film tackles the incredibly ambitious task of making one tongue out of two. Sometimes switching back and forth between the film languages of two continents, sometimes blending them, her movie gives us a full-blown musical fantasy about arranged marriage within Ontario's Indian diaspora. Using a luminous cast of Bollywood stars and veterans (including Rahul Khanna as the man resisting his family, and Lisa Ray as a gorgeous *anime*-proportioned escort who drives the narrative forward and steals his heart), Mehta contrives to embed directly into the film's schema the happily familiar clash between traditional old-country values and the corruption of Westernization, even going so far as to include onscreen kisses between Indo-Canadians – 'The kiss of all kisses!' as it's called in one of the picture's numerous playful subtitles.

The movie is very willing to be wild: Jessica Paré is killed in a levitation plummet while trying to be Indian, Khanna's father appears like Hamlet's ghost spouting baseball aphorisms as guidance to his confused son, another man obeys like sacred texts the plots of classic Bombay studio productions. Mehta even hires a bunch of white Torontonians to dance to original Mumbai beats composed by the ingenious Sandeep Chowta. (When it comes to this music, it's true that white men can't dance.)

From the title alone, we are told that Mehta – who was born in India and raised in Toronto – has set out to create a tension between the American and Indian storytelling styles, but, god bless her, Mehta is more Canadian than American, and the stuff that ain't Bollywood feels unmistakably Canuck. There's a delectation on the director's part in the more languorous Western sections that even remind one of Atom Egoyan, a tribute to this great director that goes well beyond the handful of direct homages paid to him in the story. At these times, one might wish for the thunderball of South Asian musical craziness to drop, but I suspect the director's love for the cherished movie conventions of her birthplace is tepid.

Bollywood/Hollywood is a sweet-spirited thing, peppered with occasional vicious gripes about sexism and shots at braggarts with small dicks – what about us sensitive, innocent men with small dicks? The two cultures swirling around onscreen produce a kind of motion sickness, perhaps the same feeling Mehta herself has experienced as an assimilated Canadian – the story seems as true as the most durable of melodramas. The sometimes maddening nature of this unique movie hybrid is more than just a clash of vocabularies, cultures and eras; it's a brutal 401 collision of aesthetics, a twisted fender-bendered spectacle the viewer is compelled to stare at, to think about in circular, dumbstruck ways. A Westerner may always feel like a tourist watching real Bollywood, and that's fine – admit when you're a tourist! – but viewers will need no passport to watch this rare object of macabre beauty and discomfort.

HAPPY EVER AFTER

I first met Noam Gonick in my apartment here in Winnipeg some twelve years ago. I was throwing a party and he was stealing books from my shelves and extending his search to jewellery. I instantly forgave the little charmer, figuring any book thief is a true charismatic. I was right. Inevitably, Noamie started mesmerizing the young pretties in our hometown with his movie camera. He quickly established himself as a perfervid reconfigurer of all things.

His first short, *1919*, depicts our city's historic general strike of that year by wafting so much bathhouse steam over the labour strife one can barely tell the knob-gobblers from the picketers. Next, this clever young son of a Communist professor at the University of Manitoba made *Waiting for Twilight*, an hour-long doc about one of Winnipeg's better-known filmmakers – me, actually. Ever the mythmaker, Gonick portrayed me as passive aggressive and self-pitying – a remarkable editing feat! Now comes his first feature, *Hey, Happy!*, an outrageous staccato burp of amyl nitrate images from Winnipeg's propped-up and overripe rear end. I recently spoke with the director over tea in my library.

GM: Dear Mr. Gonick. I know while you were shooting *Hey, Happy!* you were making a story about characters anticipating the much feared turn of the millennium, an apocalypse that eventually failed to show on time, but now when I watch this picture shot in our Winnipeg, I see a landscape that looks and feels more post-apocalyptic than anything out of sci-fi. Did the doomsday that missed the rest of the world somehow lay low our city through the magic of sound mix, colour timing or some other darkly mystical post-production process?

NG: Winnipeg is by its very nature apocalyptic. Floods of Biblical proportions annually threaten our home, the rivers swelling up with sewer effluent and drowned bison. And sometimes you wonder if there was any logic in inhabiting this landscape in the first place, if it isn't some kind of failed experiment which the gods want to terminate. I was in that four percent of the population that believed in Y2K, the biggest hoax ever – I guess I like getting spooked. We originally called the film *Fuckfest 2000*, to play up that millennial angle and refer to the protagonist DJ Sabu's life mission of fucking 2000 boys, but since the shoot was mere months before New Year's, we thought the title might be a bit passé by the time it was finished. The film is shot entirely outdoors (except for two washroom scenes), porn stores situated in wheat fields, beauty salons in junkyards, all shot in a jaundiced CinemaScope – in many ways the world of *Hey, Happy!* has already been squashed by an undetermined socioeconomic collapse when the story begins.

GM: Yes – Y2K! I'm already nostalgic for that sweet little impending annihilation we all trembled at like Boy Scouts around a late-night campfire. You've somehow welded together homos and end-times in your picture.

NG: I can't take full credit. Here in the Bible Belt, homos and end-times are bound together with fire and brimstone, and I thought instead of denying the connection it would be fun to embrace the mix, to say, 'Yeah, homosexuality is rampant and this does mean the end of the world,' kinda like Jerry Falwell after 9-11.

GM: You do have Happy, perhaps your most sympathetic character, torching an American flag. Do you deserve castigation for this very unprescient script blunder?

NG: According to my distributor, yes. I was trying to make a very casual anti-imperialist gesture, perhaps best understood after smoking a bowl of hash. Faggot utopias like that found in the denouement of *Hey, Happy!* are built from of the ashes of today's empires.

GM: Perhaps true evil is represented in your film by Spanky, the most petulant he-pussy ever invoked by the occult art of filmmaking. I know I do most of my casting through the local phone book; where did you find this boy?

NG: I was producing a series of after-hours parties and Clayton Godson, then aged fourteen, was found passed out in a puddle of his own puke, makeup splayed out around his candy-raver lunch-box purse. He had just been sprung from juvie hall, and within days he was performing with a cucumber for my twenty-fifth birthday. He's like an inverse Divine – stick thin, but still intent on being the grossest person in the world. Bruce LaBruce, on meeting Clayton, said he was a young Jerry Lewis. We presented the film together on opening night of the New York Underground Film Festival, and I think he alienated the audience, screaming, 'Who wants to get fist-fucked?!!' into the mic. I would think that would go over very well in New York, but I guess they've already dealt with Lydia Lunch. You've got to be ready to fight or run at all times when you're in public with Clayton.

GM: In spite of all the toxic puddles, vile language, glory holes, a gut-eating sequence, and a drowned dog, your movie has a totally charming sweetness. All this mean spirit dervishing around such a cute soul. How did you pull off this little miracle?

NG: Watching the finished film, I was actually embarrassed at how romantic the Sabu-Happy love plot is – verging on sappy – but I guess that comes with the Astro-Camp territory. I patched genres together recklessly. I wanted to provide a well-balanced diet, make the audience laugh, cry, get an erection and then throw up in their laps – isn't that what entertainment's all about?

GM: I did throw up once, but only in my mouth. Let me comment that, even with your apparent dog's breakfast of intentions, and all the abounding mayhem, the overall trajectory of the picture is so sensitively suggested – such a gentle takeoff, flight and landing. This certainly isn't off-the-rack camp. Are you trying to sucker-slap what's left of the camp crowd? Just who is your real or imagined audience?

NG: Very naively I designed this movie for the fevered suburban multiplex of my imagination, thinking that Spanky and Sabu would be great role models for truants who play pinball in the local mall, dodging security guards. Of course the film buyers at Sundance didn't see it that way, and alas this movie will be taking a very circuitous trip into bedroom communities, hopefully inspiring clandestine basement circle jerks around DVD players. We're just blowing the heads off old dandelions, and wherever the spores land we hope they take root.

GM: I love the movie's rave scenes. It's nice to see breakdancing made it to Winnipeg before the end of the century – at least according to your mythic view of the city. How important is mythmaking?

NG: I look at *Hey, Happy!* as a big future-tense creation myth. In the end, the DJ is adrift alone on a flooded planet, spinning cabalistic charts on turntables, pregnant with an alien love child, which might repopulate the planet. Sort of a new Book of Genesis.

GM: A new boner-filled Bible?

NG: With cum-stuck pages.

YOU GIVE ME FEVER

Anthology Film Archive's 'Halogen Canticles' program presents a rare chance to see three staggeringly unstable movies – chlorotic, tumescent features made in all good faith by clammy journeymen gone mad in high fevers – and, programmed alongside each, the landmark short films derived from them by back-alley emulsion doctors with secret, sadistic needs of their own.

Joseph Cornell's *Rose Hobart* (1936) is an enigmatic, mischievous rearrangement of shots culled from George Melford's lush compost heap of tropical jungle-adventure tropes, *East of Borneo* (1931). Perfervidly obsessed with the peculiar deciduous fineness of the movie's lead, actress manqué Hobart, Cornell slices out all obstructive plot from *Borneo* and transforms it by the camera obscura of his famously boxed-up brain into a glorious parade of decontextualized portraits of his lissome fixation. By this method, virginal Cornell desired 'to release unsuspected floods of music from the gaze of the human countenance in its prison of silver light.' The boner quotient is indeed high in this primitive and loving ejaculation from America's most important basement boy.

If not actually the very first found-footage film (Chaplin must have reconfigured some actress screen tests for personal use years earlier), *Rose Hobart*'s wondrous brilliance has undeniably inspired thousands of filmmakers to try their hand at this sometimes fecund practice. Pity, then, to take the contrarian stance that Cornell committed an act of butchery rivaled only by that of RKO's upon *Ambersons*. *East of Borneo* is sublime in its original, unmangled form. See for yourself the seductively engorged hybrid of an early von Sternberg love triangle (Hobart sleeps in drag within a tent of mosquito netting stretched across a crocodile-infested equator of the mind) and the Halperin brothers of *White Zombie* vintage, whose willful use of rear-screen, impenetrable murk, stock footage and music loops conjured aromatic continents that *National Geographic* could only expose as banal disappointments.

In *Her Fragrant Emulsion* (1987), American filmmaker Lewis Klahr immolates himself in the androgynous presence of another marginalized actress, nitro-burning funny-car diva Mimsy Farmer (*Hot Rods to Hell*, *Riot on Sunset Strip*), whose smile Klahr was seduced to regard as 'a little too believable,' convincing him that Farmer was 'genuinely wild and having too good a time' onscreen, and that this quality sealed her fate as a B-movie actress. He decided to stalk her, retroactively, through her filmography. Admittedly inspired by Cornell, Klahr's methods differ decidedly. He glues onto clear film leader tiny sliced strips and celluloid shrapnel bits of Her Mimsiness clawed and gouged out of the 1969 shot-in-Italy hippie-noir incest-o-rama feature *Road to Salina*. The images in *Fragrant Emulsion* barrage the viewer exclusively with elusive and erotic glimpses of this somewhat Sebergian former star of what can now be wistfully called skin flicks. The 8mm textures and enervated color of the serrated images rip open a piñata of sad nostalgias, and the oft-repeated sight of Farmer springing nude from a beach into the sea evokes the slippery sensation of struggling to remember all at once every lineament of a dead beloved. A most ardent necrophilia of a still-living actress.

The ninety-six-minute *Road to Salina* features a Murderer's Row cast of Robert Walker Jr. (the skittish look-alike ghost of his own father, remembered from *Strangers on a Train*), Rita Hayworth (a confused ghost of herself wandering around in another woman's body, only the voice consistently recognizable from when she lived in *Gilda*), and mealy-faced über-Borgnine Ed Begley. Its groovy film vocabulary defining the era, this is a picture Spike Jonze might have studied compulsively. An orgy of zooms!! Brazen dubbing – even the cars seem to rumble out-of-sync in a foreign language!! Hardcore spaghetti-psychedelic score!! Free love, with your sister!! Rita Hayworth smokes a joint and boogaloos with Begley!! (Fred Astaire always said Hayworth was his best partner. Perhaps already suffering undiagnosed from the Alzheimer's that killed her, Hayworth is rumoured to have preferred Begley.) A spectacular vintage car wreck of a movie.

Influenced in turn by Klahr, Austrian Peter Tscherkassky has made two films cannibalizing Sidney J. Furie's 1982 Barbara Hershey horror film *The Entity*, the story of a woman who is continually assaulted and raped either by real ghosts or by awfully adept repressed traumas. Furie's original feature, to be screened in a freshly minted print, is a crude and sometimes stupid contemporary of Tobe Hooper's *Poltergeist*, with Val

Lewton allegorical aspirations and lurid lapses in taste – all of which make it damned disturbing. Incest and spousal abuse invisibly haunt the house in which one views this movie.

Tscherkassky's two short glosses on the picture are respectfully unworshipful of the tortured pre-collagen Hershey, but of all the females under scrutiny discussed here, certainly no woman's face is offered up more intensely than that of this woeful victim, the former Miss Seagull. The screen literally explodes with a tumult of Hershey faces, shattering Steve Burum's original cinematography into shards of frightened eyes, trembling hands and violent outbursts of self-defense, presented in multiple exposures too layered to count, too arresting to ignore. Each frame is further entangled with details revealed by a jittery effect (a primitive travelling matte?) which spills fluttering ectoplasmic light pools from one cubist aspect of the woman to another. The filmmaker mimics the action of nightmares by condensing the original imagery of the feature and displacing it into a new narrative – as in dreams, a narrative not explicitly linked to actual events, but emotionally more true than any rational explanation. Tscherkassky's shorts are actually considerably more terrifying than the original material.

So it is that from unstable, unloved, unremembered films come even more unstable and obsessive and timeless works. Now fully inspired to participate somehow in the thread of history so unspooled by the Halogen Canticles, I shall plop on my filmmaker's hat and wait some ten years before releasing my own reassembly of *Undercover Brother*, featuring the long-overdue coronation, high upon the gilded and jewel-encrusted found-footage throne, of luminous and deserving Denise Richards. Long live the queens of Cinema Rejecta!!

THE WOMB IS BARREN

In spite of how much I thirst for living my life – and BOY! do I thirst for some kind of life! – I'm not really going anywhere fast. As if on a breezy Sensurround Stairmaster, from a stationary position I churn thoughtlessly through my time spent here on Earth, past the vistas and plains of my outer landscape – Winnipeg – and the sheer accumulation of insignificant memories left strewn across my inner landscape by a life lived with glacial slowness. If I set the Stairmaster in reverse, I can prove that this strong sense of inner landscape dates back to my earliest days, and even before.

Imagine the biggest womb in the history of childbirth – it sat ten thousand people. This glorious and most-missed locus of pre-natal paradise was the Winnipeg Arena where, during a game between the local Maroons and the Trail Smoke Eaters, I came into the world, quick-slipped out of my mother onto the trainer's table in the Maroons locker room, delivered by team doctors Cuthbert Handford and Fusi Taylor. I apparently made no obstetric cry at the time – the real shock of birth never hit newborn me until I was removed from the actual building. The blast of wintry outdoor air made me chronically nostalgic for my erstwhile comforts inside, and, as soon as I was able, I made my way back into this womb – the Winnipeg Arena – and there spent a most glorious childhood.

In the Winnipeg Arena, my inner and outer landscapes were one and the same thing. My five senses gorged themselves in the place, and were felt up in return. There isn't a sound or shadow from one of my alleged movies that I didn't get off the rack at this great store of memories. And most importantly, my Moral Code, by which I've lived my whole life, and by which I've judged all my friends and acquaintances and found them to be sadly corrupted people, was handed down to me at the Arena by both its immortal and mortal occupants. And now this Moral Code – or set of filmmaking commandments – is what shapes EVERY one of my little moral melodramas on celluloid, and so EVERY one of my little movies is a direct reflection of my time spent in this temple, the Arena. To explain this literally, using explicit examples, would be too painful, too revealing, too incriminating, too litigious. Let me just waft some sense samples your way, little spritzes free of charge, and hope you can smell the connection between my geography and my movies – assuming hopefully that someday you'll actually see one of the movies.

In those days, the Winnipeg Arena was like the Wrigley Field of hockey arenas. It was a building that fit hockey like a skull around its brain: a Gothic structure, dark in every aspect, a vast mildewed cathedral. The building was peopled with lurid throngs, somehow culled from the *noir*, grotesque files of police photographer Weegee. The fans would freely fill the building with their cigarette smoke, and life in the building was very rich and strange. Large swarms of bats would issue from the black infinities of the rafters and catwalks that teemed with shadowy lurkers above. There was a giant pipe organ, bigger than the one in old Chicago Stadium, that seemed to play nothing but the blackest dirges – none of the Gary Glitter stuff that diddled the ears of hockey dilettantes in other cities – and the games themselves were played by men helmeted in a thick protective gloss of Brylcreem dripping down over their lumpen faces, which were cross-hatched by the wounds of many years played. Players just looked different in those days: a twenty-year-old player would took about forty-five. The fans were selected from the same Weegee demographic. Everyone in the building was involved in some unknown crime, mug shots in a gallery. The seats were pregnant with corruption and profanity drenched in aftershave. By the third period of each game, these hockey-loving malefactors would be effaced by the thick clouds of cigar and cigarette smoke they produced to conceal themselves. Smoke actually billowed down to ice level, and on some occasions the players were forced to bluff about where the puck and other players actually were.

One game in the early WHA (World Hockey Association) days really sticks out in my memory. The Shrine Circus, eager to set up following the final buzzer, had lined the area around the rink with its exotic animals, so for this game the human faces were actually replaced by lions, tigers, elephants and giraffes watching from rinkside cages. Errant pucks often went rattling into the depths of these menageries, and the groans and cries of bestial pain would bellow back to the players and up into the empty seats on high. My friend Jeff Solylo (my future art director), used to sell popcorn at the arena at the time, and the popcorn-loading station was right by the elephants. He told me that whenever the elephants urinated they would send a golden mist over all the popcorn, which was promptly sold while it was still warm.

I enjoyed a special privilege in the Winnipeg Arena because my dad was the treasurer for the Canadian National Hockey Team in the sixties. He had enough celebrity status to get me into Jets games for free when the WHA started up in 1972. 1 got to go into the dressing room where I'd be stick boy either for the Jets or the visiting teams, and I'd slice oranges for the players and quite often – in a rather charged atmosphere, I realize now – I'd sometimes lather up the backs of the players. I remember lathering the great goaltender Gerry Cheevers when he played for the Cleveland Crusaders. I remember squeezing the juice from the orange slices into the months of the players before they went on the ice as part of a good-luck ritual. Jets trainer Bill Bozak once confided to me that Jets centre Ulf Nilsson had a more womanly figure than Zsa Zsa Gabor, whom he'd also rubbed down on occasion. Next time I was in the changing room I decided to check Ulf out for myself, and it was true. He had such a slender, beautiful midriff and wide, child-bearing hips, and a near total absence of body hair.

The players' wives had their own anteroom where they used to breast-feed their children, and as a kid I was the only one allowed to run back and forth between this lounge and the players' acrid changing room. I loved the olfactory shock of passing from this chamber redolent of wet diapers and breasts swollen with milk into a room of damp men, the dubious smell of athletic supporters, unlaced skates and drenched jerseys, the soapiness wafting warmly from players hollering in the showers. I remember, during an NHL exhibition game, standing among the men and regarding, at eye level, the makeshift fig-leaf contrived out of suds by future Hall of Famer Gump Worsely, who taught me everything I know about modesty and indirection.

When the Winnipeg Jets left us, the tragedy shocked me into adulthood. There was a civic funeral at the arena; 15,000 and change showed up, and all the players came out and waved goodbye. Thomas Steen's sweater was retired – whatever that means when a whole franchise is dead anyway. Today, my old womb is home to the Manitoba Moose, whoever they are. The arena is gussied up with modern surface stuff, cosmetically painted with a mortician's clumsy hand. The upper balconies are hung with black crepe, completely covered by it, to hide the seats the desiccated old place can never again hope to fill. THE WOMB IS BARREN! I'll not go back – not literally. My mother won't let me.

Whenever I aim my camera at something, however, the same mists that filled the old rink steam up my lenses, the same rancid eroticisms arrange themselves like rotting Rodins behind these mists. When writing a script, I can't think of a dramatic character who doesn't think in the simple sports concept of 'us versus them,' who doesn't seethe with a delirious competitiveness, and who doesn't need a great deal of liniment rubbed on his chest. And I can't conceive of these naked warriors without their beautiful women, together in a nearby enclave, a little gynocracy smaller even than Vatican City, where these wives are sexy and mothers, too. And so, in my interior there will always be a man and a woman and, over by the sliced oranges, a baby. That's before more men and women wander in to complicate things. That's how I started out, and that's how it shall always be.

VERY LUSH AND FULL OF OSTRICHES

I can never read reviews of my own movies. I'm terrified to find out what the barbaric world thinks of my trembly filmic dreams and, by extension, my overly frangible soul.

As a hedge against catatonic depression, for years I gave all the print reviews to my nonagenarian Gramma, who would translate them out loud into Icelandic to her big brother Hjalmar, who in turn would promptly translate them sentence by sentence, with a shrill dental whistle, right back into his own archaic approximation of English, while I listened in a cold sweat.

By the time my review went through this two-stage process, it no longer frightened me, having acquired the flavours of a bowdlerized Nordic folktale. Most of the cruelties were recouched in quaint hearthside metaphors with more charm than stomp. Even better, the not infrequent praise warbled out in the singsong falsetto peculiar to Icelandic typically depicted me as a mighty storytelling slayer of Hollywood ogres, a fair-haired god with wisdoms infinite, or some kind of mischievous lava sprite – all good things!

I never suspected generous mistranslation, but when these two handy ancestors of mine recently climbed up to Valhalla, I hauled out my clippings to reread the encomia. Without fail, I was shocked at the sorry level of writing in the original English text, film journalism as sloppily hammered together and painted as a kid's klubhouse – no grace of line, no awareness of harmony, no evidence of an eye. And this was the positive press! Really! (I've actually received very little, or no, bad press that can't be easily explained off as reviewer's insecurity.)

If this well-meaning but unfortunate scrivening is the best America's top film critics (some of them very nice people) can come up with, and if I want a fair shake in the press, then I am left no choice but to review, with great reluctance, my own movies, starting right now on the eve of a mini-retrospective of my four features, along with a short, at the Brooklyn Academy of Music.

Made while he was practically still a child, *Tales From the Gimli Hospital* (1988) is Guy Maddin's primitive first feature. Setting out to be not juvenile but wilfully childish, Maddin shot the movie in the vernacular spoken by film in the year of its own

91

glorious second childhood – namely 1929. He mixes black-and-white with toned sequences, mime with talking, locked-down expositional tableaux with bumpily fluid musical numbers. His moral sensibility is strictly precode. His mono soundtrack drones and hums out a comfy wool blanket of ambience – the viewer can sense his own mother tucking him in beneath a sweetly decaying quilt. The director eschews sharp focus in favour of oneiric portraiture and dismisses the literal mindedness of continuity as inimical to dreaming. He seems always careful to throw the picture together carelessly, with the delirious glee of a finger-painting preschooler.

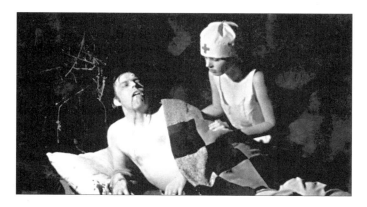

Gimli's story takes the director back to his own ethnic prehistory in a nineteenth-century Icelandic settlement in rural Canada, where an epidemic (cleverly unnamed to invite comparison with AIDS) has paved the pioneers with unsightly fissures and landed them all in a makeshift hospice shared with invaluable heat-generating farm animals. Here, in the titular hospital, dark but bouncy tales of death and jealousy exchanged between two men eventually pit the endomorphic raconteur Gunnar against the necrophiliac Einar in a buttock-shredding climax that is probably the most autobiographical moment of Maddin's career.

Though finding a Canadian Ned Sparks or Guy Kibbee for this project proved impossible (virulent strains of Berkeleyism infect almost every frame of the picture), the filmmaker did find a stalwart actor in Kyle McCulloch, whose ability to pitch his mannered performances perfectly to each anachronistic script won him the starring roles in this and the next two features.

The fluency with which Maddin speaks a dead movie language suggests he suffers from a most plangent nostalgia, that he has spent most of his life looking backward through misty eyes and with absolutely no idea where he is going. Travelling through a film in this fashion, he bumps into and rearranges much narrative furniture, often standing still to weep while he and his viewers get their bearings.

In *Archangel* (1990), all of Maddin's backward-gazing characters grope about in the murk of their memories in a sad attempt to regain loves and comforts lost. *Archangel* is a full-blown amnesia melodrama set deep in the confused winter immediately following the Great War – the last war designed exclusively for the pleasure of children. (The uniforms worn in battle made all the combatants look like scaled-up toy soldiers, and Maddin himself described the movie as a 'Goya painting etched upon a child's windowpane in frost.') Another part-talkie, this is Maddin's most delirious feature; there is a narrative, but it lies buried somewhere beneath a fluffy snowfall of forgetfulness. All the characters, being amnesiacs, have forgotten the war is over, and between naps continue to fight. They fight painful facts, they fight the love gods, they fight through thick mists of Vaseline. (The *Archangel* camera crew went through a whole keg of this unguent.) Soldier and viewer alike fight confusion, unsuccessfully. This is said to be the director's favourite among his movies.

Careful (1992) is a pro-incest mountain *traumerei* shot in the two-strip Technicolor used in that holy year of 1929. Maddin's most fully realized project, it's also his most accessible. His longtime collaborator George Toles was possessed by a high-altitude Hamletism when he wrote the meticulously detailed script as a mad tribute to Herman Melville's *Pierre*. (*Careful* is actually much closer in feel to its source than the recent adaptation by Leos Carax.) Prairie-bound Maddin was obsessed by mountains, which he had never ever seen, when he shot it. McCulloch gives his strongest performance as a Butler Gymnasium student who must endure paddy-whacks of Oedipal privation to win his beloved's heart. Both violent and cozy! The colours are extremely lurid.

Twilight of the Ice Nymphs (1997) drifts away from the familiar confines of the archaic film (it's shot in 35mm full colour with a contemporary aspect ratio and nary an intertitle) and into the deep waters of language, and therefore decadence. The dialogues are drawn from the ascetic Knut Hamsun's *Pan*, then corrupted by dollops of *Prosper Merimée*. The theatrical decors are inspired by fevered Gustave Moreau. Toles gave actors Frank Gorshin and Shelley Duvall plenty to say, and Maddin let them say it all as musically as possible. Very lush and full of ostriches! Has the strongest final reel in the auteur's filmography.

Running before each feature at the retrospective is the five-minute agitprop pastiche *The Heart of the World* (2000). Some have described this frenzied feature-compressed-into-a-short as a call to arms meant to topple the complaisantly flaccid cinema of today, a plea to reinvent movies from scratch, or a reverent myth which finally places film at the very centre of the universe where it belongs. Maybe Guy Maddin, that great lava sprite, has been expressing all these impassioned sentiments since the very beginning of his career. Who am I to say?

GUILTY PLEASURES

I don't know if these are my 'desert island' movies, but my world would be an arid wasteland indeed without these lush little oddities I've discovered during my years crawling from theatre to theatre.

The Fleet's In (Victor Schertzinger, 1942) Schertzinger not only directed this naval musical – that most outré of genres – but wrote the melodies as well. This movie is too queer to fathom, boasting three of the strangest women in pictures: the debut of oddball Betty Hutton, freakish mug-puller Cass Daley and dancer Lorraine, whose contortions are almost sickening. For would-be cinephiles this movie is a very brisk hazing, and Eddie Bracken doesn't make things any easier for the uninitiated. When she premieres 'I Remember You,' the usually iffy Dorothy Lamour looks as if she's been filmed by von Sternberg.

Ace of Aces (J. Walter Ruben, 1933) Absolutely perfect low-budget fighter-pilot picture that deserves the same reputation as *Gun Crazy*. Wearing his blasted soul on his middle-aged face, washed-up Richard Dix plays a pacifist sculptor who goes bloodthirsty on account of a woman and shoots down as many teenaged Germans as the Kaiser can put into biplanes. Unique aerial sequences! The picture starts off with charming ineptitude, then picks up speed, confidence and genius as it divebombs through its seventy-seven minutes. Dix is a forgotten American treasure.

Road to Glory (Howard Hawks, 1936) Hawks's maligned diamond. A gorgeously mudded-and-mustard-gassed and outright oneiric war melodrama that crams every human fear and desire into the baggiest jodhpurs ever worn by a Hollywood leading man. A blinded and atrabilious Warner Baxter commands his own elderly father (Lionel Barrymore) to join him on a suicide mission to atone for the latter's cowardice. When Barrymore asks his own son permission to toot on a little bugle seconds before they know they're to die, he seems to be tooting for all the great impotent fathers of all time. A very mean script by Faulkner. Surrender to it!

The Naked Jungle (Byron Haskin, 1954) An opening title sets this Technicolor movie in 'South America.' Charlton Heston is a plantation owner cuckolded by his wife before he has even met her – he has married vavoom Eleanor Parker by proxy and had her canoed upriver for the honeymoon. The always-grimacing Heston is troubled by armies of red ants, even before they literally arrive by the millions to raze his property. The brooding future Moses responds with Old Testament intensity, destroying everything he owns to re-virginate his bride. I feel like Haskin has been reading my mail.

The Devil's Cleavage (George Kuchar, 1973) Kuchar's epic black-and-white 16mm tribute to Douglas Sirk weepies, with the lurid and the rancid aspects somewhat heightened. The almost nonstop dialogue seems like it was cut-and-pasted ransom-note-style from a thousand old movie scripts.

From Munich to Berlin (Oskar Fischinger, 1927) The premise for this three-minute film is so simple I want to make a hundred of these myself. Oskar took a walk from one city to another, shooting everything he saw along the way – each shot is less than a second long, but stays in the memory for months. This silent travelogue is the most beautiful cine-poem I've ever seen.

Bill and Coo (Dean Riesner, 1947) A garishly shot circus love story acted out entirely by trained birds. This fluttery and perplexing *film maudit* so charmed the Motion Picture Academy that a special 'bird Oscar' or something was invented to salute the enormously exhausting achievement of its quixotic maker.

The Face Behind the Mask (Robert Florey, 1941) Peter Lorre has never exploited his sensitive face to more heart-breaking ends than in this tragic noir about a recently arrived immigrant watchmaker who turns to a life of crime after severe facial burns leave him unemployed and unloved. When a blind girl – yes, MELODRAMA! – falls for him, he tries to sneak back out of the criminal underworld and into a redeeming love nest. The script has fresh twists galore, and no false moves, in its remarkable sixty-nine minutes.

Hell's Angels (Howard Hughes, 1930) When he made this, Hughes was only twenty-five – a Wellesian and Eisensteinian age for debuts – and parts of the movie are as brilliant as anything by the more regarded neophytes. The young millionaire and eventual collector of his own urine was a perfectionist obsessed with aviation when he shot the spectacular dogfights that zigzag across this photoplay. There are two-strip

Technicolor scenes, both silent and talkie episodes, tinted sequences, even a disarming strategy in which English intertitles are used, before subtitles had been developed, to translate the German heard on the soundtrack. Most awesome, however, is the lengthy zeppelin setpiece, which only a possessed man could have created, and which is more shimmering and architecturally immense than anything by Max Reinhardt. Whenever a movie is set in a zeppelin, you know things not originally intended to be ballast will eventually be tossed overboard in desperation to keep the gasbag aloft. When stolid German soldiers the envy of Mel Brooks volunteer to make their death plummets for Gott und Vaterland, my goosebumps rise in chilled admiration for the audacity of young Hughes – long may his toenails grow! The other worthy entries in my 'Lighter-Than-Air Trilogy' include Capra's *Dirigible* and DeMille's *Madame Satan*.

Thunderbolt (Josef von Sternberg, 1929) Part-talkie crime film featuring immortal Canadian Fay Wray. I love this movie, even though I've never seen it. If anyone out there has a copy of this rare masterpiece of film history, I will trade you my VHS copy of *London After Midnight*.

Hello, Sister (Alfred Werker, 1932) The picture that resulted when Erich von Stroheim was removed from the director's chair of his only talkie, *Walking Down Broadway*. Did I really see this on a late, late show years ago? Or did I dream it? There's a great shot where only the heads of two innocent-faced young lovers are visible poking out through a skylight into the starry night air; in the next shot we see their indoor nether portions, standing tippy-toe on a table – a dog sniffing up under the girl's skirt sees what the twinkling stars can't.

A final recommendation: Watch as much Carl Dreyer and Joan Crawford as possible. I currently teach an advanced university course entitled 'Dreyer & Joan.' Until you've seen *Ordet*, you can't really understand *The Female on the Beach*.

SWORD PLAY

Here's my chance to atone for years of sloughing off a grave responsibility, for which I've felt deep shame for the longest time. No sensible force ever prevented me from watching Akira Kurosawa's *The Seven Samurai*, the centerpiece of the Japanese master's spectacular career, certainly no fear that my jaw would unhinge itself from painful overyawning if I ever tried. I've watched many other Kurosawa films with sublime pleasure. *The Bad Sleep Well* (1960) might be my favourite movie, but something always stops me from embracing *The Seven Samurai*.

Several times I've gotten as far as popping this mega-hit from the Art House Golden Age into my VCR, only to be frightened off by the Sumo-squat of my television set. Ineffable dread simply closes my eyes to the promised pleasures of any more than six samurai swinging swords at each other. My inexplicable behaviour reached its shameful nadir when I was at the Tokyo Film Festival and my guide pointed out Kurosawa himself, not ten feet away, and I refused to turn my head to look – my only chance to see the aging legend in person before he died.

With ultra-girded resolve I intend to ride out this troubling pathology, to eff the ineffable. The process, as suggested by the editor of this therapeutic quarterly, is simple. I shall be tied to a *Cinema Scope* office chair and forced to watch the cursed work, then, with one hand free to grasp a pen, simply recount the experience. Wish me luck!!

Opening credits. A title card informs me that a seventeenth-century samurai civil war is to be the story's backdrop. The familiar dread swells my chest close to bursting. Won't these credits ever end? Finally, images – hey, beautiful images! This looks just like his other pictures of the period, better even. What grey-scale! Depth of field! What lyric nimbleness and economy of control displayed in limning a mythic landscape!

Now, Toshiro Mifune starts into some comic antics. He's like one of the Ritz Brothers! I never suspected this horror. I've been tied into the Death Ride seat. Lighten up! Admit this is better than *The Magnificent Seven* (1960). You like comic relief in Westerns. You like it when Walter Brennan scolds John Wayne like an angry spouse. You like it when a sugar-crazed cowpoke steals up to a chuck wagon, trips, knocks over some pots and pans, and starts a tragic cattle stampede. Why can't you like it when Mifune grunts and struts and, sporting only a thong, catches a fish in his bare hands? Okay. I do like it. This is just a western.

This is my way into this great movie. Sometimes it's like a western. And sometimes, when the characters are defined in a single brushstroke, it's like an epic poem from ancient times. It's *Tristan and Isolde*! This take makes me weep at the film's genius. Thank God Kurosawa tackled the themes of old sagas. Only the *Nibelungenlied* contains as much passion! Except there are no women in *The Seven Samurai* – not in its first eighty-five minutes anyway! No wonder my anxiety has shifted down to my trembling prostate.

And now Mifune is at it again. I had no idea John Belushi had been so spot on. The dread!! The dread!! For the love of God, untie me!

Calm yourself. If irritating performances don't kill a picture, they make it stronger. Think of Eddie Bracken in *The Miracle of Morgan's Creek* (1944). That's right – this is like Sturges! And now there's even a girl, with a haircut like a tomboy's, even though she's fiercely in love with the cutest samurai. It's Angie Dickinson in *Rio Bravo* (1959). I weep tears of pride for Kurosawa. This picture is so many things!

But it's not short. I must gravely report, the samurai are into their third hour of planning their defence. Endless, endless meetings. It's the Wannsee Conference, but with the Ritz Brothers. A recipe for unsuspected dreads.

Suddenly I awake and the movie is over. Nodded off. Kurosawa, that purblind doomster, finally crushed me into unconsciousness. It wasn't the boredom; it was the stupidity of the villagers. More than *Yojimbo* (1961), *It's a Mad Mad Mad Mad World* (1963) comes to mind. In spite of the ropes cutting painfully into my wrists, the film sucker-sapped me into merciful slumber. I missed the famed action sequence, with all the battle scenes. Would have been like *Saving Private Ryan* (1998), probably. Which is why I have fallen on my sword. As soon as my ropes are cut, I'm checking out of this clinic, out the window if I have to. Like Rock Hudson in *Magnificent Obsession* (1954).

HOLD ME, THRILL ME, KISS ME, KILL ME

When on a shopping spree for anguish, rapture, martyrdom, comas, counts, rapes, bastards, orphans, dogaressas, philtres, sirens, suicides, mistaken identities, flower festivals and sudden fatal loves – even a tattooed baby – one need look no further than the Italian Diva Film, a vast clearing house of art nouveau decors and nineteenth-century melodramatic devices still in wondrous working order.

Anthology Film Archives is opening up the gaudy inventories of 14 such movies, which flourished on the continent between 1910 and 1920, and which starred cinema's first divinities: Lyda Borelli, Pina Menichelli, Francesca Bertini and other Olympian ancestors of the merely mortal stars of Hollywood history. (The series was a New York Film Festival sidebar last year.)

Gathering into one deeply conscious glance all the beauty scattered so sublimely through that last hour of the fin de siècle, the Italian film diva is both the movie's centre and the movie itself; she is the eye and the hurricane. Indolently we bathe in her fragrant mysticisms and sensualities, while all about her, rent hearts and havoc are strewn with the violence of Armageddon. Even she is consumed by the force of her own storm – babies are ripped from her arms, leering roadmen are thrust into their place. She is buffeted by betrayals. Her purses are torn away. Her hands are pelted by ducal kisses innumerable.

Savagely lashed by her own tresses while Destiny blasts her soul, the diva cries out for vengeance, cries out with her entire body, and this is what is most spectacular about the diva film – the vocabulary of the body! Aided only in part by as many as thirty drool-inducing costume changes per film, the diva's body twists and ripples in endless metamorphoses expressing wave upon wave of inner tumult. Ever so slowly – for the film's time is the diva's time! – and in a fashion completely alien to our New World eyes, do the torso and its limbs strain toward an unprecedented posture of prurience enmarbled, and upon achieving this shocking pose, move on to the next astonishing attitude, unfurling the fingers first, languidly allowing these digits to splay about the face and the bosom of the diva and in so doing inscribe upon those marvellous surfaces the plots of all stories from all times.

During the screenings you can't help imagining you sit next to Wayne Koestenbaum, that great curator of history's taxidermied opera divas, chronicler of their conduct, and exegete of their every signifier. You pretend you've introduced him to these florid films and by doing so you've struck him dumb. The cine-diva's vocabulary smites him with its vastness, strangeness, and uncanny accessibility – like hieroglyphics made suddenly readable.

Penny-dreadfully named – *Satanic Rhapsody*, *Royal Tiger*, *The Painting of Osvaldo Mars* – and aggressively assembled by genuine but forgotten Italian auteurs, the diva films at Anthology are hugely watchable. Packed with melodramatic non sequiturs, dazzling and long-abandoned editing tropes and sometimes outright peculiar toning and tinting strategies, these compact little dramas—most of them run under an hour – induce the most arcane intoxication.

The films' morbid and degenerate yoking of sex and death, and their closety devotion to costumery and decors, spritz the bruised-fruit aromas of Decadence from one end of the program to the other. One can feel in all the scenarios the pervasive influence of Gabriele D'Annunzio – a kind of Italian Walt Disney of his day. It seems plausible that D'Annunzio, the great sensualist author and poet, ghostwrote the screenplays, and with his one tin eye shining, oversaw the production of these movies like the construction of so many death-rides at a great Liebestöd theme park.

While the cult of the diva grew within the Italian populace, Mussolini could perceive the fevers of degeneracy in this great film genre. Preferring more subservient women for his country's ideal, he especially disapproved of an art form that celebrated the fearsome power and savage suffering of the feminine. After his rise to power, the diva film went into eclipse.

Now, exalted by the imminent return of the diva, if only for the duration of the Anthology series, I'm determined to throng her portico with the other ardent suitors. Then, at first sight of her and her heartsick entourage, I shall toss my unworthy self headlong at the hem of her dress, hoping to plant there just one kiss before being swept into oblivion by the delicious fury of the Divine.

HOW DO YOU SOLVE A PROBLEM LIKE MEDEA?

The recent release on DVD and video of Lars von Trier's 1987 made-for-Dansk-television production *Medea* alerts us to the thrilling awareness that Carl Dreyer still walks among us, albeit very slowly, long after his passing, and sets us to looking for his blessed footsteps in the darnedest far-flung corners of the film world. Von Trier shot his movie from a script written by Dreyer, found among what must have been the most austere and orderly finds of personal effects in the history of Death.

One needs to see only the first few images from this version of Euripides' classic – the never-been-topped account of a jilted woman's fury – to wish he could get a lot more Danish TV stations from his satellite dish. The first shots of Medea's (Kirsten Olesen) tortured, expressionist hands clawing the brack of a North Sea tide pool prove that Greek melodramatic agon can travel to Scandinavia without suffering any jetlag. Soon, von Trier's camera is tilting down from the fire-lit face of Glauce (Ponds-lovely Ludmilla Glinska), at her hair-brushing toilette, to reveal her complete, painterly and full-frontal nudity. I wonder what the Danish Match Game '74 used to look like.

Everything looks painterly in this taut, exhilaratingly inventive seventy-four-minute masterpiece and curiosity (a curiosity because one can never stop wondering how much credit should go to old master Dreyer). There's a strange, rough canvas texture to every shot. Claustrophobic theatre effects – shadow-play and projections – are merged with the raw marshy *Hamlet*-y outdoors to make all of Denmark into a wild wind-torn stage. How does the director get his mise en scène to appear woven out of virgin wool and other natural fibres native to his region? Turns out he just shot it on crummy old video equipment. Is the gossamer soul von Trier managed to convey with this clunky analogue gadgetry simply inherent in this previously unloved, grotesquely under-appreciated technology? Is *Retro Boogie Dance Party* really deserving of the exaltation it, too, produces? Yes and yes! Please give me one of those old video-cams. I can't believe I once derided the look of this medium. As usual, we're moving in the wrong direction – with its every step forward, digital video feels like it's leaving something wonderful behind.

In Dreyer's wilfully laconic script, Euripides' torrent of hysterical apostrophizing is reined in, muted and replaced by cruel, quiet and implacable natural elements. The blond hair of Jason's slain children shows up in the wildly flapping field grasses that lash the flanks of their father's horse as he drives about in a silent, fruitless attempt to outgallop the pain brought down on him by his vengeful ex-wife. Viewed from above, from a god's point of view, inaudible Jason's (Udo Kier) wretchedly crazed zigzagging is about as insignificant as a fruit fly's. Von Trier honours the script by pacing the high-strung insanity of the story as an inevitability, as a horrible turn of the millstone, as just one unit in a cycle which must endlessly repeat in all families to come. If hysteria is what makes Euripides so surprisingly readable, then Dreyer, and ultimately von Trier, eschewing it, have found a hyperborean equivalent – Nordic brooding – which is just as electrifying, and maybe more cinematic. When expressed using the tropes found in this amazing picture, the result is some kind of odd relation to the Dreyer family, second cousin to Euripides, once removed.

Which puts me in mind of another curious kin of Dreyer's worth a closer look. Robert Aldrich's *Autumn Leaves* (1956) seems to be constructed out of plot elements wildly torn from the Lutheran jasper's masterpiece *Day of Wrath* (1948), and rearranged in a terrifying collage of hysterics rivalling the greatest of ancient Greek hissy fits. Joan Crawford, whose long career as one of the screen's great sufferers and avengers would have made her a perfect Medea, stars instead as a lonely Sirk-aged woman who makes a devilish deal with herself to marry a much younger man (Cliff Robertson). His head is a hornet's nest of pathologies because, in one of many brilliant inversions of *Day of Wrath*'s storyline, he was once being cuckolded by his robust father (Lorne Greene, for Christ's sake). When Joan's husband tries to kill her by bashing her head in with a typewriter, you know that Aldrich has taken all the wool battens off Dreyer's staid hatches and instead decided to honour the foaming hatreds of his classical Mediterranean master. You get the feeling that the Furies themselves, and not stage hands with fans, are whipping up the titular leaves into the tornadoes of rage and revenge that lay low all the characters by the end of this mad tale, one more bastard offspring of the great, celibate, procreatively prolific Dane.

SAD SONGS SAY SO MUCH: THE MAKING OF
THE SADDEST MUSIC IN THE WORLD

Day One. For months I'd been planning to mark the inaugural day of production by planting an elm tree. There are trees planted by Victor Hugo strewn across Paris, bulging with more lore than deciduous rings. Similarly, 200 years from now, I want this, the picture I've been waiting so long to make (with a $3.5-million budget, a twenty-four-day schedule and real movie stars), to be remembered in the towering, tortured, mossy limbs that will welcome visitors to the place where *The Saddest Music in the World* was shot.

The day was to start with this simple arboreal event, then proceed to the first scenes in the schedule – a couple of Two-Strip Melancolour funerals featuring Maria de Medeiros and Mark McKinney. But when we went to fetch the elm sapling in the backyard of my birthplace, we found the ground so hard with permafrost – the overnight low had bottomed out at $-44°$ – no amount of work with pick and shovel could so much as chip the soil. I called for the art department to arrive with blow-torches and chisels, which eventually loosened the soil but also charred the roots of the slender, slumbering treelet. We tried tree after tree in this fashion, but always burning, hacking or snapping them off short. Late in the day, we finally got a frozen lilac bush out of the ground – it had been my Aunt Lil's – and,

105

wrapping its roots in a burlap bulb, plopped it into the shallow grave that we were able to claw into the tempered tundra of our studio grounds. There was no time left for shooting, so we decided to start fresh tomorrow. Now I've got Auntie's old bush, already grown to full height, planted to commemorate not the first day of production, but the day before. At movie union rates for all the would-be tree surgeons, I don't even want to think about what this has already cost.

Day Two. Yesterday forgotten. Morale high among cast and crew, probably because we all wear hockey jerseys donated to us by the Burtonians, a beer-league team whose devotion to Winnipegger Burton Cummings, erstwhile lead singer of the Guess Who, reached apotheosis in their silk-screening his locally mythic face across the proud chest areas of their uniforms. Rehearsing and lighting, we strut around in these things with sheer sassitude! Feeling that happiness depends on structure and hierarchy, I set my rank as director apart by donning jodhpurs and an imposing fez.

Cameras ate up those colour funerals like so much popcorn. The sun we needed for our slow stock streamed in through the skylights all day long, and we simply followed it across the sky by rotating our little cemetery set upon the lazy susan, some forty feet in diameter, that we had built specifically for this project. We'll soon be ahead of schedule. Even had time left to pull the drapes over the skylight to shoot a little night scene.

This movie, about a competition to determine which country has the saddest song in the world, is my first musical, and even though we don't shoot any numbers for a few days, the studio is teeming with artistes who lurk deep in the shadows of this cavernous space and practice endlessly their various laments. Trying to get them to stop playing when we're shooting sound is difficult. First, you've got to find these guys. Spent about ten minutes today tracking down a Norwegian who had hidden himself behind some broken crates to play seafaring songs on his accordion. The mariachi band has really hit it off with the klezmerim, and they jam for hours on the only song they both know, producing an infectious hybrid gem out of Engelbert Humperdinck's 'Spanish Eyes.' We're all crazy happy. But tomorrow, things will be different: Isabella Rossellini.

Day Three. We're terrified of Eeez-uh-bellllll-a, as she mellifluously pronounces her name. If I were named Isabella, I'd never have the poise to str-e-tch my name out so gloriously. I'd somehow cram all those letters into one abrupt, sheepish syllable, like I do with the name I use now. Gosh, she's wonderful! Disarming and unpretentious. She arrived at the Winnipeg airport wearing no makeup and expressing a sincere wish that she'd saved us money by flying economy. This is her Scandinavian side, I'm thinking.

Why are we terrified? Because she's been photographed by the top hundred photographers of the last half-century, and now I have to face her with my little Super-8 camera – it's hard not to think of all those who came before me. I've warned her my camera is small, and she seems understanding, but now comes a love scene between her and Mark. Must just jump in. But I can't. My equally intimidated cinematographer Luc Montpellier can't either. My producer Jody Shapiro lights upon a great solution. Since the love scene requires very tight shots, why not just give Isabella a camera and let her photograph herself while acting? And so we did; we put a wide angle lens on it to keep everything in focus, and Miss R. simply held it in one hand, pointed it back at her own face, while she acted opposite Mark with the rest of her body – and all her soul! The extension of her camera-toting arm is explained in the reverse shots, where her ardent hand, now free of the camera, clutches at her 'lover.' Pure movie magic! Now she gets a camera credit, too.

To give an idea of how daunting is Isabella's legend, even our stills photographer (a veteran of some forty Hollywood superstars during a half-decade of snapping in Vancouver) refused to face off against the ghosts of Herb Ritts, Mapplethorpe, et al., and Jody had to hire a courtroom sketch artist to take her place. So what if I have no publicity stills? Every director has those, but what charming souvenirs these drawings shall be!

Day Four. Jody says we have to suck it up and film Isabella ourselves, just like other film crews do. I know I'll thank him for this edict someday, but I sure didn't like his bossy tone this morning. Eventually, we warmed to the day's work, mostly because we were wondering how to amputate Isabella's legs on film. Eschewing digital effects as grotesque artifacts of the present, we had all sorts of Méliès-era tricks up our sleeves, but no one knew how they would turn out. Eventually, in a way I cannot, under my producer's gag order, reveal, we removed her gams and replaced them with beer-filled, glass prosthetics, as per the script. Remembering that her famous father Roberto used to direct inexperienced actors by tying string to their toes and tugging whenever it was their turn to speak, I had Larry and Speedy tie a little fishing line to Isabella's glass toe. I felt this filament somehow tethered me across time and through his daughter to the father of neorealism. I was instantly pebbled with goosebumps. I delighted in pulling at this thing to make her kick at me over and over while Luc filmed. I guess I did it too much, though, because soon the beer in the long glass legs started churning up and spilled up a yeasty froth over her garters and into her lap. Speedy daubed away at the extraneous head, according to him one of the worst cases he'd ever seen. Why does directing make me despair so much!!!

For years, I've been meaning to put into practice my *Anatomy of Melancholy* approach to directing. And now I finally get to! Having already copied out on index cards various descriptions of depression gleaned from Burton's ancient tomes, as well as some forty synonyms for sadness culled from a thesaurus, I now start each day by dealing out all fifty-two cards, face down, on the breakfast table full of actors who are to work that day. Each performer has a different, sometimes fuzzy idea of a word's meaning – for instance, lugubrious or throboxyc, which is sadder? Actors love restrictions, and why not restrict them in the only fair way possible: with a lottery windfall of commands drawn randomly from a reference book?

The results have been sensational. The trite and the clichéd don't stand a chance under such an acting system. Dialogue clunks from one line to the next with a fragile-X clumsiness, scenes unfold with a Ritalin-thirsty zing! Most importantly, the work done is in the same tenor as my planned super-primitive rip-and-paste editing style. I want to unlearn how to watch movies; I want to flip dyslexically the images of my film to jangle their readability for the viewers; I want to re-create the thrill I felt as a boy when I finally recognized three words in a row!

Day Five. Today I paid a scenic painter $2,000 not to sleep with the Polish soprano who's been singing in the lunchroom the last three days. I have absolutely no desire to sleep with her myself; I think I'm going crazy!

FILM COMMENTS: DVD REVIEWS

If, as Wayne Koestenbaum says, Jackie Kennedy was the mute 'sphinx that brought order to chaos,' then her televisionized version, Mary Tyler Moore, as sexy and coutured as any Bouvier, playing Laura Petrie on the Camelot-era *Dick Van Dyke Show*, opposite a Kennedy-coiffed and nardless Dick, gave an accessible voice to a trendy brand of sex symbol – the married woman – and even galvanized the chaos in that comforting, ingenious sitcom. When Jackie later shocked America by going Greek, Mary reacted by donning a delicious nun's wimple in *Change of Habit*, the last of the ill-advised features starring likeable schlub Elvis. As a singing doctor, Elvis leads a few jamborees (hard to believe a summer of love was happening somewhere nearby), cures an autistic girl in five minutes, cops a few nunnish gropes, and most importantly, introduces police lieutenant Ed Asner to Mary. A year later, Asner would create one of many immortal characters in arguably the best ensemble sitcom ever, *The Mary Tyler Moore Show*. The first few minutes of episode one seem to be set in more primitive times, in Ralph Kramden's apartment maybe, but things get top-notch in a hurry, and soon the open-faced, prêt-a-porter Mary, like the secretive, hounded Jackie, glitters deistically, durably, many glorious seasons ahead of her in her life after Dick.

❧+❧

In *Cinemnesis*, a collection of three shorts, Austrian experimental filmmaker Martin Arnold reveals the hilarious, erotic and elegiac dreamlife of films like *The Human Jungle* and *To Kill a Mockingbird* with his trademark strategy: he selects a brief passage and optically prints little broken-record skips into it, stretching a few seconds into fifteen minutes. The repetitions isolate and fetishize tiny movements and magnify them into bizarre onanisms and droning concussions. By obsessing on cinema's secret nanoseconds, compelling new melodramas are reconfigured from indifferent fare. Arnold can find the twenty frames of truth – the film hidden within the film – in an otherwise completely dishonest performance. In the best, *Life Wastes Andy Hardy*, Mickey Rooney's always eager and somewhat pornographic face machine-guns a chaste peck into his mother's neck, deeper and deeper each time, while his filial squeeze of her flabby triceps is elaborated into a full-blown molestation, her dentures clicking like an aroused Geiger counter. In Arnold's crazed, stuttered reincarnation of her, film history's forgotten Mrs. Hardy is given all the awesome blasting force of a Clytemnestra brought to life. Fathomlessly strange, beautiful and spit-sprayingly funny.

✳✦✳

Herman J. Mankiewicz's 1963 *Cleopatra* still stands as the most expensive movie ever made – its $44-million budget solves out to almost ten times that amount in 2001-adjusted dollars. Producer Walter Wagner determined a wilfully un-DeMille-like approach to the picture, choosing Shavian ideas over corn, and just about proved old C. B.'s genius as an entertainer in the process. Seemingly released in response to *Gladiator*'s success, this expansive three-disc DVD set features almost ten hours of material, including a fantastic two-hour doc on the insanely profligate production of this cursed epic. The picture itself is a fatally sexless four hours of pyramids, orgies, elephants, Rex Harrison in a breastplate, and a braying, already Woolfish Liz Taylor – all lusciously lensed by the immortal Leon Shamroy. Liz threw up in humiliation at the premiere. Spectacular!

✳✦✳

Lewis Milestone's clever and likable *The Garden of Eden* is a 1928 romantic comedy written by longtime Lubitsch collaborator Hans Kraly and designed by the immortal William Cameron Menzies. Its once-famous stars are sadly underrepresented in film restoration – leading lady Corrine Griffiths, as gorgeous as anyone in the twenties, was known to millions as the 'Orchid Lady'; Lowell Sherman was every bit the roué that Adolphe Menjou was, at least until he dropped dead in the middle of filming *Becky Sharp* in 1935; and the weirdly pie-faced Charles Ray was a once-beloved, suaved-up prototype of Franklin Pangborn. Bonus features include a fascinating 1927 travelogue of Hollywood architectural curiosities and a rapturously strange silent Technicolor gloss on *The Little Match Girl*.

※+※

As in Daniel Clowes's original comic-book version of his screenplay, *Ghost World*'s anagrammatically named Enid Coleslaw (Thora Birch) is a proud geek-chic teenager who fiercely fends off conformity in her generic American city by posturing herself through a series of arcane fashion and music tastes, and by deriding anyone who falls to match her genius for creating an outré persona. Almost Chekhovian in his fairness, director Terry Zwigoff masochistically adds an alter-ego in nerdy middle-aged record collector and nostalgiaphile Steve Buscemi. Never has art direction – with its orgy of vintage designs desperately summoned from the past to supply individuality – so specifically and painfully defined characters in a movie. Smart, cruel and hilarious. The DVD includes the entire Bollywood musical number over which Enid obsesses – incredible!

※+※

During the hot summer of 1968, East German auteurocrat Joachim Hasler decided to make his own Iron Curtain Funicello and Avalon beach comedy. *Hot Summer*, a kind of Baltic *Beach Blanket Bingo*, involves the collectivist tribulations of eleven teenaged comrades and their attempts to remove the Brezhnev designer summerwear of eleven little suntanning Ninotchkas. One would think a hormone flood great enough to wash away all German guilt would result, but after thirty-six years of Nazi and communist dictatorships, there were no Jewish lyricists nor gay choreographers left in this dour neck of the woods to get any mischief off the ground. Teeming with hilariously robust ideologues horny only for five-year plans, this Cinemascope and Technicolor sand putsch is decidedly undecadent – another failed attempt to overcome America and its heavily funded Lawrence Welk program in the sixties taste race.

※+※

Incubus. Acting in this horror-fantasy just one year before framing his face between James T. Kirk's much-beloved sideburns,

William Shatner seemingly steals a march on UNESCO in the first feature shot entirely in Esperanto, the artificial language of utopian peace. The apparent lack of contractions in this tongue produces a forest of wooden performances that Shatner charmingly overtops with sporadic Zorba outbursts. The story concerns a flower-child daughter of Satan who seduces a brother away from his sister during a brief solar eclipse. Shot in black and white by future Oscar winner Conrad Hall, this hippie tingler uses natural light and California locations to create atmospheres that eerily anticipate the 'vibe' at the Charles Manson commune. One actor in particular, Milos Milos, later murdered Mickey Rooney's wife Barbara before killing himself, thus dealing Esperanto cinema a setback from which it has yet to recover.

⚓

Legendary Parisian exile and cigar-chomping crustcake Samuel Fuller's last picture *Street of No Return*, a kind of follow-up to his *White Dog*, is a co-production involving so many Mediterranean countries that the American-set race riots at the centre of this crime melodrama seem to be fought among rival factions at a Pasolini cattle-call – terrifying Euro-sissies. David Goodis wrote the original story which recombines elements of his earlier *Shoot the Piano Player*. Keith Carradine plays a pop singer who dresses like Siegfried and Roy, until his throat is slashed and he becomes a mute Neil Young look-alike wino who sucks grape only from broken bottle shards; the gorgeous and almost always nude Valentina Vargas plays the girl over whom the musician must fight gangsters. Fuller himself makes a memorable cameo as a grumpy silhouette. And, yes, the castration scene! A thirty-three-minute documentary with much interview time devoted to the most affably bilious director of all time makes this disc a must for Fuller cultists.

⚓

Time travel isn't kind to actor Guy Pearce. In Simon West's *The Time Machine*, stripped of the tattoos, rages and noirish suavities of the icily contemporary *Memento*, and thrown into

Victorian-period garb, he's an awkward doofus with a Wilde play clenched in his glute – impossible to see him as the same hottie. Cooked up for undiscriminating SFX geeks, this groan-inducing H. G. Wells adaptation has DreamWorks' fingerprints all over it, especially the charmless off-the-rack digital effects, the listlessly whimsical Jiminy Cricket presence of Orlando Jones as a gay hologram, and the epidermal John Williams psychology present in Klaus Badelt's fulsome score, much of it seemingly padded with canned orchestrations from TV's *Survivor*. Irish pop star Samantha Mumba looks great in her chain-mail maillot, but I'd rather pay money to see Ray Harryhausen pelt Steven Spielberg's bare behind with balls of plasticine.

❧+❧

Twin Peaks: Fire Walk with Me, David Lynch's big-screen prequel to his hit TV series *Twin Peaks*, was panned by just about everyone upon its release in 1992. But the passage of years and the recent creation of his masterful *Mulholland Drive* intriguingly contextualize this earlier welter of gratuitous ugliness made before the director worked his way out of the mire and refound the dreams that mattered most. As a valuable bonus, a fascinatingly lurid documentary on the DVD revisits that once-beloved hip cast of hotties years after the series phenomenon, and finds them in various states of Lynchian confusion. Clear-headed Peggy Lipton describes the movie's problems most aptly by comparing unfavourably its in-your-face aggression with the TV show's beneath-the-surface quiet. Meanwhile, the dwarf in the red room collects palindromes: 'Go hang a salami, I'm a lasagna hog!!'

JOURNAL TWO
(1998 – 1999)

29 June 1998

ameron's fifty-second birthday, we think. No one in our family can remember the date exactly – yesterday, today or tomorrow. It always got mixed up with and lost in the excitement at the end of school and the start of vacation. I too could never remember, what with Harmon Killebrew's and Dr. Handford's birthdays somewhere in this June-end. I spiritually vote for today, because last night at midnight, while lying half-asleep in the veranda at Loni, I felt, for the first time – and twenty-one years and four days late – the terror, sheer terror in my heart, that I should have felt when I heard Amma's voice summoning me to Chas's deathbed. I know I have delayed reactions to huge events, and I've been dealing with grief on the painless installment plan for decades now, but I'd forgotten about terror. I'd put off making any of the fear payments on my father's death, and last night the collection agents, perhaps led to me by Cameron on his birthday, made a chilling call on me to demand a long overdue sum of dread. And my soul seared out through my mouth and back in again, branding my entrails, etc. – lots of intense stuff – until I summoned the forces of repression and called off this whole Grand Guignol flashback as preposterous. There's little to be gained by confronting these horrors now. What's the exercise worth? Will it make me more capable of feeling terror when it's appropriate? Why would I want to? This is not even worth mentioning except that it is Cameron's birthday, and, in some kind of account-balancing, Chas must have felt the terror that was the end of Cameron. I remember complaining thirty-five years ago that Cameron had ruined my birthday by dying. Did Chas feel terror on my birthday? By this kind of triple-entry bookkeeping, Cameron must have felt terror on one of Chas's birthdays (March 29th). Perhaps specious reasoning, since the fatal terror of Cameron visited him sometime between 16 Aug 1962 and 16 Feb 1963. There must be at least one other sufferer in our birthday equation. Who else is in our loop of cold-sweat trepidation? No thank you. I don't want to figure out a foolproof system of divining all future days and times of terror.

Came out to the lake on the bus last night. Read George's *Edison and Neemo* last night and today. It still takes me two days to read a script; what's the matter with me? Normally this would be a sign of a bad script, but George and I have made great

116

headway lately, and I see all the 'through-lines' more clearly than ever, maybe even for the first time. (Fuck! You actually start talking like a script doctor when this subject comes up!) Zella now has a character. Neemo is scared of venus flytraps. Faraday is a moth. This will help when I get the script from 135 pages to 95. George has written so much dialogue that is musical, but perhaps too sweet, too conflict-free – like that fucking awful scene between Clooney and Lopez in *Out of Sight*. Shite! Also, the action's set in places extraneous to Edison's world, i.e., libraries and trees. Elise told me the script was pure crap, but she's jealous and evilly motivated. It just needs surgery. I was bracing myself for a huge war with George when I raised all my concerns, but lo, the calendar flipped back a decade! We worked in total harmony, and George came up with many improvements and trusts me to make the rest. I daresay I believe the second draft will actually be tons better, just a final pass away from something really special. But I must make this next pass good enough to send out to Fabrice, R. Frappier, Alliance and Keith Griffiths. It must be finished in eight days, for I fly to Victoria – and Jilian – on July 8th. Sorry, having pronounced myself ready to write, I must confess to a dangerous lassitude: a bone laziness, closely akin to depression, which threatens my entire filmmaking and any other-making future. I can't seem to shake it. These sentiments are very similar to those I suffered through prior to *Twilight of the Ice Nymphs*. Nothing galvanizes me. I seem to have no reason for making a movie, any movie, let alone this really cool story of George's. I used to be able to trick myself into finding reasons for, or at least fun in, my actions.

30 June

The pressure to start this second scribbler with something of significance resulted in a clumsy and morbid gesture: a charmless ramble on Cameron. I just want to free myself from the pressure to write well. Then perhaps I will give myself the pleasure this is designed to trigger when I reread this thing at the end of my long life – for I will have written in complete liberty, and thus actually have written honestly and well. Since I speak of honesty, these journals (or notebooks or whatever they now at last plurally are) are designed to help my daughter Jilian –

who has given me reason to live these last twenty years – a chance to know me (if she can make sense of or even hack her way through these accumulations thicker than *Moby Dick*) as most kids fail to know the secret half or whole of a parent. And I surely know Jilian barely as much as I want to – except for the fact she has all my love – for I have too many regrets to count about how much and what kind of time I've spent with her these past two decades. But I'm afraid I can't allow myself to think of Jilian reading this while I write because this future fact mutes me, reluctances me, slows my hand – and I must be honest. As I recall, my writing in the fall of 1997 and early last winter was full of pointless self-censorship. End of aside.

This being June 30th, today is the last day of school for all the kiddies in Winnipeg. Seeing the sunny and happy *tabula rasa* faces – nothing but two months of empty daybook on each uncaring visage as I cut through them in my Grey Goose bus this morning – brought me back to my favourite June 30th. The one in 1970 when it was hot and sunny and windy, a great combination, and I got home to 800 Ellice but just couldn't go inside because the summer was so splendiferous and, so far, completely unused. I went into the backyard and found old blind Gramma, ninety-one years old, white hair flapping as breezily as her wonderfully simple cotton sundress – a floral print sweeter to see in the backyard than our own lilacs. And she sat in a lawn chair drinking in the wind in those huge drinkable gulps which summer makes just so perhaps one day a year. By the end of the day we were all gone to Loni, leaving Gramma to enjoy the entirety of the summer in private. Of course, she fell down the stairs, suffering mortal injuries, at the very end of summer – her last summer. But on the occasion of that brief moment in the backyard everything seemed full up to the tops. I have no recollection what we spoke of on that floral day, probably next to nothing – which is enough, more than enough, to create lifelong unseverable connections to a pointless moment, to a meek and invisible person, to a bundle of love.

Back at Gertrude now. Having just entered my back door into the coolness of my kitchen from the afternoon heat, I notice my apartment has its own, pleasant even, summer holiday city smell – as distinct from all the other months as the air conditioned and shade-drawn summer months at 800 Ellice were. This new smell in a relatively new home, aided by the simple purring of a large window fan and the sub-aquatic murk of an apartment at dinner time with no lights on gives me the first hard experience of something I'll be trying to remember properly for the rest of my life. The breeze from the fan smells a bit like root-cellar earth: clean and dark and cool. The fan is also blowing in microscopic insects, sucking them in through the screen and speckling my face with them. This page, too.

2 July

I'm forty-two years old, and I'm as lazy as my first report card said I was. I have until July 8 to redraft George's script – twenty pages a day – and I've done nothing the last week. Soon, I'll be up to sixty pages, 120 pages a day, then just forget it; another act of completely depressing torpor. Completely inexplicable to all others as well, considering how lucky a position I'm in as a self-employed artist with some sort of crummy international following. But I fritter away everything.

I would like to live life to the fullest for twelve months. What does this mean? This: I would like to exercise as much as time permits. I would like to read voluminously. Most importantly, I would like to work hard hard hard on film and all related areas. Finally, I would like to solve my long-standing problems with loneliness. I've always had too much or too little company by way of lovers, and always the wrong person, and never fit them in relation to work or pleasure in any satisfactory way. If I'm working hard, I do so at the expense of diet, exercise and relationship. If I exercise and address loneliness, reading pays for it. Reading pays for everything, as a matter of fact. If I could design my life to fit everything, and in such a dynamic that all the components drive each other in turn – for just twelve months – I would have 'smugness' and 'happiness' momentum for a lifetime. Perhaps it's just faith that's needed – faith that by applying in all categories I will be rewarded in all categories; that loneliness will be taken care of by all the other areas. I think the first step though is to decide what kind of people, lifestyle or even city I want associated with my remaining years. Then actually act like I'm a decision-making mammal paddling about in the real world; perhaps then everything will be swimmingly fulfilling. At least until the inevitable cancers, crutches and amputations visit me. Can I also add that I wouldn't mind earning my own living as well, and paying taxes, and finding and learning to love the right person? (Did I mention that?) Please grant yourself these wishes, or self-fulfill them. Cancer warms up in the on-deck circle. Twelve months of this isn't too much to ask. Consider it a boot camp or a jail sentence, a tithe to Father Time. Self-help. No wonder it's a perennial growth industry. All my hopes are as banal as TV and *Cosmopolitan* put together. Why not add multiple orgasms to my wish list?

Okay, okay. It's 10:04 p.m., and I've come up with more work-avoidance tactics than I could imagine. To avoid spontaneous combustion from self-loathing levels unprecedented, I'm removing the most urgent deadlines from my daybook. But I am pledging to start the 'golden twelve-month' – that should be in upper case – on the 4th of July, and I shall dedicate it to Aunt Lil, who died on that day. And I shall live and love purely and honestly and correctly until the following 4th of July, if I live that long. I shall live according to my long-standing expectations of, and hopes for, myself. I shall work in private and with others. I will do favours for many, but know how to say 'no.'

I shall resume learning and producing. I will be as fit as a Nazi youth, as freewheeling as Neal Cassady, as observant as John Ruskin, as decadent as Huysmans, as witty as Oscar Levant, as well-hung as Ron Jeremy, as sensitive as Nikola Tesla, as honest as George Washington, as gregarious as Shirley Temple, as guarded as J. Edgar Hoover. All this starting day after tomorrow: The Golden Twelvemonth. Le Douze d'or? L'An d'or? I'll learn French while I'm at it.

Jilian might, just might, come and live with me. I just spoke with her on the phone. She's struggling a bit in Victoria. God, would I love it if she came and lived with me, just for a while since she's twenty already. If she really came and made my address hers, it would be the first real living together in an indefinite arrangement since 1979! Maybe my life can be saved! I'm a sort of Glidden, without literal sphagnum moss, but with something rotten about me, who can be redeemed if I'm reunited somehow with my daughter.

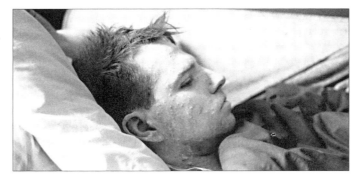

4 July
Day One. Awoke at 8:00 a.m., clicked on the loaded coffee maker, took all my pills and vitamins, and toted a steaming cup back to bed where I read George Ade for an hour, fell asleep for another hour then reawoke to read DeQuincey till 1 p.m., sorted bills and receipts till 2:30 when Steve took Carl and me swimming at Pan Am and to coffee on Corydon. Ate grapefruit, cereal, skim milk and vegetable soup, and now plan on a simple pasta, stewed tomato and wine dinner, with more readings – probably the BFI *L'Age d'or* study – before going, in the first blemish on Lil's Year – to Carla's, a destination in my plans but

not in my heart. I owe it to the memory of Lil to clear up – er, end – with tact, but muscular honesty, my relationship with this perfectly wonderful girl.

Darryl Kinaschuk (or deco dawson) came over to show me his third *Film* – beautiful, about shoe polishing. He made 380 shots in one day, and cut them to some Philip Glass. He's really a great editor. I showed him some Watson and Webber, *King of Jazz* and *Napoleon*, and he was suitably aroused. We also watched the disappointingly dark transfer of my *Archangel* trailer, and he went beyond himself in enthusiasm, the little genius.

My world reeks of pineapple sweetness. I leave a fresh pineapple on my silver plate-warmer by the kitchen window fan, which blows the tropical aroma clear into all the other rooms.

15 July

When Jilian was about nine years old, she and I went for a ride with Ian the day he tried to kill my mother. Ian had already told me about the day he killed three things. In the morning, he euthanized a suffering bird (windowpane) by stepping on its head with his work boot. In the afternoon, he dispatched a house pet (roadkill). And, in the evening, at Aerotrades, he and John Harvie flew a mercy mission to a reserve to bring an elderly woman down to a Winnipeg hospital, and Ian mistakenly re-loaded onto the plane the empty oxygen tanks instead of the full ones – and the woman suffocated on the flight. On the day he tried to kill my mother, events unfolded something like this: Jilian and I were strolling after dinner down Lake Avenue in Loni Beach. Ian drove up to us in his truck and wordlessly – wordlessly! – signalled for us to hop in the back of the pickup. We wordlessly complied – how else? Now the Loni mosquitoes were blasting harmlessly past my daughter and me as Ian accelerated to joyous hair-whipping open-air speeds. Then we spotted my mother, Jilian's Amma, wobbling her seventy-one-year-old way on a twilight bicycle ride right at us. From behind the rear windshield Ian looked back at us, said something mute, then white-knuckled the steering wheel, and, as if fixing Herdis in his crosshairs, floored the gas pedal. My mom saw the pickup bearing down on her. Jilian saw her grandmother growing larger and larger through the windshield. I nervously looked back and forth between my shaky, cycling mom and the hell-bent Miu, racing to eat up the distance between them. Jil screamed something, mute as well, tears flying from her eyes. Herdis moaned something mute and succumbed to horrified indecision. Ian bore down with a death-camp deadpan. At the last second, he swerved; Jil broke through with a rasping sob; a blast of mosquitoes peppered my face; and Amma, surrendering to death, simplying rolled her big ass and two bike tires into the air – a perfect header into the ditch. Ian stopped the truck and tried to figure out the etiquette for the situation: what to say to an elder whose life you've nearly taken. I tried to convince my septuagenarian mom that my good friend didn't mean anything by his joke. Jilian tearfully kicked the repentant Ian in the shin. If one wishes to break new comedic territory, one needs to take risks.

26 July
Recently read: *The Unknown Quantity* by Hermann Broch, *Father and Son* by Edmund Gosse, some of the pallid *Waterworks* by E. L. Doctorow, *Woman Without a Shadow* by Hugo Von Hofmannsthal. I've still not even started writing a second draft of George's script, and, now, so close to Jilian's arrival and Islendingadagurinn, I'll probably hold off for another eight days. Let's say I'll start on the Tuesday morning after Icelandic Day – computer on the dining-room table. In the meantime, I should read more – great lateral-thinking endeavours which are focusing the script's more free-floating aspects into something I might see as photographic subjects. Perhaps this last sentence touches on why I have trouble adapting a script written by someone else, even my best friend and soulmate; when I write alone or together with George, I allow only scenes I can already see. Making them visible after the fact is an overwhelming ordeal for my extremely narrow abilities.

27 July
Rage-thought to live by: in *The General*, Buster gets so annoyed at his girlfriend's stupidity for stoking the engine with tiny pieces of wood, he facetiously gives her little toothpicks – which she dutifully feeds into the fire. He then stares at her in disbelief, then delights in her anyway and leaps at her with a kiss. Sweet axiom!

14 August
Finished *The Blue Flower* by Penelope Fitzgerald. Started *Little Apple* by Leo Perutz. Turned down trip to Sitges to avoid exhaustion and inevitable cold picked up by sneezing fuckers sitting beside me on long plane ride. Watched *Shadow on the Wall* with Steve S. and George Toles at my place last night, screening out phone call from Elise – who I feel has committed too many crimes. Watched Stanwyck's *Ladies of Leisure* (great work by Joseph Walker) at George's the night before. *Edison and Neemo* (or *Brand upon the Brain*) grows point by point in these dog days. A little black cat chases a butterfly in the smoke and Mister Bowel has summoned me for the third effort of the day – by 10:30 a.m. I'm going back to bed right after.

15 August

Went to Cinematheque to see Keaton's *Blacksmith* and the nightmarish *Man on the Flying Trapeze* with W. C. Fields, with Carla Mundwiler and deco, then to Cousins, then home to watch *La Jetée* – obviously very strong, a compelling DVD host to *Odilon Redon*.

23 August

Jil and I at Second Cup making quick list of remembered smells: 1) Hot day, grass hot and freshly mowed with hot oil and gas of mower and the freshly chopped open steaming dog turd, also just mowed open and hot as a baked potato. 2) The smell of a childhood playmate's house. 3) The smell inside Amma's musty drawers at the beach. 4) The surprisingly strong smell of old, very thick nautical ropes – very greasy. 5) Lilacs on spring Sunday afternoons in backyard on Ellice, the intensity of their smell somehow tied up with the short time of blooming and Sunday night being a few hours before Monday morning classes and their purple colour being the colour and smell of twilight. 6) The smell of shampoo being rinsed down the black enamelled shop sink by the joint efforts of a black rubber hose and my mother's knuckles, which hurt my wimpy scalp. 7) Morris Block's caboose at Loni. 8) Rotting fishflies. To be continued.

What an overwhelming and simple pleasure it is to live with Jilian, and even with Kessa. Both seem totally comfy in the home I have made. Kessa even seems to love the apartment. She's out right now, getting in her last few days of the outdoors before going down into her basement prison – all furnace and litter box – in Aurora till next summer and two months again on the Channel Island in Lake of the Woods. While I finish jotting these lines, my parents' old alarm clock, set to wake me for my morning swim, noisily churns out time like a nearby factory. All else is a quiet Sunday night, 12:45 a.m. A fire engine chirps and speeds by, a few tires unroll themselves a mile away, strangely audible. A twig snaps in the front yard and some leaves rustle and other than a spoke pinging and a pedal spinning, there are no further sounds of human wakefulness. I shall rise and call Kessa in and she will sleep purringly either on my Morris chair, Lil's comfy chair, on the back of my chesterfield or, most happily for all three of us, with my daughter, who loves Kessa very much and who misses her and who sleeps in my porch now listening in her sleep to a U2 tape and who alone makes my porch a room. Jil and I have actually stayed in two nights running. Last night we watched *Philadelphia Story*, and tonight we channel-surfed until we started, too late for our sleepy heads, to watch *Strangers on a Train*. (Got halfway through.) We swam for thirty minutes today, with Steve, at Sargent Park. Yesterday, we swam at Pan Am pool for thirty-seven minutes; the day before that Jil and I swam for sixty minutes.

I've learned how to love people while I'm with them; nostalgia for the present, George would call it. My eyes tear up when I think how much I love my daughter. She rollerblades alongside my wobbly old bike (from Uncle Laurence) up Arbuthnot and down Scotland on our way to the pool. In the water I watch her as she swims beside me. Once, when we were both 'Australian crawling,' I loved her with my eyes, and my eyes swelled up and throbbed like a proud and lovesick heart. Jil's stay has been full and great and strength-giving. We even wrote in our journals together. And she took an interest in Sei Shonagon's *Pillow Book*, reading a few passages aloud. I gave her this book, bought in Edmonton originally to give to Sabrina, but it is Jil's now and perhaps it will be a tuning fork for her journal-writing tone from now on. We've had wine together, watched *The Balloonatic* together, looked at my old photos. Jil wants some snaps copied, including my pig-slaughtering pics and one of Phil Silvers. She found photos of Chas with Fran Huck that she wanted, and requests a copy of Cameron's obituary. Kessa has happily eaten a whole tin of salmon over the last three days.

27 August
Encountered a heartbreaking sight last night: a dead chipmunk upon a tree stump. I looked away with the deference and disgust I have for dead animals. But, as always, a clinical curiosity took over and my eyes were back, fixed on this ex-varmint, who turned out not to be so grossly mutilated as I first feared. After all, there are no roadkills on tree stumps, only little chipmunk diseases or heart attacks. This one had a head gash, one inch long, from which a brown resin had leaked. It oozed like sap. But there was something mangled about its body. Wait. It had two bodies. It was a squirrel, in fact, locked onto the chipmunk, eating it, a kind of cannibalism. The squirrel more or less sucked slowly on the little creature as a boa constrictor would upon a pig, taking it in slowly. Both predator and prey seemed entranced, sexually mortified. Was the chipmunk alive? I knocked the squirrel away with a stick. The squirrel, when untangled from the furry confusion of the scene, turned out to be a raccoon, and the chipmunk was indeed alive, awakened from its debilitating trance, only slightly injured. Shaking off a few head bites, he seemed fine. Fine, I say, because he was a tall boy now, naked in the woods, bloody, tousled, staggered, then recovered, happy and gamboling. Gamboling away into the shadows of the ferns and stalks.

3 September
John Harvie's sudden and permanent excommunication of me as his friend so many years ago may well have come about because of a pair of shorts. I've spent years wondering what ended the blessed spell of time Harvie and I spent together as companions, a time when Harvie buried the calendars in musty amber, submerged himself five decades deeper than everyone

else and comported himself down there in a nimbus of Brylcreem and flashing spats. Simply put, we all wanted to be with him in this rich world he improbably constructed out of desultory readings during a childhood spent in Prince Albert, Saskatchewan. John was nothing less than the doorman to the Hollywood Canteen, and, with his permission, the chosen were allowed to enter the choice decades barred forever to everyone else in the world. A handful of Winnipeggers, in love with Harvie the way girls loved the young Beatles, lay palm fronds in the path of this patent-leather hothead in hopes of catching an errant treasure: a charismatic sentence fragment spilled from a calculatedly careless conversation over-brimming with mint-condition anachronisms.

Harvie had great baggy navy-blue shorts cut from old military tarpaulins – or, actually, they were simply purchased from United Army Surplus. Shorts such as those weren't just different from early-eighties Speedos – those silky, nut-hugging little thong bikinis worn by most men – they were different from all other shorts in the world. These were the zoot suits of the shorts world. A statement that said: I don't want to be with you, I want to be by myself – in the shorts department, at least. (In 1998, all shorts are this size.) They seemed an ingenious move, and I thought they looked great. They bestowed a special, insightful status on whoever wore them. They were as uniquely enchanting to me as Jamie Handford's schizo-Popeye mutterings had been when I first fell in love with him. The shorts were the official uniform of a club of one.

Jamie had happily made his club big enough for two and we thrived. I must have been thinking like this because I bought the same shorts, and showed them to Harvie in a spirit of celebration. I stormed his club of one wearing his shorts – a heinous fashion crime. I realize now what I'd done to Harvie, barging in like that and standing before him as a shabby, unshining reflection of his own glossy person. Triple-harumph! I'm a thief! And I've lived all these years well past any statute of limitations, in complete freedom, shorts flapping in the wind, alone!

6 September

Carla and I watched *Leaving Las Vegas* last night; the obnoxious Sting soundtrack could be justified only by fact that Sting is a bigger loser than protagonist. Fell asleep early enough without difficult labours expected. Carla and I slept in Aunt Lil's bedroom, right down by her big picture window. Deborah Axelrod tended to Lil's garden – I actually gave Lil a strawberry plant for her eighty-fourth birthday, when she had little over a year to live (sheesh!). Deborah came very close to the window, without actually seeing me in bed just feet away, and I was able to watch her bend and flex her sculpted body in gardening exertions. Deb's boyfriend Mark appeared, noticed Lil's windows, which now seemed as transparent as air. Not knowing whether or not there was even glass in the window frames, Mark threw a stone toward the pane, knocking a big hole out and sending sugary pieces of glass onto Lil's carpet. I picked up the shards, at the last second stopping myself from just chucking them back out through the hole onto the lawn. Mark, apologetic, tried to help. His way of checking for the presence of windows by using stones infuriated me. A dog licked up most of the glass before I could get it out of the deep pile of the carpet. Lil was in her mother's bathroom when I dumped the pieces into the kitchen garbage. I had to think hard about how she had once died, or almost died and then made an enormous recovery which left us exhausted with gratitude. Now she was sick again; the once-ravaged bowels were all over again full of cancer. She relieved herself loudly and without shame, hoping perhaps to pass all the tumours no matter what the cost in pain, while I picked ever-tinier pieces of glass off my hands and dropped them into the pail under her kitchen sink.

LIST OF DISTINCTIVE VOICES:

Colin Clive	Katherine Hepburn	Alfred Hitchcock
Ned Sparks	Bette Davis	Miriam Hopkins
Clark Gable	Greta Garbo	Frederick March
Cary Grant	James Cagney	Walter Huston
James Mason	John Lodge	Al Jolson
Rock Hudson	Herbert Marshall	Nelson Eddy
George Saunders	Claudette Colbert	Jack Webb
Peter Lorre	Ronald Colman	Tony Curtis
Bela Lugosi	Gary Cooper	Burt Lancaster
Boris Karloff	Joseph Cotten	Dean Martin
Dick Powell	Eric Blore	Marilyn Monroe
John Wayne	Edward Everett Horton	Claude Rains
Buster Keaton	Franklin Pangborn	Lee Marvin
Groucho Marx	Cecil Blount De Mille	Raymond Massey
James Stewart	Marlene Dietrich	Adolphe Menjou
Woody Allen	Kirk Douglas	Clive Brook
Andy Devine	Margaret Dumont	Robt. Mitchum
William Demarest	W. C. Fields	Agnes Moorhead
Lionel Barrymore	Henry Fonda	Kim Novak
Maurice Chevalier	Glenn Ford	Gregory Peck
Fred Astaire	Tom Neal	Edward G. Robinson
Robert Stack	Orson Welles	Slim Pickens
Jack Benny	John Garfield	Walter Pidgeon
Humphrey Bogart	Gloria Grahame	Linda Marr
Charles Boyer	Conrad Veidt	Thelma Ritter
Marlon Brando	Charles Laughton	Richard Widmark
Walter Brennan	Tippi Hedren	Cesar Romero
Vincent Price	Charlton Heston	Robert Ryan.

13 September 12:11 a.m.
Start French lessons tomorrow. I'm very concerned I will drop
out and shame myself. Was feeling lonely tonight. Couldn't
work up the enthusiasm to make dinner for myself so I went to
Dutch Maid and they made dinner for me. Four griefcakes with
sausages. Boredom, laziness and poor diet. Remember: Year of
Lil. Did I mention I weigh over 200 lbs now? Just like 99% of
dieters, I gained back all I lost and I'm still gaining.

Barbara Stanwyck   Erich von Stroheim   Robert Walker
Lorne Green   Robert Young   Basil Rathbone
Brian Kieth   Gene Tierny   L. Bacall
Joan Fontaine   Rosalind Russell   Carole Lombard
Jean Arthur   Vivien Leigh   Elsa Lanchester
Olivia DeHavilland John Barrymore   Sean Connery 1960's
Dick Burton   Ed Wynn

14 September

Autumn! Autumn! Chilly morning before my first trip to school
as a pupil in twenty-five years. Leaves fermenting in yesterday's
heat, sun rising from gutters in steamy spirals from tobacco-ish
shreds of deciduae. Shadows sharp in the nostrils, sunlight in
high contrast and gauzed over by peat smoke. An apple is
polished. I'm nervous about new classmates; could anyone be as
beautiful as Karen Smith was on the first day of school in 1968?

16 September
Il y a neuf étudiants dans la classe Française. Ira est un masseur.
Tracy est une serveuse Canadienne. My Art of Film class has
fifty students – only one empty seat in 2UC38, but such empty
seats are a rapidly spreading disease. I rode home on the
omnibus with George last night. He had stayed out late rehearsing *Speed the Plow*. In the crammed bus we sat opposite a woman
who shall be forever tattooed upon my retinas, or so it seems.
Diyah Doe-ness, and coincidental and hope-giving eye contacts
of the nanosecond variety, along with slouchy fleshapods gauzed
up poorly, made a recipe for desperation – my first after a long
day on the crowded campus. Normally a hormonal chaos but
strangely unaffecting this year, until the tattoo artist. Diyah lives
again!!!

2 October
Last night – a celebrity dream!
    I dreamt of Hitler, that I met him one-on-one in a long
encounter that evolved slowly into a situation of such terrible
gravity, which eventually dragged my entire family down – the
whole thing unfolding in what seemed like 'actual' time, and for
the entire episode (about four hours) I was thoroughly
convinced that I was actually experiencing this encounter. So
undreamlike was this episode that I never thought once to
escape the dream, but only thought desperately and impotently
to escape the situation.
    Quickly, Hitler and I chatted; I was Jewish – we both knew
it. I joked obsequiously. He was affable, dull, insistent and
omnipotent. I was to drive him to my family, to the lake where
they dwelt at the cottage, so they could be registered. I suppose
I felt I could reason my family to safety because I drove Adolf
to the lake, conversing all the time, suffering the Führer's dull
gags. At the cottage, Hitler informed us we would all be going
with him – to some ominous and obvious destination. I had a
twelve-year-old son who would be coming with Amma, Jilian
and me. 'At least you can't take Aunt Lil!' I countered when
Hitler read her name off a list, 'She's dead!' At that point, Aunt
Lil emerged from her bedroom, sick with stomach cancer but
disturbed by the ruckus. 'Get out of here!' I demanded of her,
while a distracted Hitler looked at my record collection. I shoved

the dying old sweetheart out of the cottage. 'And never come back!' I begged her, banishing her to the bushes to shiver and squirm with stomach tumours.

The lake clouded over darkly as we all piled into the family car. I drove, Hitler rode shotgun, Amma and the kids in the back. My mind spun with fruitless designs. How could I crash the car and not hurt the kids? Should I just crash and kill us all?

6 October

First good lecture in 'Art of Film 1' this term. *Citizen Kane* covered in twenty-five highly caffeinated minutes, my hair standing on end. Only some students pointlessly adversarial: 'No one would throw Rosebud in the fire! Don't they read the papers?' But other students jumped to the picture's defence, and I feel at least some of the students were amused to see me attempt to pack, speed-lecturing style, all the info in under the ten p.m. deadline. And, if not amused, at least relieved the lecture was so short (owing to fact I showed Berkeley's 'By a Waterfall' beforehand, along with the challenge that one would notice spectacular camera work or make an appointment with an eye doctor). Next week, I'll endeavour to dovetail my take on Berkeley with Paglia's on *The Birds*. It might be wise to bring in a tape of a Leafs game to keep some students awake. I think seven out of forty-nine students made the correct distinction between 'distinterested' and 'uninterested' – an assignment left for them. Students' bluff answers make for hilarious reading. 'Disinterested is when someone is bored with something. Uninterested is when they don't even care to be interested.'

7 October

French lessons in morning, then, leaving my office key with Steve Burke, I play hooky from teaching to take up my prestigious duties as Honorary Chairperson for the Manitoba Schizophrenia Society's first annual Voices (in the Head) Film Festival. Never before have I agreed to do such a thing about which I know so little. A complete impostor! I interview a psychiatrist specializing in 'Antistigmatization of the Mentally Ill'; I try to sound like I know what I'm talking about. I steep myself in the jargon of mental wellness. The audience is full of heartbreaking and humorous consumers of mental health services. I discuss not 'schizophrenics' but 'those who live with schizophrenia' or 'psychiatric survivors.' One tortured consumer mumbles into his breast that he's scared of clowns. 'Who isn't?' I ask back, using the safest route for a big laugh – which comes instantly and loudly, and that scares the poor twisted consumer, too. But I got my laugh, which emboldens this impostor more still. By the end of the two live onstage interviews (the other one with an educator and dramatist who directed a play created and performed entirely by consumers) I feel like a mixed success, a bit like Charlie Rose. Could I do this every night? Chat with people by blowing huge billows of bluff off a sheet of questions written by some researcher all the while looking for gag ops? You bet!

11 October
Steve tells me to write about walking alone at autumn. An immense writing task, but here goes my puny effort!

In autumn, one's memory is sharpened by the tiny little bites taken out of one's nostrils by the cold, strict air. One no more walks in autumn than one cuts through golden frigid blocks, like a swimmer leading with his nose. 'Yellow!' we scream, and the frosty precipitate is shot through with a warmth shaped like fork lightning. Lightning which hangs there and dissolves into us, onto our suddenly closed eyelids. 'Who can dare to look at the heartbreaking sunlight of autumn except through closed lids?' And verdant potentials lie roasted in hot, yellow tatters as dead as hope; but we are lucky because no one can remember hope. And yet we stare at the end of it all as amnesiacs, all context replaced by veil upon veil of smoky confusion. Made stupid by the smells of autumn, we decide everything is beautiful, then we wonder why we're unbearably sad. The sky hangs low, or rings bells, or fills ears with frigid stillness, or chops itself into black furrows then turns itself around and chops itself into squares. And the squares descend, one to each city block, descend like hair dryers onto the uplifted branches of black trees. When these cubes are lifted, the trees have been wildly coiffed, backcombed, teased unhappy with the wizened, scared and poultry aspects that they now present to each other. And, stupid with smoke and veins of warmth, we again confuse these shocked and varicose and denuded faces with beauty, and our eyes moisten and our bosoms ache as if we were sad, for the simple reason that we are sad. Sorry, Steve.

15 October
Second Cup. Steve says I'm to write of any childhood hunting or fishing trips. Did me father ever take me fishing? I DON'T THINK SO! I went fishing a few times, each time resenting the disruption of my routine of incredibly lazy solitude. I preferred spending mornings at the lake crouching in silence by the water, daydreaming about how next school year would represent a massive romantic turnaround for me. No turnaround ever occurred, but I was compelled to visualize this possibility. And being yanked away from these vague strategy studies just to fish off Gimli pier seemed to doom me to yet another kissless and caressless winter. Winter after winter, as a matter of fact, when not one girl could bear to look at this trembling Fejjoid. And I can't blame them, certainly never blamed them.

No, my father didn't insist. Rob and Reynold, two brothers who always wore glasses, hard-ons and rolled-up jeans, virtually kidnapped me into their angling hours – the baiting and elaborate hooks, talk about stink-fingers and fucking and cumming. While I brooded about Valentine sweethearts, they cast about razor-sharp lures with dangerous disregard for where the barbed projectiles flew. Who can scour from his head the fear of a fish hook grabbing into one's eye or face when running the gauntlet of the asinine rod-whipping sportsmen on any pier, real or imagined? They made me fish while they tortured, with needle-nosed pliers, whatever they caught. I got a little perch, just once, as puny as my hairless dick. While Rob and Reynold, throbbing pricks livid and tumescent with fishing excitement, conspired in blue plots that outstripped in evil even the most ingrown and lonely lucubrations of my worn-pillow nights. This one little perch, too small to keep, but also too small not to torture, I cut from my little rod by severing the line with scissors. Some line still dangled from the little flipper's mouth. I operated on pure instinct, and placed the puny guy into a dry baggy. Or rather rolled the baggie up over the fish, sealed it with a twist-tie, and threw it back into the lake, upon which surface it floated out of sight. The first and only fish I ever caught. Murdered in a to me puzzling way. Rob and Reynold were in jail a few years later, busted in a huge drug sting.

17 October

Painted living room yellow-gold, brown and a putrid green last night while listening to Korngold and Offenbach. Four hours total to remove furniture and queeny knick-knacks, paint, then replace all the shit. In bed by three. Wonderful.

Steve says to write on Vigo and my love for him. My receptivity to Vigo was primed by watching early Fleischer Brothers cartoons, which I did every day since before I can remember. Somehow, on two continents, unaware of each other, and having only transatlantic zeitgeists and the film chemicals of the thirties as the thinnest of shared influences, Vigo and the Fleischers produced works of uncannily similar mischief, bounce and density. Vigo's works, smudgy as the grease pencils Max Fleischer ordered for his artists, are cross-hatched by shadows, wrinkles and clutter all Rube Goldberged together into rhythmically jiggling frames where the decors are as alive as any actor. They move in subversive loops, these backgrounds, as do the highly detailed frames of a Boop or Popeye, whose peculiar mumbling gaits stamp out the meter to which all passing decors must perform: autos must bounce upon their tires, clocks must tick, policemen whistle and birds flap their wings in time to the swinging of Popeye's forearms. Cats must swarm, teem and spill out of bunks, closets and portholes to the measured cooings and hip-swingings, but always, over all this looped anarchy, there is the free jazz of mumbling. Popeye or Pere Jules. Which one is the greatest improv soloist? The greatest sailor? Each the champ of his continent, they were never to meet.

24 October

Went out to Loni with Carla and swam after dark (very cold, to be sure), then walked to Pizza Hut for beer and dindins. To the pier, then back home for wine from the Schizophrenics Society, drunk beneath the extremely twinkling stars and northern lights, which domed over the rotting picnic table, the now-precious and rarely seen sandbars of Loni, and the screamingly yellow trees of our own yard. Said trees went Ektachrome in the morning when the sky couldn't have been more azure. My yard resembled the Rock Hudson gardening scenes from *All That Heaven Allows*. Saw a fox go into Snidals from beach.

Darryl Kinaschuk has finally fired me up to 'omnivorous' status concerning the Soviet silents – so much flavour to add to *The Branded Brain*. Watched *Mother* by Pudovkin last night; rented five other Commies for the week. Deborah Axelrod just popped her beautiful beamer into my back door to rip off an almost healed scab before dashing off to a Royal Winnipeg Ballet matinee of *Dracula*. Deborah looks great in Darryl's movie, by now in its semi-fine-cut stage. No one else in 'Filmmaking 349' has even mailed off their footage yet, far as I can tell.

28 October

Gave a not-bad *Léolo* lecture last night, preceded by a speech about how to kill our fathers, and the clip of Dorothy Malone dancing Daddy Hadley to death.

Darryl Kinaschuk's fourth *Film* with Deborah Axelrod is absolutely wonderful; it's reinfused me with the movie-making tingles. Axelrod is the new Kiki, with an eau de Falconetti. None of the dancers – Deborah, Erin, Sherri or Shaun – knew what to say after its screening, so conversation quickly went shop. Is this how they'd have it after one of their own performances? I've often found dancers to be the most literal-minded of film viewers – strange for those who perform poetry.

Got *Dishonored* and *Shanghai Express* back from Richard Ott yesterday, a lend-out that had lasted a year. And now my video collection needs only one errant sheep – Dreyer's *Joan of Arc* – to reunite the entire flock. (No, *Leech Woman* is with George.)

Steve is attempting to find one American movie from the sixties he can bear to screen for his 'American Cinema since 1950' class. He's tired of Peckinpah's slow-motion violence and misogyny; he's nauseated by the slick sixties agitprop of *Bonnie and Clyde*. The sixties really were a terrible decade for movies, says Steve.

31 October

I don't want my Dead Father dreams to end, but by now I'm wondering what's up with me. Last night, Uncle Ron turned into Chas. The sight of this perfect transformation to vintage '77 Chas brought the sobs bubbling out of me, and with tears soaking the face of Ron/Chas, I planted a few kisses on the masculine, unshaven cheek of my father. Yes, by now he was simply my father, and I felt the bristles of the five-o'clock shadow on the turned-away and uncomfortable face, glass eye staring blankly in confusion at my pressing face during this unprecedented act. Not only have I never kissed my father, nor he me, I've never dreamt about it, nor even perversely thought of it for any of the eventually unavoidable reasons. Not even to ward off an urgent pleasure with an enervating taboo. Sob, sob, sob.

6 November

I'm sitting on AC 718 (Ken Griffey Jr.'s final home-run total?) to La Guardia. Three nights in New York. Lucius Barre and Gariné ... great. I love New York, but I'm unexcited about this trip. I'd much rather spend the weekend at the cottage with a bottle of hooch and the little galaxy of Onan in which I find myself these days.

Watched *Les Anges du péché* by Bresson last night with Carla and George, who is a huge nun-o-phile. He was initially thrilled by the wall-to-wall wimples, then fell prey to Bresson's tardy pacing and went into a deep nap, only to wake up shrieking during the movie's last seconds, hallucinating that someone was standing next to the TV. This morning at 6:30 a.m. I watched the rest of the super-exhilarating *Arsenal*, which I scored myself with my Korngold. At times, this music works so well with the movie, I weep or get chills.

My crushes are very tepid these days, nothing to compare with the old days of Sarah or Deborah. I think my body is beginning to know what I can't make my head realize, and I fall asleep before embracing my pillow on most nights. Food is the thing in which I overindulge, and it hasn't betrayed me yet, performing on command. Of course, I may not be able to afford food much longer, or the kind of food I hang with will kill me some day. Right now, it's just making my thighs rub together.

Amma turns eighty-two on Monday. She celebrates by going out for lunch with that old snake-in-the-grass Mel Wilson! Mel jumped on a fumbled football for a touchdown in the 1939 Grey Cup and has been lying down ever since.

9 November

I found no time to write about the trip while actually on it (there's no Steve Snyder in NY is my only explanation), but now from gate A7 at La Guardia, I can begin scribbling. Friday: took cab to West Park Hotel. On the way, the cabbie showed me a picture of the sixteen-year-old babysitter he's been fucking. We hit it off just fine. He sent me off with seduction pointers: 'Just look the girl in the eyes, the tits, then the pussy. She'll come right up to you.' This guy fucked the bride just moments after the groom the night of the wedding where he was best man. He doesn't even know, or seem to care, if he's the father of this latter woman's children. I shall try his strategies; they seem to work.

Emily met me for Italian at some down-and-dirty restaurant. I strolled to Times Square and back, stopping at Coliseum Books (*Dreamland: America in Photographs 1900–1910*) and Virgin Superstore. Lev Kuleshov's *By the Law*, Harry Langdon's *Short Pants*, and Gabriele D'Annunzio's (title anyway) *Cabiria*. On Saturday morning, I walked to Gotham Books (41 West 47th) and bought Pater's *Renaissance*, Canetti's *Agony of Flies* and Osbert Sitwell's little book of friends' portraits. $US 140.00 or (@1.51/1) $211.40 CDN. Then cabbed out to Astoria for an AMMI screening of the Jock Sturges flaying *Art for Teachers of Children*. Hung out with Todd Haynes (fresh from his *Velvet Goldmine* premiere, but forget to collect his autograph for my book) and David Schwartz (director of AMMI). The gorgeous black woman who works in the foyer remembered me from spring and made sure I got free food and drink. What a beautiful smile. I was so staggered by her beauty I forgot the hack's game plan and looked only into her eyes. Ah, but what a sweetie, anyway. Met Christine Vachon, Todd's producer, and Todd Solondz's producer as well. I ditched everyone, surprised to find myself unwilling to join Gariné and her new boyfriend for dinner. Instead, I strolled for miles before catching the late screening of Solondz's *Happiness*, which I didn't like that much.

Shit! I forgot to buy one of those graphically beautiful Heimlich manoeuvre posters from the deli next to the hotel. A very stylized fish bone curls over the text, as strong as Soviet agitprop. A graphic success, but a safety precaution failure, one's eyes refusing to assimilate the text in such a gorgeous design.

Watched *Irma Vep* properly at AMMI yesterday, with much pleasure actually, then nervously (why was I so nervous?) introduced *Umbrellas of Cherbourg*. My big gag gambit, which dismantled itself before harvesting many chuckles, concerned the movie's wallpaper, which always seemed to match the clothing worn by the characters, and how I loved this strategy so much I was attempting the same thing in my own home. Oh, well. *Umbrellas* was incredibly moving for me on this my third viewing. I had to think of maggots near the end to keep the tear-streaks off my face at the illumination of the house lights. I was very pleased when the large audience laughed in unison at the most conspicuous specimen of costume and decor colour-agreement: Guy's betrothal scene with Madeleine, when she wears an orange dress at an all-orange café.

After the movie, a good time as always with Mike Rubin and Su Patel. Gariné took David Schwartz and me upstairs by the second-hand nuts to look at the 16 FPS ceramic movie. I met her current sweetie, a vaguely continental DOP for Bruce LaBruce. I hugged Lucius Barre, nodded at a few familiar faces with forgotten names, chatted with Emily Russo's perfectly sweet Peter Aaronson, snapped wet towels at Kino's Nicholas from the order desk, sparred for some reason with that DOP chap, went out for Greek with twenty of these types (oh, David Sterritt showed up with his two new books – on Godard and on the Beats – to introduce *Irma Vep*). Then, bidding goodnight to all, including Adrian's charming wife Geneviève, rode back to Manhattan sharing a cab with the drunk and hiccuping Adrian. Gariné looked beautiful but contrived, not unearthly as I'd thought once before; perhaps my eyes were filled with bile, perhaps she's losing it. Perhaps I even made her a bit sheepish – this I really doubt. For the second straight visit, Gariné piled up the bindi between her eyes, wearing these gold-and-red coloured plastic buttons in a vertical column and some cardboard teardrops in the corner of each eyelid. She was reasonable, sweet, quiet, barely there, but gracious. What do you want from an ex?

12 November

Yesterday a wonderful, peaceful, snowy Remembrance Day – the first day of winter – quiet as snow itself. Took Amma to the new Pavilion restaurant in City Park – a giant glass atrium, surrounded by bright clouds on all sides. A sweet visit with my very pleased mother, with whom, for once, I communicated honestly, freely, guiltlessly. I also actually paid for her lunch, her birthday treat, and she actually ate a red pepper, a vegetable usually designated too spicy and thus verboten by her hair-trigger sexual principles. (Was this lunchtime lubricity because of her date with Mel?) She had her beloved pickerel. I picked her up an hour early for the 11:30 reservation, then drove around the park and Charleswood, chatting, waiting for the eatery to open, checking the time every two minutes, and we arrived right on time.

Rewatched *The File on Thelma Jordan* at George's, napping a bit in the middle of this great Siodmak noir. Then ate drive-through McDonald's for bowel-masochism – which arrived an hour later. Please, never again! After a nap, I actually called Carl to come over and keep me company while I painted my kitchen. Amma actually phoned me at nine p.m., and in a good mood too, to say she found the interview with Lindy Vopnfjord in the *Sun*. Carl and I painted, drank wine and listened to tapes: Hermann's *Psycho*, *Swing Street* (with Maxine Sullivan), *Musical Bits 1* (with 'St. James Infirmary Blues') and Arthur Tracy – amazing! Finished kitchen at 2:00 a.m. and slept straight through to 9:10 a.m. A lovely little day to remember.

15 November

Gramma and I always ate lunch in the darkened living room. Being blind, she never turned on the lights; being lazy, apathetic and slow, I never did either. With no windows letting into this room, I could barely make out the shape of this shrunken, soft-voiced tiny woman. Nor could I make out the food she rendered for me out of the unlikely ingredients gathered together and boiled up without the advantage of eyes. The identical size and shape of the spice tins led to spectacular errors – and results – on the lunch table. Powdered milk boxes the same size and weight as powdered potatoes led to nutritious but unpalatable substitutions. We sat together, next to the huge circular mirror, a wedding gift to my mom and dad, which reflected our darkness, actually reflected nothing back to us. The mirror was as blind as my grandmother, and in that room I was as blind as both.

I had become obsessed with palmistry at school, embroiled at every recess in competitions over the length of our lifelines, over the inscrutable value of our heart-lines. No one could agree upon which line was which. I had a cocksure friend, already tall and pubertal, whose lifeline stretched way off his palm and well into his wrist. My palm was simply creased by three or four lines, and the rest of my handflesh was as character-free as silly putty. We shoved our hands in each other's faces, and I smelled the doomed futures of these core area kids – futures reeking of boiled cabbage, floor wax, bubble gum and itchy, poorly wiped asses. There was no denying the long lives they all held in their hands, but there was no denying the stink of these long lives either. I was intoxicated with these competitions, for my future had no smell and looked like the best possible future of all to me.

At lunch, in the dark, I held my Gramma's palm up to my face. By stretching my young pupils open even further and turning her hand just so, I could almost make it out. And by palping it with my own homogenized hands and staring long enough, a vague vision of her fingers emerged, like a kind of thermograph. I found her palms, plunged into their warm and bulbous veins, little nosegays of bones and tendons her hands were, and so netted with the wrinkles of her ninety years. I was as lost as a person could be on the palm of a hand. 'Where's your lifeline?' I asked my Gramma, and suddenly, my parents' mirror could see. The mirror showed me Gramma, her white hair standing on end in the black, holding two transparent and luminous hands up to the face of a young boy. 'I don't think I have a lifeline anymore,' my Gramma lamented, and in spite of my desperate contradictions of my Gramma's sad realization I knew she was right. She had every line a life can acquire, and all these lines, bunched densely into crepe, had left no evidence of the lifeline. We returned to our unseen food, something thick and warm from the blender, not one lump in our lunches, no clues as to what we ate in the dinner of the mirror.

The sleek mirror's glass had no lines of its own, but its life ended very ignominiously decades later. In a delirious and unsentimental moment, I took it down off the wall and cemented it into the bottom of a movie set, and made a fake pond of it. Photographed it once, then let part-time employees smash it with hammers while they hurriedly demolished my decors so a new tenant could move into my film studio.

18 November

Last night: *Nights of Cabiria*. I screened it on a good 16mm print for my class, but the throw of the lamps was so dim, and the P.A. buzzed out shrill orders to murder our parents. So I had the projectionist take the film off, and I showed *Un Chien*

Andalou, a picture in a very degraded state, but at least the P.A. didn't rive our heads in two with its CIA-designed frequencies.

After class, Launi Davis, one of my best students and easily the sexiest, waited for everyone to leave before asking if she could write on *Gummo* for her final assignment – the bathtub spaghetti-eating scene. Launi's face was strangely a dark red; she's either been skiing on some windy slope, unlikely for this time of year, or was blushing like a woman in Tolstoy. I refuse to believe she was blushing.

Tonight is the big screening night in 'Filmmaking' – the students' first films. Steve Burke wants me to get drunk, and he'll pour me a big whiskey, but I've got to stay sober. There is no joie de vivre in this class, no spontaneous ejaculations of glee, applause or wakefulness. If Steve and I drank, we'd be the only two drunks in the class, a rancid scenario.

Carla and I had a talk about my lack of passion. I'm the thermostat in this chilly little relationship.

Mark and Deborah have yet to finish watching *Careful*, after numerous tries spanning five and a half months. Now they want to borrow another one of my movies. Am I supposed to give them *Archangel*? Instead they went away with *Sweet Smell of Success*, *Notorious* and a plunger, none which they have returned yet.

22 Nov
Grey Cup Day. Steve says I should write about the first time I heard 'vintage' music. I owned two 78s as a toddler, and, in spite of never being warned about their brittleness, I never broke them. For I loved them too much to be rough with such strange playthings, and never allowed them into the hands of any of my dim-witted friends – future suicides one and all.

One 78 was Arthur Godfrey's 'The Man with the Weird Beard' with 'Heap Big Smoke No Fire' on the flipside. The 'Weird Beard' song evoked mysterious bushes of hair and an inscrutable, perhaps powerful, man, with the kind of impulses one finds or feels or fears in big bushes. 'Heap Big Smoke' was an Indian complaint about male impotence or, as I understood it then, about an Indian brave who made jokes when kissing was preferred – a strategy I noticed Chas deploying around Herdis, and one that has served me well to this day. The other 78 was more ancient, mildewy and alien: Harry Lauder's old Scottish music hall pasquinade 'Stop Your Ticklin' Jock' – lots of *echt* Scottish creepiness in Lauder's accent and the tortured drones of those detestable bagpipes. Lots of boozy forced laughter, and jokes too cheap even for Chas to recycle among his pals. On the disc's flipside there were no more jokes, just a smooth surface, as if it hadn't yet dawned on the makers of phonograph records to use both sides, thus dating this song somewhere in my mother's prehistory even. I played these records almost round the clock one winter. Until I was informed of their inestimable dollar worth by my parents, and I took even more precaution against the bumbling of my huffer friends and played the tunes only in private. Thirty years later, with yet three more decades of appreciation accrued to their market value, I saw other copies of these discs for sale at Lee's in Minneapolis. Each one was worth two dollars. Monuments of credibility, my parents had been bang on again.

Perhaps the first vintage recordings I embraced as an adult in a fresh listening situation were the early works of Bing Crosby and Dick Powell. (Of course, like everyone my age and younger I had already assimilated every note of *The Wizard of Oz*.) Dick Powell came to me through the eternally cutting-edge couchmares of Berkeley, which I watched off Steve's living room wall as often as I could in the winter of '81–'82. We must have worn out the last reel of *42nd Street*. The Crosby came to me courtesy of that be-spatted arbiter of the acme in anachronistic arts, John Boles Harvie. With patent-leather hair, gleeful bounce and the affected bug eyes of Eddie Cantor, whose photo he carried on his person for comparison purposes, John ginnishly lindy-hopped to the *King of Jazz* discs, clanging the imaginary triangle with one of his remaining fingers whenever Pops Whiteman had Ferde Grofé do the same. Especially animated during 'I Want to Do Something for You' (or to you, as John quipped with perfectly stale-dated saltiness).

24 November

George has remarked, after admiring Matthias Müller's *Home Stories*, that a similar montage could be made of people throwing drinks at mirrors or through windows. Ah. Where's Müller's phone number?

I write this page in the U of M bar an hour before teaching *Possessed*. Joan! Oasis plays on the jukebox – actually, no, it's someone better. Whatever. The ambience is so beer-swilling and undergraduate. I'm in a great mood! (Though a little anxious because there is no woman on any backburner.)

Jilian sent me her short story 'The Happiest Day of My Life' – her account of our ritualized trips to Gimli. Very funny. Very closely observed. Nice unforced metaphors: 'Boondoggles was about the size of a powder room.' There's the touch of Sei Shonagon. 'Most hateful.' Surprising details in the memories: the lilac bush at 800 Ellice; and a nice twist of the recollection into a new situation: the sudden need to do this ritual alone and how happy it made her feel. This was so naturally written that I'm proud to tears. When Jane and I split up years ago, and it seemed like she might win sole custody of Jilian, my first thought, or terror, because the best times I'd ever had with Chas were the trips in the car down to Gimli, was that I'd never again get to drive there with my little daughter. And now comes, nineteen years later, my daughter's first short story sent to me, about the twenty years' worth of car trips to Gimli, and how ritualized these trips were, and how, when she finally got to make the trip by herself it occasioned the 'happiest day of her life.' So the rituals prove they have a strength of their own. I hope she drives her children there someday.

30 November

Careful plays tonight at the Cinematheque. I admit I would like certain people to see this movie, but I was too undevious to plant any promotions. Darryl's going, which is very loyal, or enthusiastic, or even smart, of him. During screening read Gogol's 'A Terrible Revenge' at the Fyxx.

6 December

Last night, Ross and I took Amma to Earl's for dinner and let her pay. At home, I read Jean Paul Richter's *The Comet*, drank wine, ate even more, fell into a belly-groaning sleep of much fitfulness and now, as I race through these last lines, prepare to speed off to Van Sant's *Psycho*.

Back from *Psycho*. Not at all wrath-inducing, but not much else either. Very strange, but the script is so well written, and the camera placed so well, that even these shabby simulacra re-enacting the parts down to the last mince don't entirely ruin the picture. But then, back home, one watches Janet Leigh in her white, then her black bra, and wonders if Anne Heche, in her scraggy little Sandy Duncan full-colour red bra, is somebody's idea of a joke. The movie's not sexy, even though Vince Vaughn is quite nice.

10 December

Just got up at 6:35 a.m. with a splitting headache that was torturing me with endless, ridiculous dreams – signing a deposit slip in thirty-seven different places and counting when I awake – remembering that I forgot to drink coffee last night, hence the headache. So, two Japanese oranges later, and with that cup of coffee by my pathetically addicted side, I sit in my Christmasy kitchen, with waves of headache receding painfully.

How did I 'forget' my coffee last night? Big workout in the afternoon, 110 minutes, straight home to make dinner – clam chowder, bean salad, steamed vegetables, and hummus with tomatoes on Ryvita – and Carla, who came over to convince me to let her back into my life. She was gracious all the way really, and made no real fuss, just little tears running down her cute face. And I was really happy to see her, but I have to be alone, alone, alone! She went off just in time for me to get off to school for my filmmaking class – the screening of my students' films in a three-hour ordeal. Running late, I answered the phone to reassure what had to be a concerned S. Burke, but it was Elise – oh, how stupid am I, having just given her my new phone number – who phoned to call me a raving idiot, or she was a raving idiot, I can't remember. I got into my car, late, and coffee-less, got to the university just in time, and in a monstrous, withdrawal-aggravated mood, sent Eddie Powell, a student from last year who wanted to talk with me about a feature script, to Gene Walz; then announced that Melissa B. got a zero for her late film, the whole class listening and even laughing uncomfortably, and me wondering why I hate everyone when it's really just, furious Elise side-swiping aside, lack of coffee. The last delicate moment after dinner was an agonized Carla contorting her face against her pride, lamenting that breaking up with Jeff was no problem but that this breakup hurts, and I not being able to help in any way except to go back to her – which, in her matter-of-fact words, I am 'determined not to do.'

S. Burke and I complained crabbily in our office about the mirthlessness of the filmmaking class, which really meant, and we admitted this, that no one in the class *liked* us. They didn't laugh at our jokes, didn't express any interest in us personally, didn't stop talking when we spoke and didn't learn anything that we endeavoured to teach them. When the last class ended, we were *not* invited out for drinks, thank god, and I went straight home, snacked and went to bed about four and a half hours ago.

At first, my dreams were wonderful. I had a long, detailed dream about a dinner at 800 Ellice. Dad was the most definite presence, sitting in his place at table's end, picking over one of my Mom's ancient recipes. I sat in Lil's chair, on my knees, leaning onto the table like an unruly twelve-year-old, a teenage Janet sat kitty-corner from me (I sat on the right-hand side of Dad!), and Lil sat ectoplasmically somewhere at table, a very pleasant presence. Mom worked through dinner down in the shop; Ross was off married somewhere; Cameron rested in his grave; Gramma and Toby made no mention of themselves in this playland, either sitting on their blind-chair and heating vent respectively, or reposing in death, fully off the premises.

I think I blended an actual occurrence into the program of dream features, remembering to ask my Dad, for the very first time in his life, how old he was. He pretended not to be sure before revealing forty-seven as his age, as I completed a loving pencil sketch of him in profile, a very convincing likeness as I recall. This pencil-sketch/age-revelation occasioned my first realization of my Dad's mortality; I asked him if forty-seven was very old – he joked that it was, then reassured me it wasn't – and I asked if he had long to live. Long to live, I was assured. Then Dad grabbed his twin-pack of Old Dutch chips, and went of to 'work' for a few evening hours, probably in one of his procession of Dodge Darts, setting me to worry about his proven-fatal diet and his itch to get away from us. But still happy that we'd had perhaps the largest group dinner in our family history – about five minutes. Off he went, deserting us but at least talking to us, making excuses for his imminent absence.

Afterwards, Janet and I lay, stomach down, on the couch and watched TV. In full *Untouchables* configuration, but feet-to-feet instead of head-to-head, Janet and I reflected on this just completed dinner. 'Wonderful, just to be here, like this, for dinner again, at 800 Ellice,' she opined into the hand she rested her face upon. I proclaimed through the fissure in my heart that it was the most joyous idyll in my history – a dinner AND conversation with my night-beloved, and very little rejection. Oh, how I loved the dinner! Warmth, warmth, sweet family warmth, and the warm tears filled up in huge bosom reservoirs, but I held them back with sublime and hurtful restraint. The ache in the over-stretched tear flasks, as stretched and rubbery as hot-water bottles, made me as sensate as I've ever been in a dream. The pain migrated north into my head, commencing the fitful, coffee-dance dream portion of my truncated sleep.

It's a new day: Mark and Deborah have just clumped down the stairs and driven off to Mark's work. Deborah will soon return and climb back to her bed, and I, weary of this sterile flirtation I had with her (on my side, anyway), will go back to bed, unable to assign any romantic identity to the larger, more huggable of my two pillows. So loveless am I that no face will stick to this pillow, and a lifelong practice seems at an end.

Reading Rilke's *The Siblings*. Watched *The General Line* with George a couple nights ago. Bought, with the last of my cash, a Gustave Doré collection, and Mandelstam's *Moscow Notebooks*. I really want to order Starewicz's *The Cameraman's Revenge*!

23 December

Very busy. Finally got weight under 190 – did it by walking. Almost finished Joe Roth's *String of Pearls* (very *La Ronde* and Canetti). Caelum and I drank a toast to bachelorhood last night – a pair of double Wild Turkeys clinking at Bar-I. Caelum said 'uh-oh' and Carla appeared out of nowhere, sent a frost wave my way, then disappeared again. I'm secretly house-sitting George's place for the next nine days (Toles family in Hamburg). Will I be able to use the place to soothe my aching breast? I don't know (and that's the 'fun'). I've been swimming forty of the last forty-one days, but it was the long walks I took while Xmas shopping – for myself – that burned off the lard. My thighs still rub together; I can't remember the number that I have to hit to make the chafing go away. It must be 180; nine lbs to go! I'm switching to fish and lentil (with wine) soup, plus raw vegetables the Xmas week. Skating (it's so cold just one week after Winnipeg was Canada's hot-spot), and walk will do the rest. I still have many papers to mark, a script to finish, two movies to edit and even make pickup shots involving Darcy and – Deborah naked? – and I have no income. Hardly the Year of Lil, but here goes!

26 December

Just back from Noam's annual Boxing Day Boyopolis Extravaganza. I'm drunk on Stoli and Chartreuse, and incredulous that my answering machine is as empty as my bed. At least I played my first two hockey games of the year today and yesterday. I'm stiff. Oh, the Chartreuse is making me sick. Disbelieving my own age, I see it on my contemporaries and even on my juniors and am horrified on my own behalf.

Laura Michalchyshyn gave me an eighty-year-old case of glass eyes she bought off Walter Luek for thirty dollars on a Christmas Eve shopping spree – sixty-two glass eyes in total. I finished Roth's *String of Pearls* and have started Voltaire's *Candide*, and intend to read Voltaire's 'Huron' story and D'Annunzio's *Idolaters* next. Karen F. looked very beautiful in her dead-girl way tonight and Carl noticed this too, seemed to project something special our way. But she retracts cruelly whatever she sends out with caustic precision. I had to opt out of conversation tonight; my bosom literally rent by her acerbity.

Carla came over, as a 'friend,' last night to return my fireman's helmet, my sword, my sweater. We watched *The Goat* by Keaton, and then she left – with a wake of regret a mile long. So it goes.

2 January 1999
The world can be lonely, or at least I can. I can't make myself visit my mother, even though I can feel her loneliness. I can broker phone calls between her and Jilian, whom I miss and feel growing up and away more each passing day. And I've tidied up my busy life from a few girlfriends and countless acquaintances to zero girlfriends and two or three friends. And now I find my evenings full of night, swallowing up a brief visit to Bar-I, where I am surrounded by the familiar faces of non-friends.

Jilian is committed to moving back to Victoria, to her sweetie, much against her mom's wishes. Jane wants her in school, ready or not, an attitude I remember in my own family when I cheated and sloughed through the undergrad years wasting everyone's time. Jilian is in love. A loneliness has taken hold of her. The charm of her Toronto acquaintances has been drained from them like pigment, and she sees them differently – with poor results.

Lately, I've been trying to sort out, to make sense of, the experience of my dead loved ones. This is not really a recent activity, I know. I'm forty-two. When my Dad was forty-two, he made the legendary phone call from Czechoslovakia, taped by Cameron around Christmas and New Year's of 1960. I remember my Dad jitterbugging wildly, hilariously, with my mother at parties thrown during these years. Clearly an excellent athlete, sedentary Chas quickly lost breath after about thirty-five to forty-five spectacular crowd-thronging and thrilling seconds, sagged into a chair bemoaning how he could no longer do this, having given up totally. Putting it so completely into the past, so Old Testament-y and adamantine had been the warning signs of his heart, his arms all achy, all dancing seemed to have been done so long ago, so permanently finished. As it indeed was since angina was diagnosed and all physical activity except rage-filled snow shovellings (when little lazy Guy should have been out there instead of growing his hair) was dropped from the regimen and replaced with more smoking, chip-eating, griping and half-assed escaping. At least I'm still playing hockey at forty-two.

And Aunt Lil. I've tried to find counterparts to Lil in my street life. Big Nancy Fullerton, single and running her own business, hard-working and good-natured, reminds me a lot of my auntie. Someone to track for years to come as an ersatz method of watching Lil age, and coming to a 'felt' understanding of how she got where she ended up as my beloved and aged spinster aunt! I recently dreamt of Lil bathing, in lingerie, in a tub, at an indeterminate age, possibly in her eighties. The body she splashed was not the toe-twisted, veiny one I remember in waking hours, but one I had managed to will into something sensual. Very old, but dignified I supposed, with something suave and translucent about the thighs, which she wetted with scented bathwaters, her back revivifying as I watched, everything reassembling itself into its carnal potentials. To be born to old parents is to be given the gift related to nostalgia; one has to work that much harder, look backwards so much further, to make real as people one's parents, grandparents – even pets! God bless you, Chas and Herdis, for your belated, fumbly conception of me at the new beach cottage! And God bless all my ancient dead loved ones!

A new beauty has slid nearer my back burners. She must be made a movie star, and I must make a movie – thus the birth of movies. She's a dancer, name unknown, all doe-like, etc., who works at the Second Cup, and I've had a couple of successful conversational snatches about bagels and weather with her so far – which have daubed catnip on my heart!

4 January
Jalapeño bagel and glass of wine at 4:25 p.m. Canada beating Sweden on CJOB 68 to advance to gold medal game in World Juniors. Just came from Bar-I, where Deborah, fresh from her duty at her grandfather's shiva, dropped her knitting to ask me, more ebulliently than ever, when she could pose nude for me. Now she writhes nude in my head, sits smugly on the other back burner – no, all of a sudden at the very forefront of my thoughts.

I'm just going to finish reading D'Annunzio's *Orsola the Virgin*, then tomorrow I shall write one page of the 'final' draft of *Branded Brain* – my new title for the feature. (How about *Burnt Blood*?)

I invited Tracy McCourt over tonight to join Enright, Meeka, Noam, Snyder and me for my second Monday salon. Tracy replaces Laura, who co-hosted my groaning-goldeye first salonette last Monday – very drunken and spewing night during which I finally got to play my Cantorial 78s on my wind-up gramophone (Rabbi Pinkosovitch, not Eddie Cantor!). I'm very happy (though poor) probably because of the Flirtation Walk I made on Corydon, speaking to a bon vivant's riches of attractive women in a ten-minute span there; ego stroked to bursting nearly.

Canada has won, 6-1. A Monday afternoon sell-out at the Winnipeg Arena, a white-out, the old Jets' P.A. announcer. I could almost smell, over the radio, the toasted dogs and the unique trough urinals. A happy day with all of cold, cold, cold January stretching endlessly ahead with all its hockey for me to play. Yesterday, I lifted weights and swam at Sargent Park for ninety minutes, then played half-court shinny with Rob Shaver and Bob Bright for ninety minutes. (After: chicken breasts and baked potatoes and a guilt complex at Amma's, and a video – *Angel Face* and *The Making of The Searchers* – at George's.) This was my first two workout day since 1974, when I ran stairs at the arena with the Flying M Track Club, then flew through an afternoon hockey game at Willie O. Was that the game with Bones Raleigh and his daughter on my line? No, I remember the Standall brothers instead. It's great how you can remember little stand-out, almost classic, personal athletic triumphs. My six touchdowns – I scored every point for my team – at Neil Young's Earl Grey circa 1976. Certain dekes or passes sprinkled over the decades. Yesterday, playing with the sublime Shaver, I was the recipient of blissfully accurate passes from that meticulous man. One pass of his I won't soon forget. Unable to see the puck on his stick because of traffic in front of the net, I merely placed my stick on the goal line, the puck came through, hit the tape on my stick and went in. I almost fell in love with Rob. Every needle-threading pass he completes must trigger the release of highly addictive endorphins. He passes off the way a junkie cranks up. This shall be a wondrous, bachelorish, shinnyish, bookish and writerly, downright boob-squeezing winter. I'm happy!

5 January

After La Salon des Clips, Bar-I again, with Noam and Steve;
Tracy bowed out, and, in her absence, was exposed by Noamie
as being 'interested' in me – a fact he gleaned from girl talk.
Tracy is fun and beautiful, but ... Then Deborah came in,
sitting as far away as possible, her face reduced to the size of a
winter sun. She radiated all that was life-giving to me in this
room, and I caught her eye a half-dozen times without the
precautionary welder's glass. Finally, she came over to the table,
removed her sweater to reveal the musculature of a trapeze
artist, and propped her feet in between the coffee cups. I let
Noam operate the bellows of Guy-inflation for a while – a valuable man that way – then died and squirmed and died again,
exquisitely.

Later, Deborah and I descended stairs on opposite sides of
a house owned by a very creepy man. We left at the same time,
but on either side, on a pair of strangely identical and symmet-
rically arranged stairs, arriving at street level together. We had
been up there to see a dead person, or at least the spirit of a
person long dead, and while I never saw this man, his presence
was so strong I felt I could describe him. Slightly threatening,
he'd had a very malignant life. Deborah had the same feeling.
The owner of this haunted house awaited us at the bottom; his
spirit, though still in his body, seemed more timelessly evil. He
pestered us as we walked away, or rather pestered Deborah,
taking huge bites from her neck and scalp, pawing and scratch-
ing at her. The red lights took forever to turn green as we
attempted to shake this guy. Finally, our steps took us into the
back lane behind 800 Ellice of all places – familiar turf. I lunged
for this maniac's head while Deborah fled up Home Street. This
cretin went down with surprising ease, and I pounded his head,
gripping his hair in my hands, upon the cement of the back lane,
until I'd broken his skull open. The Ellice bus, detoured for one
block down this lane, wheeled around the corner, and I dashed,
just ahead of its headlights, into my old backyard, then cut up
Home Street and sprinted with a fear and vigour I hadn't felt
since childhood.

Deborah's been staying in Leo's old house – the very house
where Leo once put me on his bed to play for me a Reveen
record, to put me under (to molest me?). Now, years later,

Deborah was taking a break from her boyfriend at this address. When I knocked on the door, I couldn't help feeling Leo's long-dead mother Vega would answer, but Deborah let me in desperately. I didn't dare confess to her I'd just about killed that guy. No matter how much I could've rationalized it, I didn't want her scared away by my capacity for violence, which scared even me. And this is where I had my best opportunity to come clean to everyone – especially the police. Everything was so close together: Leo's house, the crime scene, even the victim's haunted house just on the far side of the 7-11 on Ellice. Footsteps in snow, witnesses and all that stuff, began to plague my conscience. Deborah and I had the added guilt of conspiring against her boyfriend, who moved vaguely in the corners of the musty and starkly lit rooms of this frame house. Our conspiratorial whispers filled our ears with warm moist secrets pitched at such intimate volumes, a great deal of inadvertent palping transpired between our dizzied bodies, agitated by the excitements of our recent foray into the paranormal and the subsequent street violence.

Steve wanted to see this haunted house. I wanted no more part of it, but knew I would have to show it to him to deflect suspicion from myself. I couldn't come across as inexplicably afraid to recross my steps through the innocuous lane – by now, I feared, a police crime scene. I took Steve out, leaving Deborah behind, which made me sad, showed him the 'Green Cabin': an old peeling garage visible from the sidewalk. Across the street, I thought, from this cabin, was the haunted house. But I wasn't thinking right, and when I walked Steve closer it became obvious that my fear had confused me, that I was lost. We cut through the darkness of a museum ready to close, down some stairs into the subways, whose tracks we cut across to right our way. I'd never crossed subway tracks before; it seemed stupid to do so, but I was inexplicably rushing to show Steve this house, to show off my ignorance of the crime it seemed I was already sought for, that my behaviour alone would convict me in everyone's eyes. Now I can only lie at home, alone, and hope no one comes to my door. I shall be lonely indeed, but I won't clumsily incriminate myself. I can even hide under my bed if I have to!

9 January

Watched *Nightmare Alley* at George's two nights ago. Last night, watched Fritz Lang's *Blue Gardenia* there, then came home at midnight and watched the restored *Nanook of the North* by myself. Watched Bob Mitchum and Jean Simmons in *Angel Face* at George's last Monday. My life consists of watching great movies at George's, being tortured by a pretty girl – Deborah these days – and ignoring my aged mother – which will torture me forever.

Jilian moved back to Victoria yesterday. I hope she's happier now. I hope to hear that happiness when I talk to her on the phone.

Great piece by Ethan Coen in the *New Yorker*; also 'Sea Oak', a promising 'Aunt Lil' story by George Saunders. I shall finish reading it now with my coffee.

17 January

I played Wednesday. We laced up outside in our cars, with the doors open and a cruel windchill, snowdrifts on the ice and no shovels. I drove Jason Holt, an affable Philosophy sessional with dark-rimmed glasses and a Sartre ciggy going in the middle of his balaclava. Bob wears a Gore-Tex *Silence of the Lambs* face without a hat – little frosted beard bits surround his on-ice ciga-rette. Rob never ices up, just makes passes that seem like wish-fulfillment. We played again yesterday. Six on six. My team skated into the low sun – blinding. Carl played a while, unchar-acteristically sulked, stabbing his chest with his index finger to indicate he needed the puck more, and went home without saying goodbye to anyone. I finally got my legs and surprised even myself by skating, almost flying, faster than ever in my life. All those leg presses are paying off. A very competitive lad of twenty or so drove me full-speed into the net, knocking it with my hurtling body out of the deep hill the metal frame had made in the soft ice. The temp was about +1 °C. Wonderful game, wonderful. Only hockey can satisfy in this fashion, and make this land fully habitable.

I did pick-up shots with Darcy earlier in the day, and have some fingers crossed somewhere I guess. Then went out to Noam's Psychic Saturday Night at CKY, where I hung with Tracy McCourt, who wouldn't mind seeing me, according to

Noam. She was there with a date whom she ignored for two and a half hours afterward at Bar-I, while she talked movies with me. For years, I couldn't get a drop of conversation out of Tracy. Now I sat with the faucet broken off in my hand, and talk compulsively flooding from the girl onto me. I would really like to snuggle with her, but little else. One of these Monday nights might do it.

On Friday, Deborah phoned to invite me for a drink, and I spent eight hours with her at various cafés, bars, bookstores and concerts. Not quite connecting, not thrilled but definitely not bored – though I probably bored her. When we first met up at Carlos and Murphy's, she stood for a hug, and I bent for a kiss on the cheek. But, with her sprained neck, she rose with an automaton's posture – and a very long, very white neck, which I accidentally kissed. And then, for some reason, held the kiss for a very personal duration, which I didn't mind, and, if she did, she pretended not to. Eight hours later, she said goodnight with that branding eye-stare of hers. I can't remember what evil food I shoved in my mouth at that point; ah yes, a quick drive to McDonald's for three cheeseburgers and small fries. Food has replaced all libido now; what a fucking baby-boomer! Then I drove out to Darryl's at three a.m. for three games of pool, returning with light meter and light an hour later.

20 January

Now I have this nervous stomach. I've taken four or five mini-poops this morning. I have no appetite for lunch. Why? Because Deborah phoned. Maybe I should welcome the return of this completely hopeless, completely irrational, unrequited crush scenario, and use it to lose weight and start work on film projects. My date with Tracy, as sexless as it will be, is later today, after hockey, and both these things make me nervous. Boy, Deborah's neck felt great! What an old geek I am. Paraphrasing Tyrone Power in *Nightmare Alley*: 'How does one get into this geek racket anyway? Are they born into it?'

3 February

Some ten days ago, I spend seven hours with Deborah, helping her into makeup, long raven wig. Then shot her with a little camera geegaw, a Bolex, and she wore a dress that was not only as transparent as glass, but shredded, torn and poorly laundered – so shrunken the hem fell slightly about her panty-less bottom. I shot in quintuple exposure: I shot her crawling, running in circles, clutching her bosom, swooning, writhing, and, finally, just clawing her clothes off in a flurry of feathers. I reloaded in the dark on a little two-seater bench, shuffling over in case this nude Venus wanted sit next to me. She did. I put film spools on her very empty lap in the dark; I groped around and found them again. She leaned toward me in dimly haloed outline, to let me look at a loosened fake eyelash. Face to face, nose to nose, eyes to eyes, in the dark, my lungs swelled up like tires in a pit-stop. I was professional, and repressed everything till I was home. Later, alone, I ignited like a match head.

Earlier, on Tuesday, I earned a painful but desperately needed $750 for a one-hour lecture on Canada's cinema century – showing clips from the two great Canadians: Lipsett and Lauzon. Then, clips from *Leave Her to Heaven*, *Written on the Wind*, *Strange Illusion* and *Dishonored*. Canadian cinema has been a history of absence. This is what we missed!

Wed: no hockey! My fifth consecutive night at Soup Pierre. Lamb chowder. Finally, my date with Tracy. *Tarnished Angels* and a skate on my Duck Pond. Splendid!

Thursday, amid much pleasing afterglow, Noam and I planned a pyjama party at my place. I dug Jilian's bed out of the frigid veranda for myself; Noam was assigned the capacious pond. But Noam, the wild cat, dragged home a little half-dead bird as an offering to me: twenty-year-old club kid Felicia, a thoroughly narcissistic coked-out cutie who promptly removed her pantyhose. Noam dived into Jilian's bed – 'My blessings on the both of thee' – and Felicia staggered to the pond, slithered onto its tyger-stripes and disrobed, leaving a cute little heap of undergarments on the bog, before pyjama-ing herself and launching into a discussion of her sexual hegemonies. I soldiered on awhile but never felt so old. Toting a pair of wineglasses I always keep in the nearby duckblind, I felt like a post-stroke Hef. She made like the deli counter, and I pulled a Bob Nixon, and soon, somehow, in a swirl of disappointments, bitter, bitter, Felicia and Noam spooned with the ducks, and I slept without dignity beneath my fax machine. Which sent noisy missives down to me from France as I dreamt of paper cuts on my face.

'Bi for 99' was Noamie's morning mantra as he emerged from the marsh wrapped in nothing but the tyger-skin. Felicia emerged and showered for work at some makeup counter. She is smitten with the gay man. At least she has agreed to my gluing sixty-two glass eyes to her midriff and thighs and snapping a couple shots for the Floating Gallery Camera Auction.

Friday, a quiet night of wine drinking and weight-shedding calisthenics with the truly wonderful Tracy. Deborah's rushes returned, and they look quite good. Now I'm back in the groove. All fruitless crushes forgotten.

Sat morning I shoot a roll and a half of Mark Olsen as Darcy's double – a jarring continuity gambit which I just know will be cool. At three p.m., another two hours of hockey, another great hockey Saturday. Last Saturday, Tom McSorley played outdoors for maybe the first time ever. A perfect Prairie boy's day. This week, I had my legs, as fast as ever, and not even tired!

On Sat night, I was Wayne Baerwaldt's substitute choreographer on Psychic Saturday; Stephen Lawson (Gigi) was back after a week's absence. A dancer named Raven earned himself some notoriety among 'St. Mary's Academy' – the adamantine, boulder-dyke friends of Mary Wilson – by bending his tight ass straight into camera one and letting the switcher dissolve Psychic Mary's face out of his sphincter. This week, Gigi kept everything classy, and I have a choreography credit on my CV. Tracy slept over after – very sweet – and in spite of a lot of digested food coiling in my bowels and ready to strike, I joined her for a mid-afternoon greasy brunch at the nook and dropped her at home by four p.m. A very long date indeed. George and I went to Raimi's *A Simple Plan* (very solid, beautiful) at Portage Place. Never once did we mention Tracy, about whom he is very protective and paternal.

Monday Night Salon with Nora Young, David McIntosh, Carl Matheson, Robert and Meeka, Darryl, Caelum, Steve, Tracy and, of course, Noam (all pin-curled for a Heartland piece). The Starewicz with which I ended the program put us in a blissfully charmed state, and we retired en masse to the Duck Pond, where I snapped an overhead photo of the Saloniers: looked a bit like the album art for Lou Reed's *Berlin*.

Last night, dinner and *West Side Story* at Tracy's. We swapped our tales of Dead Fathers and other grief-buttons, then flattened her futon while her two cats scratched at and head-bonked the bedroom door. Home at four a.m. Message from Darryl about the film he completely reshot with Sharon Johnson. Very excited puppy!

Now, I ready myself for Wednesday afternoon hockey. It's one o'clock, and I've caught you up headline-wise on a week of superficial but deeply satisfying triumphs, which kept me too busy to attend to you, dear diary, but I shall be more faithful now we've had this little talk and everything seems to be settling back to normal around here.

13 February

Tracy and I have sworn love to each other. I'm very happy with this seventeen-day-old relationship.

Hard at work on the *Edison* project. Recent CDs: Korngold *String Quartet No.1*, Reznicek *String Quartet No.1*, Gershwin rare recordings reissued, *Ultimate Dinah Washington* ('Blue Gardenia!'), Korngold *Opera Selections 1949*. Ordered videos: Murnau's *Tartuffe*, Gance's *Torture of Silence*, *La Roue*, *J'accuse* (silent), *Sud*; *Bhezin Meadow* and *Kino Eye*. Must order: Cantor's *Whoopee!* and 1930s Popeye public domain stuff.

Tracy has incredibly sexy underwear, which worn by other women would be ridiculous. She wears it like a woman. I've been with so few women. Girls are nests of stillborn gestures and hysterics. Tracy is a girl only at the dangerous moments which, at this early stage, are rare.

22 February

I have until Thursday at FedEx deadline to finish my script. Made great progress yesterday, scribbling away on old hard copy. Today, after Tracy prints up her new CV, I go at it on the computer. Long days ahead – two of them anyway – after tonight's mini-salon. I cannot afford to be hungover, or even slightly sleepy, tomorrow morning.

The last two weeks have seen me quit exercising, quit eating wisely, all in the name of writing. Even though I've done but three days work over the whole time if you add it up. It even takes me three days to *read* the script, let alone write it. Soon, that will change! It must!

How many times have I mentioned that whenever my mother says 'Okey-dokey!' – a sign of her good mood – it just about kills me because she picked up that expression from my Dad, who has been dead twenty-two years and hadn't been in a good mood for at least ten years before that.

FILM TREATMENTS

THE EYE, LIKE A STRANGE BALLOON, MOUNTS TOWARDS INFINITY

Visual Treatment

Redon worked often with charcoal. I would like to do the same.

I would like to make a mini-melodrama, very music-driven – like a Fleischer Brothers cartoon, performed by four morbid characters to almost metronomic train rhythms.

I'd like to keep the compositions tightly packed, and while the camera will probably remain mostly still, if the stuff within the frames were perpetually moving, this would please me.

The sets and even the characters might be as charcoal-smudged and as cross-hatched as Redon's work, and as oily as a train engine.

Music will be inexorably linked to the visuals: it should drive the visuals like a Silly Symphony, but with a more Poe-like dead weight.

This will be a bouncy dingy dirge sprinkled with luminous winter-night-blooming blossoms.

164

The Story

KELLER is a manly, bristly-bearded train engineer. He is very happy to stoke the furnace of his powerful machine. Everything is black and shiny, well oiled, and moves along to the soothing metronomic rhythms of the rumbling rails. The engine, and its long train of cars, move with confidence in one long solid sweep through the landscape. There is the free-breathing, beard-buffeting experience of travelling along at high speeds through the snowy slopes of someplace bleak. KELLER has always at his side his little son, CAELUM, who has a snail's curly tail where most little boys have two legs. Together, the big engineer and the little enjoy the childish freedom of their lives on the train until they witness a horrible wreck. The cars of two colliding engines twist and groan like a herd of dying creatures. KELLER and CAELUM rush to the scene of carnage, finding a little girl, BERENICE, orphaned just moments before. (BERENICE also sports the snail's or serpent's tail so common to children in nineteenth-century France.) BERENICE cries like an orphan at an orphaning crash should cry, so KELLER takes pity and adopts the little girl as his own, even though he already has a son the same age – CAELUM. Together KELLER, CAELUM and BERENICE help run the glossy black engine loved so much by KELLER the bearded patriarch. Now KELLER has found extra room in his heart where before only his son and his thundering train dwelt. His bosom swells with the wind that fills it. He names his train Berenice after the little girl, and years – dream years – do they spend as happy family traversing the continent.

When little BERENICE reaches adolescence, and steps out of her moulting tail like a little Venus on a twisted shell, KELLER suddenly finds his paternal feelings about the girl shifting gears, derailing themselves, and heading under their own steam toward more sensual, morbid and verboten territories. He cannot help but see his adopted daughter in a halo of black loco-motive smoke. He fixates on her teeth, of all things. Something has transformed her teeth into incorrect, uncomfortable, but completely irresistible, objects of desire. CAELUM, by now walking on his own two legs, also has no trouble overlooking the naked truth that his sibling connection with BERENICE is not biological; he too falls under her spell, or rather the spell of her teeth, spending long hours gazing at the profile of her mouth offered up to him in relief against a pile of coal. KELLER notices that he has a romantic rival in his own son, which at least distracts him from his own heartache – or adds to it. The older man and the younger confuse and hurt BERENICE with their new attitudes toward their close family member, stumbling as they do one over the other to display rare feats of locomotive bravery, straddling loads of lumber at high speed, entering low-ceilinged tunnels, eyes closed, while standing atop the other Berenice, the train engine. In this way, the two men hope to win the smiling approval of BERENICE's teeth.

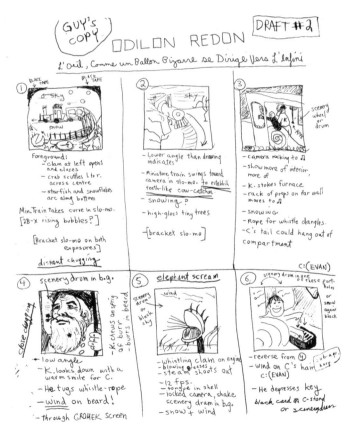

When this disconcerting behaviour, this spraying of so much familial spit, becomes too much for BERENICE, she sprouts the long dark prickles of a cactus from her scalp and runs away from her adoptive family at the first train-watering opportunity possible. She soon returns with a husband, a man even older than KELLER, and with a bigger beard to boot! This new groom wears the neatly pressed and shiny-buttoned uniform which confirms he is a ZEPPELIN PILOT. The jilted son loses his head on the spot, or rather, his head loses its body. Now the son's head sprouts from the top of a sad marsh flower. The jilted KELLER goes mad with jealousy. In a rash decision he yanks the human BERENICE by the hand onto his beloved train Berenice, and shoots off down the tracks in hot fury, scalded by his own tears as if by steam, determined to destroy both Berenices in a crash. The ZEPPELIN PILOT, so light-headed is he by the turn of affairs, rises like the very balloon he drives. Only when KELLER's train reaches top speed and the metallic Berenice is trembling with something like a fear or a passion, do the teeth of the human BERENICE, chattering like a mink trap, move into KELLER's beard – almost trimming it like a lawn mower. He knows not whether these kisses are born of love or fear. He makes a decision. He decides that love and fear are all the same to him, and definitely worth living for. He decides to stop the train.

The sudden yanking of the train's brakes lurches KELLER forward, and he is instantly de-oculated by two gear shifts protruding from the dashboard seemingly for just this injurious purpose. Terrified BERENICE flees the blinded KELLER again as soon as the train has stopped. Now all four characters – KELLER, BERENICE, CAELUM and the ZEPPELIN PILOT – have scattered to the four points of the compass. KELLER lives the life of a blind hermit upon the very tip of a frozen mountaintop.

One day, BERENICE finds her brother, CAELUM, the sad marsh flower, head hanging from its vine. She removes this grieving boy's head from this alien, botanical fixture, and with a caring caress, reconciles him to his bodiless state. Then, with a tender gesture to yet another whom she will always love, she scoops out one of her eyeballs – an organ lighter than air – and dreamily sends it up as a balloon to her sightless and lonely father, but not before attaching to this organic balloon a certain important cargo – CAELUM's head – so that neither father nor son may be as lonely as she.

BERENICE's floating eye finds KELLER in his icy homelessness, and delivers to him the head of his son. BERENICE has also pulled all her teeth and arranged them on the silver, head-carrying platter for the edification of KELLER and CAELUM. The engineer is left to nurse the severed head back to health in the clear mountain air – certainly no sanatorium could be better.

BERENICE, now a darkened and spiny cactus figure, left with no teeth and one eye, lowers her gaze from the mountain top to take in the lay of the the land on which she stands.

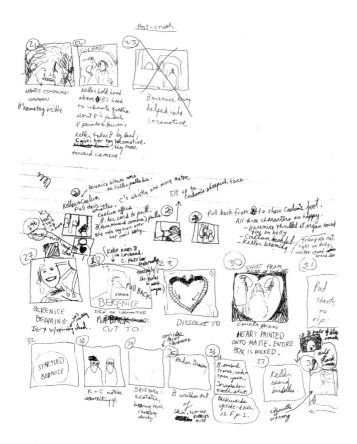

MALDOROR: TYGERS

Treatment

A young gentleman, MALDOROR, appears and opens his coat to reveal a little theatre curtain. The theatre curtain is raised by many dusty little pulleys that squeak within MALDOROR's chest, to reveal a little opera stage hollowed out of the man's torso.

On the stage, we see the story of DOL, a little girl of the zoo. The zoo is populated with the huge silhouettes of countless exotic beasts. The bars of the zoo are semi-transparent tyger stripes.

DOL lives with her zookeeper father, DELMAS. Instead of working like a good zookeeper should, DELMAS has receded into a world of his own. His thoughts are so distant as to appear absent.

DOL pleads with her father to return to her world – the world of tending beasts in the here and now.

DELMAS robotically lifts up an old animal collar from some straw. Something black and oily drips from the collar onto his hands. This goo strangely galvanizes the entranced DELMAS; he abandons his daughter to rush off to a meat-lined cottage.

DOL follows her father to this mysterious other, more-desired, place. There, she finds him sitting by the incubator of an ailing creature. No matter how clumsily DOL makes her entrance, DELMAS remains unaware of her presence, so fixed is his attention upon the occupant of the heated bed.

Now viewers see for the first time the ailing beast in the bed; it is something with the head of a moose and a remarkably human body – of withered muscle and entrails, all arrayed as if on a platter of crustaceans. DELMAS leans over this carrion-creature murmuring words of undying love.

DOL cannot understand why her father seems to perceive so many body parts stuck together and barely breathing as something else – as something beautiful, as if it were Goya's *Naked Maja* lying there alive.

On the bedstand where DELMAS sees a pot of fresh-cut flowers, DOL sees a grotesque basin of blood, tendons and digits. This horrifying tableau of father and creature sets DOL to flight.

She returns with MALDOROR, the young gentleman. By now, the beast has died. DELMAS is weeping uncontrollably upon the 'bosom' of his 'lover.' The death of this glaucous tendresse will be no obstacle for determined DELMAS, who seems to be proceeding with the relationship, in a more physical than spiritual sense, in spite of the sorry condition of his dead partner.

MALDOROR seems to understand the problem immediately. He studies the skinless creature in the bed, the lovestruck DELMAS and the hyperventilating DOL. MALDOROR approaches the bed and, methodically, almost medically, pries open the jawbone of the dead beast. Upon the tongue of the animal he finds a golden, bloodied ring. With the same motion of placing a host upon a supplicant's tongue, except in reverse, MALDOROR takes the ring for himself. This action works, swiftly dissolving the unholy bond between DELMAS and the carrion. DELMAS wrenches himself from his activities as if awakened from a sleepwalk.

MALDOROR then removes the long riding boots worn by the beast. In order to make these boots fit himself, MALDOROR whittles a bit of his own heels away with a knife, then shoes himself with a snug and shiny fit.

The ring has a long bloody thread attached to its golden curves. With inexplicable suddenness MALDOROR shoves the ring up his own nose. With equal suddenness, DELMAS throws himself at MALDOROR with rapturous intent. MALDOROR, bloody thread hanging from his nose, rigorously returns the embraces of DELMAS.

From the bed of the dead beast comes flying at the new lovers a swarm of sea urchins, weeds and crustaceans. These subaquatic creatures coat the couple like iron filings upon a magnet. DELMAS and MALDOROR are on the verge of a living entombment in these fishy little things, when a confused and disturbed DOL displays a spritely response, grabbing the thread to yank the ring from MALDOROR's nose.

DOL flees deeper into the zoo with the ring, breaking yet another spell for DELMAS. DELMAS leaves the bemused MALDOROR behind to pursue his own daughter.

Father and daughter dance around each other, amidst the orange and black stripes of a tygery place. Tygers roar and cast large shadows in every direction. DELMAS flashes predatory eyes at his own offspring. DOL throws the ring into a tyger pit.

Now DELMAS is in love with a tyger pit. He stares into its black and bestial depths, then simply lowers himself headfirst into the maw that has tygers. He is devoured.

Tyger shadows run wild. The tatters of tyger stripes rend the air. After DELMAS is eaten, for the old carrion-lover is indeed devoured, so are most of DOL's garments. DOL, imprisoned by tyger stripes, lowers herself into the pit by a rope; she is freed of her lower half by the jaws of tygers. Later: DOL, leglessly propped up in a chair, combs the beard of a goat.

The now-satisfied MALDOROR drops the curtain on this little scene, buttons his coat over the curtain, and, content with the muffled roaring that sounds from within, pats his chest where his heart should be.

MALDOROR bows as if expecting flowers from an adoring audience.

CAREFUL

Careful might best be described as an 'opera without singing.' The characters live in a stylized operatic opera – the misty crags of an alpine Germany constructed completely within a studio – and lead operatic lives roiled with the grand Germanic passions: bosom-quivering repression, homicidal self-torment and incestuous longing.

I want to make *Careful* a beautiful movie, a dream-gentle movie that intoxicates one with atmosphere and ideas. I want its look to invoke both the theatre and the bedtime story. I want the performances to be gentle, measured and hypnotic; in a word, careful.

I am weary of the garish, the loud, the violent and the gratuitous in the contemporary art-house film. I believe the viewer can best dream in a quiet setting. So I have set my story in the very heart of Quiet itself.

I have set my story in Tölzbad.

The Setting: Tölzbad

The town of Tölzbad trembles precariously on the steep slope of a mountain somewhere in the German Alps. Tiny hovels and surprising little patches of farmland nestle at remarkable angles at remarkable heights among the misty spires and snow-cloaked summits of this community.

The residents of Tölzbad must conduct their lives with *extreme care*. Narrow mountain paths must be traversed with the sure-footedness of a mountain goat, and sudden ice films can make things worse. Many a climber has felt the rush of wind betokening a death-plummet to the sharp rocks below.

If a climber aspires to heights too great, there can be another problem. Countless wooden crosses mark the spots where residents have been *von blitz getraufen* – struck by lightning!

Then, there is always the avalanche, when the snow relaxes its grip on the slope and is dragged downward under its own crushing weight. And Death throws its white shroud over everything in its path.

The slightest sound can trigger one of these deadly avalanches, possibly wiping out the entire village. The residents of Tölzbad live in mortal terror of making that fatal sound.

Obsessed with silence, the townspeople have baffled all their windows lest some stray sound escape from their homes; vociferous children are bound and gagged until they comprehend the risk they represent. Even livestock is silenced (surgically). But always there is the wild, uncontrolled sound of Nature: a terrifying moment when a noisy flock of migrating geese passes overhead. And where Death passes its hand, all will be white.

In Tölzbad, caution has infected everyone's life. Voices are low, gentle and polite. Members of the Mountain Watch carefully scan the slopes with their binoculars, vigilant against any impropriety.

Apparently, muted decorousness lends itself best to servility, and graduates of the Tölzbad Butler College are the town's proudest exports. Silent, sleek and obedient, they serve in schlösses throughout the continent.

Tölzbad's intense alpine precaution has led to a unique regional tradition. As part of funeral routine, the dead have their hearts perforated by a long nail before burial just to be on the safe side.

And there is always the avalanche, the heavy white God watching from above. Careful Tölzbad. Careful.

Careful. Careful … Careful.

The Story at a Glance

JOHANN, a butler at the Tölzbad Butler College, is engaged to KLARA, his childhood sweetheart. All is well.

One day his sunny existence is darkened when he has an incestuous dream about ZENAIDA, his mother. His discomfort about this dream develops into an obsession and he leaps to his death from a mountaintop.

JOHANN's brother GRIGORSS, a butler school graduate, now takes over the wooing of KLARA. But KLARA is not easily wooed. She has an unhealthy filial attraction to HERR TROTTA, her own father. HERR TROTTA seems to favour his youngest daughter SIEGLINDE, and a bitter rivalry exists between the two sisters.

GRIGORSS does not want ZENAIDA, his mother, to marry COUNT KNOTKERS. He kills the COUNT in a duel and flees to KLARA.

In grief, ZENAIDA hangs herself.

KLARA's affection for her father reaches a frenzy of frustration. She tricks GRIGORSS into murdering TROTTA by causing an avalanche. At the last second, KLARA embraces and kisses her father and both are swept away by the avalanche.

GRIGORSS is left alone to freeze to death. Before he dies, the ghost of his mother visits him and tucks him in beneath a blanket of snow.

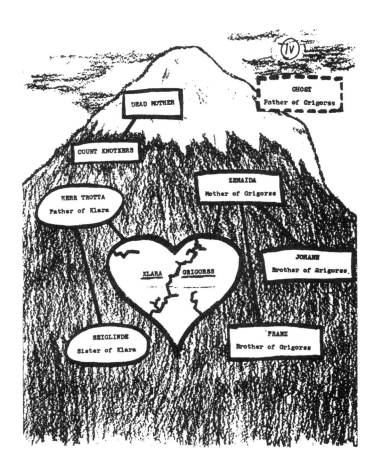

THE CHILD WITHOUT QUALITIES

*It is terrifying to think that our life is a tale without a plot or
a hero, made up out of desolation and glass, out of the fever-
ish babble of constant digressions.*
   – Osip Mandelstam

The Time and Setting of the Story
The story begins in 1960, in Winnipeg, then a senior hockey
hotbed. The Winnipeg Arena, through the lens of our memories
at least, was the Wrigley Field of hockey arenas – a building that
fit hockey like a skull around its brain. A gothic structure dark
in every aspect, a vast mildewed cathedral playground for our
protagonist, the Child Without Qualities. The arena was
peopled with lurid throngs somehow culled from the *noir*
grotesques of police photographer Weegee. The fans, and even
the players, who wore Brylcreem instead of helmets, freely filled
the building with their cigarette smoke; it always hung in thick
clouds just above the ice. Our parents belonged, in the words of
John Cheever, 'to that last generation of chainsmokers who woke
the world in the morning with their coughing.' It was a time

when almost everyone wore a hat and flirted with each other's spouses over tinkling highballs at office parties.

And from a beauty mark on Marilyn Monroe, suicide spread like a rash over all of us. Suicide, alongside its kissing cousin, Assassination, was the great fad of those years – more magnetizing than the Beatles, and infinitely variant.

Canada's Centennial splashed a brief Kodachrome illumination into the musty, secretive basements, closets and garages of our nascence. But the illumination was for us children alone, the hyper-sensitive brown studies and centennial projects within our cubbyholes remained guardedly private. Adulthood always conducted itself in adjoining rooms, muffled by a wall, maybe, but distant and so codified we may as well have been living, not without our parents, but among rooms let out to ballroom dancers. We inscribed the choreographies of our revolutionary pleasures behind our bedroom headboards, interrupted regularly from without by terrors so sudden and vehement as to flatten our lungs.

We children endure our terrors with pride – our pure, virginal terrors. We have long ago been inured to the things that frighten our parents – our stupid and cancerously loved ballroom-dancing parents.

Eventually, by the late 1970s, with our parents out of the picture, the Winnipeg Arena stands remodelled, modernized, stupid. We find ourselves remodelled and modernized as well – some of us even parents already, stupid with the delirium of parenthood. Among us, though, there are geniuses who never forget the black and mystical manifestos of our secret years. Uniformed as double-agents, children garbed in the large and flaccid flesh once worn by mother and father, they remain, nonetheless, loyal to their earliest unspoken oaths. Each wears his or her disguise like a suit of torpor, with a long sofa slid underneath oftentimes an accessory, but within each pillowed head a groggy genius wades.

It is with one such genius that our story concerns itself: namely, the Child Without Qualities.

The Child Without Qualities

The movie opens in a kind of prenatal murk, mostly black, the kind of drab monochromes officially sanctioned by TASS in the late 1950s.

On the soundtrack an ever-so-distant transatlantic telephone operator, amid the clunks, drones and whistles attending all such iron-curtain cable-calls, shouts weakly like a woman drowning amidst an audio tempest before her voice sweeps up into clear, loud nearness. In heavily accented English she instructs the caller to proceed with his call: CHAS BELLAMY does so. CHAS is calling home. It is very late at night. The little four-year-old CHILD WITHOUT QUALITIES sleeps right through the phone call. His older brother CAMERON BELLAMY, a teenage electronics enthusiast, operates a tubecrammed, stove-size reel-to-reel tape recorder wired into the phone to preserve this family event.

'Herdis? … Herdis? … Herdis? … ' we hear CHAS calling to his wife. His voice is incredibly faint. He is somewhere in Czechoslovakia with his hockey team. We see drab TASS photos of his team, married men on holidays from their families, men as scarred and muscled as Genet's sailors, posing in effulgent white rows before the black architecture of Prague. The voice of CHAS is so faint we viewers can barely hear him. HERDIS cannot hear him at all. Because of the bad cable, they miscommunicate terribly – as only parents can – talk vaguely about the weather on each side of the world, talk as if they barely know each other. CHAS's voice is dimmed at times to push its source a lot farther away than the deathly Czechoslovakia, as if the cable ended somewhere in a grave, as if the ghostly transmission were from a far corner of heaven, a heaven of grimy ghettos. We see more TASS photos of the jubilant sinewy hockey players at state banquets receiving silvery hardware and blown glass from dour and heavily moled ambassadors. The camera tracks into a photo to rest on middle-aged CHAS BELLAMY to suggest the link between picture and voice. The CHILD WITHOUT QUALITIES sleeps on in his bed.

INTERTITLE: *Things That Kill Fathers #1: A Favourite Meal*
We see a father mopping his mouth at the head of the family table. Jump-cut to whitened father lying dead, half-under table, while a paramedic pounds his chest.

INTERTITLE: *Things That Kill Fathers #2: A Clean Bill of Health*
The camera tracks in on a happy handshake between a father and his doctor. The camera pulls back on the handshake of a mourning son and a condoler at a funeral.

INTERTITLE: *Things That Kill Fathers #3: Would Have Retired in a Week*
We see a middle-aged man at work in his office.

The crackly transatlantic conversation continues over this inventory of superstitions: CHAS: 'We lost our Christmas turkey!' HERDIS: 'Pardon?'

INTERTITLE: *Things That Kill Fathers #4: New Lawn Mower*
We see a father, already quite distant, pushing a lawn mower toward the horizon.

INTERTITLE: *Things That Kill Fathers #5: Surprise Parties*
Just cut to next intertitle.

INTERTITLE: *Things That Kill Fathers #6: Watching Father Drive away without Averting Eyes before He Becomes Speck*
We see a mother and children watching something in distance past camera.

INTERTITLE: *Things That Kill Fathers #7: Buying Them New TV or Pet*

During the phone talk, it becomes known that lines out of Eastern Europe are very difficult to obtain. CHAS and HERDIS are at their communicative best when exchanging concrete information, like scores of the games for the local Winnipeg radio stations. When talk drifts back to familial areas, pauses lengthen, and thoughts unexpressed, or even unthought, stretch out between husband and wife. CAMERON fills one gap with a squeaky adolescent greeting to his dad. Before signing off, CHAS asks off-handedly how the little guy is doing. (We have already seen him asleep.) The operator's voice looms up again to put a merciful end to the call home. HERDIS and CAMERON, in nightie and PJs respectively, are left to listen as the giant tape recorder unspools the last words, buzzes, clunks, Communist dog-whistles and drones of the connection. These are finally supplanted by the more familiar, if not altogether comforting, domestic dial tone left by someone hanging up and going away.

The little CHILD WITHOUT QUALITIES lives above Lil's Beauty Salon, the family business, with his mom, HERDIS, and his high-school-age siblings: ROSS, the oldest, CAMERON and JANET. Downstairs, in an apartment behind the beautician's, live his AUNT LIL and his elderly blind GRAMMA. CHAS, the father of the CHILD WITHOUT QUALITIES, exists for the boy as a set of late-night headlights that wash the ceiling of his bedroom when the family car pulls into the parking lot in back after hockey practice. The corporeal self of CHAS is then slightly more substantiated by a small collection of door sounds: the car door shutting, the rattly turning of the front door lock and the unchanging four-beat percussion of inner and outer doors clicking shut, the long singing rills of middle-of-the-night open-doored trips to the bathroom, the fridge door closing in the morning, the toaster-oven door popping open, and the blender fixing a can of frozen orange juice before another closing of the fridge door. All of these sounds heard from the bed of the CHILD WITHOUT QUALITIES.

The consciousness of the young CHILD WITHOUT QUALITIES first awakened in the hair-chute. The hair-chute led from a little trap-door in a baseboard at the back of the beauty salon. 'Lil's' was a loud, busy factory that produced hard, heavily lacquered coiffures. The chrome domes of at least twenty drying machines bent forward in one long row to cover the netted heads of womanish forms with beneficent blasts of hot air. At least six pneumatic chairs kept customers' heads at a height just right to the wielding of electric clippers and stainless-steel shears. The phone rang out at the same steady rate as the cash register, and appointments filled the scribbled pages of a huge pink logbook as big as a tabletop. In one corner, sinks and hoses soaked and sprayed the scalps of those who came, with chemicals, dyes, soaps and waters. A huge timer, with pink numbers, ticked off the minutes hair was to spend in acidic solutions. One whole wall was filled with the pink bottles of pungent hair solvents, fixatives and conditioners. Other equipments, polishers, curling rods, irons and crimpers stood ready on pink-spangled shelving.

The plaster walls were pink and the air was pink with hairspray. The floor was of pink and grey tiles, alternating in a checkerboard fashion, and was perpetually buried in heaps and thatches of hair. As soon as a cut was completed, this pile of hair – white, red, black or pink – was swept up by HERDIS, AUNT LIL or one of the other STYLISTS, pushed over to the trap door in the baseboard and down into the hair-chute. The hair-chute led into the basement, where the trimmings collected in strange, colourful strata, hard-packed and as rectangular as the chute itself. The CHILD WITHOUT QUALITIES liked to separate these strata into little fragile and weird-smelling mats. He liked to empty out the chute, just big enough for a boy his age, and climb up its inner ribbing until his eyes came level with the baseboard trap door, which he opened as a vantage point on the ankles of the gynocracy raging above. Occasionally, the trap door was pulled open on its chain and the CHILD WITHOUT QUALITIES would receive a sweeping faceful of freshly washed hair. This is what awakened the consciousness of the CHILD WITHOUT QUALITIES.

One day in kindergarten, the CHILD WITHOUT QUALITIES unrolled his mat with the rest of the children for nap time. After the nap, one little boy failed to wake up. He was taken away in an ambulance, never seen again, and his name and existence were forgotten by everyone.

Another day, HERDIS appeared at the classroom door. This was very special for the CHILD WITHOUT QUALITIES. Someone from his home world had cross-pollinated his school world. The CHILD WITHOUT QUALITIES got to leave kindergarten early that day. Outside the school, the BELLAMY family wagon waited, loaded for the trip to the Seattle World's Fair. The CHILD WITHOUT QUALITIES saw the mountains get bigger, then disappear into a series of perfectly safe, comfortably graded roads which overlooked TV-familiar views of valleys. CHAS told stories from behind the wheel of entire towns wiped out in rock slides. But to the CHILD WITHOUT QUALITIES, it always felt that the slopes were too gentle, and the towns too far from any precipice to support such dramatic accounts, accounts which seemed to stretch history somewhat to make up for the implausibly long distance between any two points. The mountains failed to appear as mountains until the BELLAMYS were clear out of them and confronted with the ocean; then they popped up in the miniature rear-window diorama. At the ocean, the CHILD WITHOUT QUALITIES was introduced to some relatives, including CAMERON's closest friend in the family, COUSIN RONNY, whose father UNCLE ARTHUR had been killed when a tree fell down upon his head during his very last day of work as a lumberjack. At the Seattle World's Fair, CAMERON and COUSIN RONNY threw all their paper money out the window of the revolving restaurant on top of the Space Needle. CAMERON was always throwing things. He once threw a metal bicycle licence so far in the air that it disappeared.

Another time he made his own radio station out of some congestion tubes, using a metal flying-saucer toboggan as a broadcast antenna. He interrupted all the radio shows in the neighbourhood, and the police made him and CHAS throw out the flying saucer at the city dump. He once heard a speech by Castro on his short-wave and wrote the dictator a letter appealing for peace with America. Castro actually sent back a letter telling CAMERON that many of his ideas were quite revolutionary. CHAS proudly told all his hockey-player visitors about the ongoing celebrity correspondence conducted by CAMERON. But proud as CAMERON was of his friendship with Castro, he threw away the chance of a free trip to the general's palace by losing interest in writing letters altogether. Sometimes, when CAMERON became unhappy, he ran away from home, usually just going out to the family beach cottage out of season. But he always came back.

At the beach cottage, CHAS indulged his landscaping obsessions to excess. Every summer weekend, CHAS had another truckload of topsoil dumped in the yard. The job of his children was to level this soil. ROSS, CAMERON, JANET and CHILD WITHOUT QUALITIES did this by riding on a ladder, lending their weight to it rather, while CHAS, harnessed like a plough-horse to a rope fastened to each end of the ladder, pulled them back and forth across the yard until either the soil was level enough to seed or his arms and chest ached so much he had to stop.

One day, while the children were at work weighing down the ladder, their UNCLE RON delivered them the news that not only had movie star Marilyn Monroe killed herself, but that CAROL, the girl who stayed at the cottage next door, had been killed in a car accident.

CAMERON had evidently been in love with CAROL because he bolted from the mud ladder and disappeared for a day. Newspapers ran photographs of postage-stamp-size CAROL along with the much larger Marilyn Monroe, whose beauty mark – smudged newsprint – seemed to grow bigger as the newspaper was handed around the house.

The BELLAMYS returned to the city for CAROL's funeral. The CHILD WITHOUT QUALITIES was neither interested enough nor old enough to attend the service, and CAMERON was physically unable to – his grief left him unconscious in his bed, vomiting in his sleep. The beauty mark spread like a rash.

One Sunday morning in the winter, CAMERON's body rested face down in the snow upon CAROL's grave. Her headstone had been swept clean of all ice, a pillow for CAMERON, who clutched a rifle behind his back, barrel nestled into a hole in the back of his head. The smudge had grown into a bloodstain in the snow.

The CHILD WITHOUT QUALITIES awoke that morning to the sight of CAMERON's neatly made bed, something he had never seen before. CAMERON had always slept in an incredible tangle of sheets with blankets swaddled tightly around his head and over his ears, like a nun's wimple, leaving exposed only the beautiful young face. Nightly, CAMERON thrashed so in the raiments of his bed, behind a face painted always in the faint indigo of sorrow. On this morning, though, his bed was as tidy as a Sunday morning ought to be.

HERDIS was calling friends on the phone, asking if anyone had seen CAMERON. As the day went on, the CHILD WITHOUT QUALITIES lolled through some bad morning cartoons, a completely indifferent horse opera, some painfully boring country-music shows, even political talk shows and church broadcasts, all the while assuring his mom and dad that CAMERON would come home again. It wasn't until Walt Disney came on in late afternoon that the day seemed to open up a little for the CHILD WITHOUT QUALITIES. But his parents continually cluttered it up with their repetitive, circular concerns.

'Where's Cameron? Where's Cameron? Where's Cameron?'

Night falls mercifully early in winter, and soon the ABC Sunday Night Movie brought new hopes for an end to the ennui. CHAS and HERDIS now left the CHILD WITHOUT QUALITIES alone on the couch to enjoy his show. They busied themselves in the next living room – they had four living rooms in all – with telephone calls and visits. One time only did CHAS cross in front of the television, weeping with restraint, to tug at a box of Kleenex, before recrossing the line of view on his way out, having finally dropped his tedious, desperate mantra of the day. Soon after, AUNT LIL came upstairs from her suite behind the beauty salon. She put the CHILD WITHOUT QUALITIES on her ample lap and explained with a loving simplicity that CAMERON had gone to be with CAROL, where they could be in love. He would not be coming back, ever, but he would be very happy there. A woman who looked like Aunt Jemima cried voluminously – a child on her lap, too – on the Sunday Night Movie, and so did AUNT LIL, a white Aunt Jemima, as she rocked the CHILD WITHOUT QUALITIES in her arms.

The Sunday Night Movie was abandoned, and, for the rest of that evening without end, all the doors of the immense house were thrown open to allow the tireless room-to-room peregrinations of family members in search of something unfindable. The family met in small confused confabs. JANET ran, like the Olympic sprinter she dreamed to be, through the carpeted labyrinths of the giant home. Hockey players and neighbours from the beach came in through the open front door and climbed upstairs into what seemed like the beginning of a pretty good party.

The CHILD WITHOUT QUALITIES wandered into the darkened beauty salon with the idea of making a late-night visit to GRAMMA in back. Only the chrome highlights of the hair dryers, scissors and bottletops returned the street fight that came in through the closed venetian blinds. ROSS sat in the darkness, on his mother's pneumatic chair, surprising the CHILD WITHOUT QUALITIES. The little brother asked his elder if the dead could come back to life. Upon the luminous tiles of that well-ordered beauty salon, ROSS told the little one that the dead could come back to life – that CAMERON would come back. It seemed right that the question have only this one possible answer; the CHILD WITHOUT QUALITIES ran upstairs excitedly to tell everyone not to worry – that CAMERON would be back. CHAS had somehow vapourized into another place, but present was HERDIS, who now seemed to be running the party with satisfied efficiency –

fixing snacks for guests and taking phone calls of condolence with a noble acumen – and she quickly nixed all possibility of CAMERON's return. To underline this truth, she let the CHILD WITHOUT QUALITIES have CAMERON's bigger, much better bed that very night, tucking him in there when at last the party had been drained of everything but the most hermetic adult appeal. As the CHILD WITHOUT QUALITIES curled up in his exciting new bed, he heard from behind the door each member of his family – CHAS, HERDIS, ROSS, JANET, AUNT LIL and GRAMMA – one by one assume responsibility for CAMERON's death, only to be instantly refuted by all the others. Jealously, the CHILD WITHOUT QUALITIES tried to pretend it was his fault, too: just a few days earlier, CAMERON had been cleaning out his desk and had made him a gift of a bottle of ink, which HERDIS, sensing some messy accident, made him return. The ink spread in the sleepy mind of the child, and on his face the stain of night deepened and deepened and deepened.

For months afterward, every time she set the table, HERDIS got angry at CAMERON for upsetting the baby-boomer symmetry of the seating arrangement; she had worked hard to get two kids on each side, and a parent at each end. CAMERON's absence threw the dinner table into disequilibrium.

But this equilibrium had never in fact existed; CHAS had always been a restless eater, finishing and leaving the table long before anyone else even sat. Then ROSS soon became old enough to move out on his own, to accept a job in Regina; JANET went away to school to train with a better track and field coach. Those who were left were free to sit where they pleased.

The CHILD WITHOUT QUALITIES now found himself in the company of a family past its prime. These were people who had already spent much vigour clothing, feeding, admonishing, worrying over the sickbeds of, taking summer vacations with, beaming at and snapping proud birthday or graduation photos of, children who in one way or another had gone away. The last of countless family trips had been taken in the wagon. The CHILD WITHOUT QUALITIES had been lucky to go on that one, the memorable trip to Seattle. Every day HERDIS and AUNT LIL put in their long hours in the salon; HERDIS followed her day by escaping into the whirring business of her sewing room to make clothes for the billeted JANET. AUNT LIL's nocturnal escapism took the form of bus rides downtown to Eaton's, where she logged massive hours in the fanciful worlds created by that store. Finally returning late with her exotic spoils, jingling the wind chimes of the salon door as she closed it behind her in a darkness sticky with hairspray, before making her way to bed in her spinster's apartment. CHAS put in full days at the office, and then at the arena, riding home late upon the beams of his headlights. GRAMMA spent her days downstairs in her quiet blindness.

During these days, each one the same as the other, the CHILD WITHOUT QUALITIES played with his siblings' hand-me-down dolls and toy animals, some of these already played with nearly to dismemberment, all of them bearing the teethmarks and spit stains of ZERO, the family dog who grew up with ROSS, CAM and JAN, and then died before the CHILD WITHOUT QUALITIES was born. ZERO had apparently been loving and brilliant. Now there was a new pet, a stupid little DOG WITHOUT QUALITIES, years old and not yet properly house-trained, a pet who somehow didn't count as a pet, who hadn't the same compulsion to hold between her sharp little teeth these wildly mutilated toys. The CHILD WITHOUT QUALITIES loved these toys, manufactured long ago and never again, and sanctioned by the abuse of the years layered on them by his siblings. The missing eyes and arms, the soldier's head chewed upwards into a long gummy limb growing from the neck – all of these were the text of his family history. Every time he played with them, he read and learned this history: the legends of parents, young and slim, striding with purpose through bedrooms which then had a purpose; the prehistory of old comic books worn out in station wagons full of young limbs; the huge play-filled stretches of the calendar which marked out the amber years before his birth; then of the long rest for the toys while ROSS, CAM and JAN grew up in school and left all these accessories in the storage. The CHILD WITHOUT QUALITIES spread these toys out onto the clear floor of any vacated bedroom – many empty rooms just for playing! – and by arranging these artifacts there, gave shape to the story of his family.

Because of all their years' experience, these toys knew a better quality of play than other toys. And so did the old chesterfields, end tables and wallpaper in this quiet house. He recognized in the old photo albums everything in its brand new state, or early on in play-careers, being used by those three children who romped in these environs before he was born. He saw the plaster zoo animals completely intact: the giraffe with all its legs, the antelope with their antlers, the plastic camel before its head had been chewed off. Present in these photos were the missing male lion and the long-lost roof to the ark which contained the whole menagerie. What vigorous and loving play these toys and couches and radios had been submitted to before the CHILD WITHOUT QUALITIES had entered the world. Now, as a result, a residue of better quality seemed to sit on everything in the deserted house. The house held a dormancy, a potential to divulge what it held for his family before. Every object in it was full and ready to discharge its payload of history. The CHILD WITHOUT QUALITIES was permanently expectant. Everything seemed ready to move forward, at any moment, back into the time of its heyday. The unchaperoned CHILD WITHOUT QUALITIES had the roam of the house – a peculiar house indeed compared to others in the neighbourhood – with its beauty salon instead of a front yard, its two basements, its changing rooms for the STYLISTS, a sewing room full of ancient buttons, two kitchens (old and new), its four living rooms, and the blind chamber of GRAMMA. The whole works traversed by hair-chutes, laundry arteries and tiny trapdoors opening into sensual cubbyholes behind furnaces, fridges and wetbars, everything above crammed with china and chesterfields, forgotten equipment and unopened packages bought and stored long ago by AUNT LIL. The little CHILD WITHOUT QUALITIES was the happiest child in the world.

He was happier still at the beach cottage, where the linoleum, beddings and cool bosoms of sand gave vent to a rashness that made latency impossible. Everything there dissolved instantly, discharging flavour at a touch. There were so many delicious privacies and bursting pods at the beach, and a wild intemperate language of smells. If the house in the city told the CHILD WITHOUT QUALITIES his own story, the cottage at the lake sang it, and made his chest swell like a whitecap.

And so it was with chest swollen so in happiness and in happy solitude that the CHILD WITHOUT QUALITIES lived his earliest years. Sometimes he intentionally separated himself from his favourite toys, and played with the memories of them. And then played with the memories of the memories. There were inexhaustible powers of renewal within these two homes for the CHILD WITHOUT QUALITIES.

Especially inexhaustible were the mysterious blue strips of land which lined the horizon of the lake's opposite shore. The blue strips of land were serrated like knife blades; the large one, with a white scar on it, always followed by the smaller of the two, and sometimes a third, smallest strip of land, emerged from the lake to tag along behind the others.

In these early years, they were tokens of wonderment for the CHILD WITHOUT QUALITIES. One school of thought held they were islands, and that seemed quite likely. Others explained that they were the towering cliffs of such-and-such faraway beach, and various names were given to pinpoint the distant sites. But what good are names to someone who simply wants to know what such a land looks like close up?

Close up? Hah! No one could even agree on how far away they were. Five miles … twenty miles … a hundred miles of monstrously wavy waters were all frequently heard plausible approximations.

The exact nature of the blue strips was too slippery to pin down. Especially with them changing as they always were. The CHILD WITHOUT QUALITIES playing in happy oblivion, tanned and pot-bellied, would look up from the castles and buckets of his own beach to check on the fickle strips. Always surprising, sometimes they pried the whole horizon upwards and shone through, a wide crack of azure light. Other times they floated on air like zeppelins above the water, or crumbled like cookies. Often, the second and third strips would change places, or, swollen like worms, all three would embark on slow, far- ranging journeys to new resting points on the compass. On hot days, the lake held up a funhouse mirror and warped the strips into grotesque and hilarious versions of themselves; or telescopic breezes would disclose little white houses on the remote shore, but only for teasing glimpses – the tiny white squares would quickly stretch upwards like warm taffy and disappear before a friend could be summoned to witness them. As a result, the views of the strips became chiefly the property of the CHILD WITHOUT QUALITIES. He was their most devoted monitor, and for him they revealed rewards which the mere dilettantes never sensed. He actually knew their moods, their routines, and even felt their reasons at times. The unique nature of the child's relationship with the strips was expressed in their most outrageous acts: they would rise up from the water, like icebergs finally producing all of their hidden mass, and tower above the CHILD WITHOUT QUALITIES in a solid wall of blue, a Jericho which teetered and leaned over the entire breadth of the lake. They would flaunt their ridiculous dimensions in the face of an unobservant, suntanning and cavorting public. The child's mute, geographical companions may have been audacious, but still they withheld secrets. The CHILD WITHOUT QUALITIES was simply dying to know what they looked like close up! The views he did get were admittedly special, but they were not enough, and soon the strips came to visit his dreams with false solutions to their riddles.

One day, under the sway of a summer dawn, he came close to beholding their true nature.

Dawn is a proud mountebank, and anyone up at this time of day gets to keep some of this pride for himself. The CHILD WITHOUT QUALITIES had gotten up very early – the first on the beach. Amid the shrill bragging of its pink wavelets and the loud chirruping of its birds, Dawn was showing off with all its tricks, a garrulous warm-up act to the more orderly, level-headed day.

Suddenly the mountebank produced an enormous sideshow. Crowding all the clouds of the sky along its horizon, it completely buried the blue strips. But the strips were not gone; they were, in fact, presented to the CHILD WITHOUT QUALITIES in a mammoth, magnified imitation sculpted upon those very clouds, which stretched in a vista as long as the lake itself. The billowy features of that exotic landscape – revealed in detail at last – were focused into sharp relief on the clouds by Dawn's long shadows. Was this merely a vast canvas depicting an overripe hoax? Nevermind, the CHILD marvelled to see the white, thinly smeared beaches that traversed the sky. Little nacreous cottages, embedded as pearls in a dense shrubbery of crumpled silk, crowded the shore before a diorama of albino elms, wispy white spires and prodigious smokestacks folded into a populous community. Even a bright white ragged stern-wheeler lay beached at the edge of the now not-so-distant shore.

But the act came to an abrupt close. Wind scattered the scene and Dawn made a sketchy exit. Did the CHILD WITHOUT QUALITIES now know the true close-up character of the blue strips? Had Dawn shown the boy preference? The strips now sat innocently in their places while Day took over.

Such was life at the second of the CHILD's homes.

However, the third, and final, and most important home remains to be properly limned, shaded and palped. This third home, not even a home in any common sense because it probably suggested to him everything that was not home and was therefore the Outside World, but the place in which the CHILD WITHOUT QUALITIES felt more 'at home' than any other place (then why not call it a home?) was none other than the Gothic and gargantuan, the elitist and elysian, the perfumer of megalomania and melancholia, the habitué's haunt of heraldry, horror, hockey and hearses, the wonderful womb of the wondrous: namely, in a word, the Winnipeg Arena.

The CHILD WITHOUT QUALITIES was old enough to tell that his father CHAS was some species of celebrity. Almost as soon as the concept of 'celebrity' is capable of forming itself within a young mind, that was when the CHILD WITHOUT QUALITIES recognized the special features in his father. CHAS was of course some kind of important behind-the-scenes figure of the local hockey team, the Winnipeg Maroons. He was either coach or manager or treasurer, perhaps no official designations existed, but whatever he was, CHAS was well known and often given special treatment – the two requirements of celebrity. The scope of his celebrity was beyond the ken or even the concern of the CHILD WITHOUT QUALITIES. At the Winnipeg Arena, CHAS was at least important enough to get in at any time, for any event, without paying. The little CHILD WITHOUT QUALITIES witnessed time and again how CHAS used a special side entrance in the arena. This was the player and celebrity entrance, guarded by JIMMIE, the aged and one-legged goal judge, who screened all aspiring entrants with a cranky perusal. JIMMIE actually propped his prosthetic leg against the door jamb as a creepy but effective leg-gate barring all those unworthies who should really be paying their way in. These non-celebrities he grumpily sent around to the front of the building where the box office and cashier would tend to their needs. But for CHAS, and the little

CHILD WITHOUT QUALITIES, JIMMIE instantly punched his life-less leg out of its formidable position and the proud father and son simply glided in, exhaling a last few mouthfuls of frost in JIMMIE's direction by way of thanks.

The Winnipeg Arena seems like the only home once one is actually inside it. The CHILD WITHOUT QUALITIES knew and loved its every dark corner. He haunted the dark sprawl of its basements, traced drone paths through its empty seats, and perched upon the organist's aerie. Between game days, he liked to fold up against their backs all ten thousand seats in the build-ing, so as to present pleasing homogenized bands of colour to his eye. He loved the smell of the ice, the Zamboni and the acrid dressing rooms, where his father let him cut oranges for the players. The sensual intensity of the arena seemed concentrated in the pulp of those oranges, which misted the face of the child with the moist perfume of potential as he worked away.

Life in the arena was rich and strange. Giant oaks and vines grew inside and outside the building. A shallow concrete moat surrounded the ice surface, and players had to walk special gang-planks to play their games. Large swarms of bats issued from the black infinities of the rafters and catwalks. The giant pipe organ played only J. S. Bach and a few hockey anthems. The games themselves were played by men helmeted only in a thick protective gloss of Brylcreem, dripping above lumpen faces heavily cross-hatched with the wounds of many years' play with blade and cudgel. The fans seemed to be selected from the same pool. Everyone in the building seemed involved in some crime. Mug-shot faces filled the gallery, seats teemed with profanity. By the end of each game, these mugs would be effaced by the thick clouds of cigarette smoke they produced to conceal them-selves. The smoke often billowed down to ice level, where the elevated, celebrity criminals were forced to play their game with much confusion and bluffing about where the puck, or pucks, and other players (everything lost in the nebulous exhalations) actually were.

One game, though, always stood out in the memory of the CHILD WITHOUT QUALITIES. The Shrine Circus, eager to set up following the final buzzer, lined the area around the rink with its exotic animals. For this game, the human fans seemed to be replaced by lions, tigers, elephants and giraffes, watching from their rinkside cages. Errant pucks often careened into the depths of these menageries, and groans and cries of bestial pain would echo back to the players.

One day, CHAS and the rest of the Maroons held a birthday party for the CHILD WITHOUT QUALITIES. It was hard to tell exactly how old the birthday boy was; no one even seemed to care. The party started in the dressing room, but soon billowed, bellowed and tinkled its way into the rest of the deserted, half-lit seating area. Countless legs hung down from a low ceiling of smoke; the CHILD WITHOUT QUALITIES was bestowed the honour of pouring out punch into the tallest of highball glasses for the scarred faces which emerged from the clouds above. Even a chimpanzee, dressed as a cowboy and toting a pair of six-guns, attended the party. It was said he had retired from making Tarzan movies, and was now brought here specially to play with the young birthday boy. This delighted the child, but all attempts to befriend the ape were met with rudeness and stupidity. Surely it was the power of the team's celebrity which attracted this former celebrity from the animal world, but no deference was paid out by the chimp. It drank down at one draught all of the CHILD's chocolate milk – and not just one glass either. It took the entire head of a porcelain rooster pitcher between its huge black lips and gulped down every drop while the party guests howled. Later, while the simian sat at the giant pipe organ and slammed away moronically on the keyboard with its rash, elongated paws, the CHILD WITHOUT QUALITIES sat tentatively beside him on the bench in hopes of making a crowd-pleasing duet. But no duet was to take place: the former celebrity swung around, growled fiercely, knocked off his own cowboy hat, and dealt the CHILD WITHOUT QUALITIES a vicious punch to the face, toppling him to the cement of the organist's aerie.

The celebrity of CHAS was legitimized at school. Team photos of the Maroons appeared regularly in the city's sport pages, and in them stood CHAS, wearing the team blazer, with his name, but never quite his title, appearing in the legend below. The team toured to faraway places – Medicine Hat, Trail, Kamloops, Prague and Stockholm – and the media did their best to follow them in those days before satellites tightly laced our skies. The long-distance phone call, with all of its faintness and muddiness, seemed to be the reportage of choice for radio and TV stations. Sometimes CHAS spoke to celebrity sports announcers on these hookups. This also came at a time when JANET was beginning to perform quite promisingly at school track meets, so she too fell into celebrity. This proved to be contagious; a photographer friend of CHAS, desperate for a child model, acquired for a few hours the CHILD WITHOUT QUALITIES. Shortly after, the CHILD WITHOUT QUALITIES appeared, wearing nothing but jockey briefs and a stupid grin on his wide-oval head and holding a football beside similarly clad fictitious parents, in a full-page Bay Day ad in all the newspapers. The CHILD WITHOUT QUALITIES, treated to enigmatic and sometimes cruel behaviour by his schoolmates as a result, was not ready for the surprising weight of celebrity, was embarrassed and perplexed by it. He was invited by some freshly minted friends to a Saturday morning trip to the pool, where he was promptly encircled in the locker room by these new friends, who stripped naked but had no intention of swimming, only of encircling the CHILD WITHOUT QUALITIES with their bald little up-jutting and finger-like erections, threatening to pee on him if he wouldn't join them in their state of howling undress. On another occasion, the CHILD WITHOUT QUALITIES was pursued far and wide in the neighbourhood night by an older boy who wanted some dominion over the younger. In an exciting version of hide 'n' seek, with higher stakes, the CHILD WITHOUT QUALITIES spent hours crouching in garages, crawling behind garbage cans and climbing trees to elude his sadistic personal predator. At one point he made a break for home, but was caught by the older lad just inches from his own front door. The CHILD WITHOUT QUALITIES could see his mother and his AUNT LIL at work on some hairstyles just inside the salon, but was powerless to pull their attention away from their labours de coiffure. The delinquent pounded the younger's head into the stucco just beside the display window – where apparent safety was on display – then spit right into his victim's mouth before finishing things up with a winding knee to the belly. Only years later would the CHILD WITHOUT QUALITIES achieve some puzzling sort of satisfaction on this score when he noted at one of HERDIS's hair conventions that the same delinquent, as the result of some mysterious transference, had become a hairdresser.

The CHILD WITHOUT QUALITIES did not help matters at school by bragging that he was the first to own a colour TV, which was true: AUNT LIL was addicted to shopping after work and had thus purchased and installed a new RCA in her living room on the main floor. The CHILD WITHOUT QUALITIES similarly installed himself in front of this TV, whose very colours he could smell in his typical solitary pleasure. One night, all the urchins of the schoolyard pressed up against AUNT LIL's window to see the new colours; one of them made a jealous attempt to break the window, startling its lone indoor viewer and scattering all the trespassers in childish fear-fun.

All this fresh attention seemed the direct result of the underwear advertisement; the very celebrity that empowered CHAS ennervated the CHILD WITHOUT QUALITIES, and it was at this time that he retreated into the hermetic company of his few closest and most secretive friends. It was by now Canada's Centennial year, and the arcane society of these friends, three or four in number, staged some of the mustiest, most illicit and ambitious projects and celebrations that this country was to see in its basements and garages during its entire happy birthday.

The high priest of this society was TOM, a couple of years older than the CHILD WITHOUT QUALITIES. He also lived, unbelievably enough, behind a beauty salon, the rival Black Silhouette Salon – one block from Lil's. It was TOM who taught the CHILD WITHOUT QUALITIES how to play properly with the rollers, pins, clips, hairnets and bottles of the shop. In the basement of the Black Silhouette, the two children would perform their Centennial surgeries. G.I. Joe dolls were the typical patients – AUNT LIL's shopping excursions kept up a steady supply – and lobotomies seemed to be the operation of choice that year. Oftentimes, other procedures were deemed necessary, and this is where the salon equipment came in very handy. If a torture was required, a hairnet and hot hairclip were used on the miniature subject. A curling iron could melt a soldier's face into multifarious scream-agonies and raise unsurpassable sensual tingles in the two who presided. Unsurpassable, that is, until TOM discovered a solution in a dusty bottle in the Silhouette storage. This solution, when doused on a G.I. Joe, could be lit into a very exciting immolation. TOM liked to remove his pants and underwear for these immolation services. The burnings did seem like services. TOM brought a real sense of ritual to them, and with the lights off and all attention focused on the little pyre, the CHILD WITHOUT QUALITIES was put in mind of those Christmas Eve shepherd pageants at church.

The zenith of all experiments, though, involved sneaking onto the freight stairway at the back of Eaton's. Once at the top of these stairs, one has a view into a dark abyss over ten storeys deep. TOM and his acolyte took a model of Ed White, first American to walk in space, and made their forbidden stirring way into the uppermost regions of the spiralling staircase, set the astronaut on fire and dropped him into the void. Ed White floated in space for a while, as he did on his historic walk, then, with a gentle rock of enflamed terror, plummeted, face upwards all the way, into luxuriously prolonged freefall and sudden extinction. With bodies aquiver, TOM and the CHILD WITHOUT QUALITIES ran back to TOM's garage, where he produced some greasy magazines found in someone's garbage.

TOM was definitely a vanguard in certain areas of experience. Once, during a sect game of hide 'n' seek, he came screaming from his hiding spot totally naked, sporting a full erection, and laughing so hard during this anything-but-funny self-display that both farts and thick creamy snot issued from his person in eye-popping overabundance. The disgusted CHILD WITHOUT QUALITIES covered Tom's indecency with rumpus-room throw rugs.

Once TOM severed the head of a flower during some backyard play that strayed into the garden. The CHILD WITHOUT QUALITIES could sense that HERDIS had been watching from the upper back window – would she be angered by the damage done to the garden? Before this question could be answered, TOM picked up the flower head, and, in an action which proved he conversed in a poetry a few leagues above his friends, he dry-humped the blossom and discarded it like a spent prostitute. Without looking, the CHILD WITHOUT QUALITIES could sense the face of HERDIS withdraw from the shadowy window. It's hard to say what effect this incident had on either HERDIS or her son, but a short time later, in the basement washroom, beneath the stamping feet of the salon gynocracy, the CHILD WITHOUT QUALITIES put a badminton birdie on the end of his THING WITHOUT QUALITIES and urinated into the sink. Another Centennial Project to his credit.

A second select member of the secret society of friends was RICHARD K., a latchkey kid with easily broken limbs. His obese mother worked at a faraway grocery store; his mumbling father walked off to some unknown place every day, carrying a lunch bucket. It was RICHARD K. who taught the CHILD WITHOUT QUALITIES how to make simple tasty sandwiches out of just two components: bread and Miracle Whip. RICHARD K. could break his arm or leg clear through just tripping on a garden hose. It didn't take TOM long to see something exciting in all this weakness. TOM had read a human heart recipe in *Famous Monsters of Filmland* and decided that RICHARD K.'s heart could be easily obtained. The CHILD WITHOUT QUALITIES prevailed upon TOM to consider recipe alternatives, but TOM would hear nothing that could sway his course: RICHARD K. was to be slaughtered with an ice pick to his belly, and his heart would then be boiled up in a simple potage with carrots and onions. The CHILD WITHOUT QUALITIES, remembering the good in RICHARD K., and perhaps feeling sorry for him on account of all his broken limbs, warned him by phone to avoid TOM for a week or so until he got this recipe out of his head. Ironically, about a week later, it would be HERDIS who used the intended murder weapon, the ice pick, to chop up one of big TOM's bowel movements which had clogged one of the BELLAMY toilets. This incident passed without reminding the erratic TOM of his plan for RICHARD K., and the heart recipe was never discussed again.

One day, a terrified RICHARD K. came running breathlessly into TOM's garage to tell the sect of a importuning man in the bushes man who offered little K. money to put the solicitor's 'thing' in his mouth – or anywhere. The CHILD WITHOUT QUALITIES had never seen RICHARD K. this tearfully disturbed. But within a few moments the frail lad had caught his breath, announced excitedly that he was going to go back to try and find the old gent, and then indeed did dash off on recently healed bones toward the distant bushes of the Legislative Building where the first encounter had just taken place.

Later that summer, RICHARD K.'s brother FRANK K., a perpetually blinking teenager with a leather jacket, killed himself in his bedroom. Another society member, LEO J., said he saw the stretcher take him away.

RICHARD K. seemed to have even fewer qualities than the CHILD WITHOUT QUALITIES. He was as vague as vapour. He was actually present at least once, he said, at a strip poker game where the loser was subjected to genital strokings from the other players before screaming a surprised 'Look out!' and erupting like Old Faithful. Besides this story, RICHARD K.'s only proof of existence was that he always had a runny nose, which he dealt with by snorting back and swallowing. A steady dripping noise accompanied him always, punctuated by discreet little swallows in situations demanding some propriety – when talking to teachers, etc. These two qualities, the image of the viscous eruption during poker and the discreet viscous swallows, combined in the head of the CHILD WITHOUT QUALITIES to make one single creepy idea – which RICHARD K. soon came to embody. RICHARD K. and his swallows were soon banished from the company of his plagued PAL WITHOUT QUALITIES, who quickly detected a loathsome agenda in every sniffly and swallowing social contact between the two.

The final member of the inner circle was RICHARD N., a burly but gentle Japanese boy with a glass eye. He had cut his own eye out with a kitchen knife while cutting open a present on his third birthday. His parents had since filled their basement with every toy available from the department store catalogues. His inventory of new toys was so excessive it invoked only nausea among his friends instead of jealousy. Besides, his father worked a night shift and had to sleep in absolute quiet during the days, casting an unplayful pall over the entirety of the one-eyed kid's bungalow. RICHARD N. was big and submissive and loved the CHILD WITHOUT QUALITIES unconditionally. The latter took advantage of this affection to develop a slapstick routine with the former; he would punch big RICHARD N. in the stomach, doubling him over, then straighten him up with a knee to the face. Then he would redouble the big goof with another punch, and re-straighten him with another knee. This continued with cartoon hilarity until the peak of the laugh parabola had been passed, then RICHARD N., crying silently out of his one good eye, prepared himself for the next game.

As the Centennial year came to a close, RICHARD K.'s sister committed suicide by dragging a Christmas tree and its lights into the bathtub after herself. The kids at school could sense time running out, too, and pulled off an impressive last-second commemoration of their country. The two upper grades, numbering in the hundreds, locked arms to form a human chain, which stretched from one corner of the schoolyard to the other. This human chain then screamed the shrill scream of prepubescent Zulus and swept across the field toward the kindergartens and the lower grades. Like a living trawl net the line of older boys gathered up every single younger one, and trampled them under foot or pummelled them. The whole thing worked to perfection. The CHILD WITHOUT QUALITIES and his inner circle took part in this Zulu charge, but it was to be the last thing they did as a group. Who knows what project TOM was working on when he accidentally hanged himself from the clothesline in his backyard. RICHARD K. discovered the frozen body swinging in the morning frost and ran in breathless terror all the way home, but he could find no audience in his parents. They had mumbled and waddled off to work, so RICHARD K. was forced to wait until the CHILD WITHOUT QUALITIES woke up to tell his exciting story. (A few years later, one RICHARD K. story was left completely untold: he was removed from his frame house on a stretcher, perhaps the same one that took his blinky brother away forever, and his brittle bones were burnt down into a more stable compound of ashes.)

During that holiday season, the CHILD WITHOUT QUALITIES fell more and more into the company of his father. The former had been made dimly aware, during the previous months, through the CHAS half of endless phone conversations, that some sort of important hockey business was about to be transacted. Now it had happened. According to CHAS, the Winnipeg Maroons were now Canada's National Hockey Team. The CHILD WITHOUT QUALITIES was used to weighing everything CHAS said with a suspicious eye, careful to factor in his father's habitual hyperbole. But when CHAS and the little one swung past JIMMIE's unhinged leg and made their way into the Winnipeg Arena to watch a team practice, sure enough, something had changed. The team had discarded its maroon jerseys in favour of Kodachrome-bright red and white uniforms, with a beautiful red maple leaf on the chest of each. The name of the country, CANADA, stretched out above the leaf as final confirmation of CHAS's credibility. The CHILD WITHOUT

QUALITIES recognized some of the old criminals from the Maroons dressed in these new colours, but for the most part the ice was brimming with new faces, younger, more beautiful faces, faces with a less terrifying character.

Only one player wore a helmet, but there was something awesome about this player. Besides the obvious – his helmet was spray-painted a gleaming gold – this player had freshness and trickery and brilliance coruscating off every joint. CHAS explained to his son that this gilt-topped player was the famed FRAN HUCK, the newest superstar of hockey, the author of over a hundred goals in Junior last year. The son's suspicions reignited over the hundred-goals figure, but he had no doubt that FRAN HUCK was already the effulgent personification of hockey's next hundred years.

After practice, CHAS took his son into the dressing room to meet the new players. At first, the father and son had trouble getting into the dressing room – some new team official didn't recognize CHAS right away – but soon they found themselves, fully dressed, standing among the naked players in the shower room. CHAS introduced the CHILD WITHOUT QUALITIES to the great HUCK, who stood before him all soapy and steaming, smoking a cigar while the shower water beat off his back. HUCK extended a hand in greeting to the awestruck lad, whose shy eyes were exactly level with the player's genitals. These eyes could come to no comfortable resting spot on HUCK; each soapy contour sprouted surprising hairs and each new terrain of flesh discomfited the child. Finally he fixed his attention on the long, damp cigar of HUCK.

HUCK jovially invited the CHILD WITHOUT QUALITIES to come for a skate with the team. Normally, this would occasion great thrills in any Canadian boy, but a surge of shame almost smote down the son of CHAS. A previously repressed fact had just been unloosed within him – he could not skate! He had tried skating a number of times, but it had been too hard, or way too cold, and the constant pain and humiliation of falling onto the pavement-like playing surface, often cracking his already misshapen head so that it felt like an egg breaking from the inside, had made the CHILD WITHOUT QUALITIES run and hide whenever anyone suggested skating. This humiliation was aggravated by his father's celebrity status with the hockey team. How could the son of such a hockey luminary not even know how to skate? The constantly distracted CHAS did not help matters the few times he did attempt to teach his last after-thought son; he actually tied the kid's skates onto the wrong feet, introducing a new species of pain to the already unbearable rite. Only a massive repression of this incapability enabled the CHILD WITHOUT QUALITIES to burst with intermittent pride for his dad and the players. HUCK temporarily unleashed this agony, but the child was nothing if not extremely repressive. Soon, he felt only the thrill of contact with the greatest celebrity yet, a fact confirmed almost daily in the sport pages. HUCK became his. At school, HUCK became the currency with which he tried to transact all affairs. He clipped out all HUCK photos, and listened to the radio broadcasts only for the name of HUCK.

And HUCK was there for him on those radio broadcasts, which offered to the listener only cubist glimpses of the players – the blur of a brushcut, the overlapping of elbows, and the flash of FRAN HUCK's gold helmet. The games often came over from Europe, with that same transatlantic drone and whistle always associated with that continent, and they were played at such early, ghostly hours, five or six in the morning. But at that hour, the CHILD WITHOUT QUALITIES lay open like a wound. He listened amid a flurry of foreign players' names – some of these had faces formed completely out of consonants.

The Winnipeg Maroons had truly become Canada's National Hockey Team, or the Nats, as they came to be known. This had apparently been effected by some complicated bureaucratic merger with another team. CHAS was still part of the team, but in a considerably reduced role, his son suspected. CHAS still appeared in all the team photos wearing the team blazer, but there was always the impression that he had snuck into the pose. True, his name always appeared in the legend below, but always with a vague designation beside it, often with no designation at all. A sort of 'Who is this man?' puzzlement replaced the previously pure celebrity of the Maroons days. The ever-cranky JIMMIE seemed to take longer to unwedge his leg for CHAS, who had to invest more friendly chit-chat in the doorman before gaining entry. CHAS still appeared behind the Nats' bench, but there was an impression that maybe he was their stickboy now.

CHAS received almost nightly visits now from an old cohort with the Maroons, BUD HOLOHAN. Together CHAS and BUD discussed the world's ailments. In complete accord they worked into the latest hours of night, tabling plausible solutions to the problems in Russia, Vietnam, Israel and South Africa. The solution for hippies and homosexuals was decided with fairness and rapidity. Overhearing these discussions from his bed, the CHILD WITHOUT QUALITIES learned much. He dreamt up scenarios where BUD would be the president of the United States, and brother ROSS, who was in actuality an up-and-coming administrative trainee at the Bay, would be somehow the president of Russia. Together, the two gifted problem-solvers would bring sense to bear in the world. CHAS was deemed too improper to figure in this global scenario; he peppered his vernacular with unpolitical colloquialisms like 'chased him around like a fart in a mitt,' and would have to be consigned to a backroom role. Also, CHAS seemed easily angered, distracted or distanced. He did the books for Lil's Beauty Salon at the dining room table. Once, the CHILD WITHOUT QUALITIES arranged all his monster models and G.I. Joes around his bookkeeping father in a humiliating tableau vivant. Not even when the camera flash recording the event went off did CHAS raise his face from the ledger, where it remained buried long after everyone else's bedtime.

HERDIS had become very indistinct since that distant night when she hosted the party for CAMERON's death. The CHILD WITHOUT QUALITIES viewed her as he viewed all other women, as truncated legs seen through the salon's hair-chute. But a certain war, a war which raged in all the households of Canada, brought her into disturbing definition once again. This was the war of *Lawrence Welk* versus *Hockey Night in Canada*. The war between *Hockey Night in Canada* and *Lawrence Welk* was won eventually by the hockey broadcast, but the casualties were strange and unpredictable. Every Saturday night, the two broadcasts started at precisely the same time. HERDIS started slamming drawers and banging pots the instant she heard the theme song that is really the reveille summoning all men to their couches. Terrified, CHAS and the CHILD WITHOUT QUALITIES quickly switched over to *Welk*, which CHAS, drawing on his years of dance experience with HERDIS, could at least pretend to enjoy. Whenever the champagne bubbles were interrupted by a commercial, the two males would 'just check' on the score of the game, invariably returning to the musical variety show a little bit late – halfway into an Arthur Duncan dance routine, a Charlie Feeney solo or Guy and Ralna duet. The visits back to the hockey game became longer and longer with each succeeding commercial break, and finally HERDIS broke, stomping off to bed to sleep off her fury. CHAS and hockey always carried the day in this ritualistic fashion. Why CHAS wanted to watch the game at all actually puzzled his son. He spent half the time complaining about how bad modern-day players were. The new fad of excessively curved sticks and their attendant wild slapshots he equated with long hair and free sex – an equation of sheer obviousness. The simple experience of watching a game put him into furies as well. He spent the other half of his time stepping in and out of the bedroom, checking on HERDIS, who simmered sleeplessly on the backburner.

The casualties of this war alluded to earlier were indeed not to be predicted. The victorious CHAS was actually reduced to a series of vaguely sketched gripes and grouches. He seemed to fade from existence. Even during other hours he was the paltry sum of dizzy spells and car rides, only occasionally rising into substantiation by gloriously flinging large quantities of litter onto the highway, sending it into a vertiginous, spectacular spin in the wake of the speeding family wagon. HERDIS, on the other hand, learned to make herself more present by her absence. HERDIS, so strong and assertive and hard-working and fearless, now had an unbeatable strategy – and she spent her every spare moment behind the closed bedroom door. She emerged only for surprise attacks, once sneaking up behind the CHILD WITHOUT QUALITIES as he opened the fridge for a late-night glass of milk. Springing from who-knows-where, she yanked down her son's pyjama bottoms and started 'smooching her little buns.' Her son, feeling a bit like a victim of the squid in *Twenty Thousand Leagues under the Sea*, would struggle as if his very air supply depended upon it. But HERDIS was not easily pried off – her legs were strong, and wrapped themselves around her son with such thigh-bulging ferocity that her nightie rose well above her waist. Only by cork-screwing his entire body until his face lay buried in the deep shag of the carpet was the son to avoid the sloppy facial kisses of the mother. Finally, the wrestling match was called a draw and the two combatants retired to their respective bedrooms, closing their doors tightly behind them. Other fathers' headlights washed the ceiling of the son's bedroom as they drove past on their way to their own homes.

The CHILD WITHOUT QUALITIES took a new interest in his mother's work and the machinations of the salon. HERDIS had always risen early to do hair for customers who then went straight to work freshly coiffured. Five a.m. was a typical start time for the sinks, clippers and hair dryers downstairs to begin their industrial racket. The CHILD WITHOUT QUALITIES one day asked his mother to wake him at this magic hour so that son and mother might share the entire day. HERDIS crept into the lad's bedroom at the appointed hour and planted a loving maternal kiss on the lips of the sleeper, leaving a moist vapour about the two closely placed faces. THE CHILD WITHOUT QUALITIES, still sleeping, popped open his eyes and saw only the giant mask of his mother's face, horrifically unrecognizable as anything but something too big. He swung out instinctively at the nightmare and landed a solid punch on the nose of his mother, before simply closing his eyes and returning to the forgetfulness of sleep. Next morning, HERDIS started up a hurt silence and kept at it all day, closing her bedroom door behind herself as soon as possible. Her son could only mimic her powerful strategy. He found himself in bed hours before he was sleepy.

It was there, in CAMERON's old bed, that the CHILD WITHOUT QUALITIES, thinking about things, chanced upon a mortifying realization and embarked upon a new career as obsessive worrier. The realization was that GRAMMA, now in her nineties, was going to die – and probably soon. The blind GRAMMA spent all her waking hours in profound loneliness. She sat in a hardwood chair against the stucco wall of her living room, in an austere composition that would have made Dreyer envious. GRAMMA's immobility seemed to one-up that of Whistler's mother, but if one looked closely, one could see her attempting to thread a needle in her blackness. The CHILD WITHOUT QUALITIES took a frightful new interest in the life of his grandmother. HERDIS and LIL seemed to have no time for the lonely enquiries of their mother, so the grandson took on the impossible task of telling GRAMMA news from the world of light. It took great patience from the child, who sometimes found himself slipping into the shamefully snippy tones of the two daughters. GRAMMA's world was virtually devoid of event, so conversational quagmires were unavoidable. Occasionally, when the grandson came downstairs for a visit, he found GRAMMA busy at something inexplicable in the bathroom. She would open the door just a crack and extend for her grandson the familiar teaspoon and bottle of Lysol. The grandson's job was to fill the spoon with Lysol, then pour it into the warm water solution in the bulb of a large turkey baster, which was then given back to the grateful and partially clad nonagenarian, who then closed her door to work with this mysterious equipment.

Most of the visits to GRAMMA, though, were motivated soley by the morbid need to know that she was still alive. Often, GRAMMA was napping when her grandson came down, and he was compelled to tiptoe closely up to her bed to make sure that she was still breathing. This was not always easy, so great protractions of detection were exercised. The grandson, unable to perceive the reassuring heave of living breath within the chest of GRAMMA, often leant his ear right down to the wrinkly death-mask of this desperately beloved woman. Still unable to ascertain anything for sure, he would hold a mirror beneath her nostrils, hoping for steam, which the cornhusk-dry relative never gave off. Finally, he just woke her with a loud call, for she was partially deaf as well, on the pretext that he was going to the store for something, and could he get anything for her? She always awoke, alive, horribly startled to be so old but alive, and politely and gently assured her little worrier that she needed nothing. He always left her bedroom employing all the superstitions that evolved quickly out of the fear of her dropping dead. Namely, he always walked out backwards, careful never to say the word 'goodbye,' careful to turn away well before the last possible view of her (feeling that prolonging his sight of her until door jambs and corridors eclipsed it would surely kill her), and always leaving her room with his left foot first. The CHILD WITHOUT QUALITIES lived in constant fear of killing his GRAMMA by slackening his superstitious vigilance. At the beach, anytime the phone rang at any of the neighbours' cottages – the BELLAMYS didn't have a phone of their own – the grandson was convinced that the ringing, audible up and down the streets and beaches, brought tidings of the grandmother's death. But whenever the CHILD WITHOUT QUALITIES returned to the city, GRAMMA was sitting in her Dreyer tableau. The relationship between the two people was anything but active, being based solely on prevention of a superstitious sort. Little relieved was the loneliness of GRAMMA in spite of almost round-the-clock visits by her terrified-to-distraction grandson. He endeavoured to involve HERDIS and AUNT LIL more in his programs, but they had apparently spent all their energy for life-saving measures. The darkness around GRAMMA deepened. On HERDIS's birthday, GRAMMA sang 'Happy Birthday' up into the heating duct of her room, which carried the frail and feeble tune up through the vents and into the upstairs kitchen of the BELLAMYS'. HERDIS was moved enough to come down and allow herself to be maternally embraced one last time by the tiny blue arms of her former mother.

Once, after all of the grandson's preventative routines had been followed out with precision, the BELLAMYS – CHAS, HERDIS, AUNT LIL, the vacationing ROSS and JANET and the CHILD WITHOUT QUALITIES – left for a weekend at the beach. After, GRAMMA, blind GRAMMA, made her way out of her suite and into the complicated hallways leading out into the front-street entranceway of the beauty salon. She liked to fetch the daily newspaper from this doorway and leave it on the dining-room table for AUNT LIL. This time she did not make it back to the table. The sections of the paper spilled out of her soft hands and sifted their way down the basement stairs. Bending over to retrieve the pages, GRAMMA soon followed after them, tumbling down the steps and landing in a joke of a mess – black and white and red all over.

Days later, with the CHILD WITHOUT QUALITIES left at the beach in the company of ROSS, he found out offhandedly about GRAMMA's spill. ROSS, playing catch with a young woman in a bathing suit, mentioned to her how his grandmother had fallen down some stairs and landed in the hospital. This glib remark struck the CHILD WITHOUT QUALITIES like a piece of hot shrapnel. Was it true? Yes it was. No one had bothered to tell the CHILD. He knew he had no qualities, but it would have been nice to be told. Now he insisted on being taken to the city. ROSS made the one-hour drive for him a couple of days later.

The CHILD WITHOUT QUALITIES listened as HERDIS phoned the hospital for an update. The doctor assured HERDIS that her mother was doing well and could come home the next day. HERDIS gave her little son directions to the hospital, not far away, so that he could make a cheering visit to GRAMMA before she came home. All the precautions had worked after all. At the hospital, though, the CHILD WITHOUT QUALITIES encountered a completely unrecognizable GRAMMA. During her week's stay she had withered to nothing. The removal of her false teeth had collapsed her face; her hearing had become almost as bad as her sight. Her grandson tried for a few seconds to let GRAMMA know of his presence. Her toothless mouth spoke in incomprehensibilities, which was all right somehow because the grandson was startled to see in the next bed something completely comprehensible. What luck! A beautiful young woman, writhing semiconsciously, had in her delirium torn off all her bedclothes –

and her nightclothes as well. This restless, tortured, or perhaps pleasured, patient squirmed there wearing nothing but an amber catheter, while GRAMMA moaned with the weakness of wind blowing through grass. This young woman was a concentration of all the female sensuality in the world. Even this brief contact with such a concentration filled the veins of the boy with a molten thrill. He backed out of the room, staring as long as he dared, head pounding like a heart.

He flew home, engorged with new things and all possibilities. At home there was a great hubbub. JANET had apparently been ill for a few days. Now her appendix had ruptured, and she too was in the hospital. HERDIS was making phone calls to tell people of her two invalids, making phone calls preparatory to a party. CHAS watched TV with great distraction, smoking a lot of Sportsmen.

That night, the CHILD WITHOUT QUALITIES was awakened by a five a.m. phone ring. HERDIS answered and spoke with great matter-of-factness about the death. Either JANET or GRAMMA had died, and it was impossible to tell from the lengthy conversation which one it was. At times of death, Herdis got exceedingly polite, almost ebullient in her strength. The CHILD WITHOUT QUALITIES had never done a single thing to make sure his sister stayed alive. What an oversight! Soon, he found himself praying to God that his GRAMMA was dead. His whole years-old program was being junked that very moment as he trembled in CAMERON's bed. Finally, he heard HERDIS hang up and tell CHAS that her mother was dead. Prayers answered. The much-feared moment of GRAMMA's death had finally come, and instead of a complete crashing down of the sky, he felt nothing but elation, thankfulness and even an aroused longing for GRAMMA's hospital roommate. In this way, the CHILD WITHOUT QUALITIES was shortchanged of yet another simple experience. He had lost a loved one but was deprived of bereavement; in fact, owing to a series of incredible coincidences, he never learned to grieve.

The CHILD WITHOUT QUALITIES now made a simple shift of the focus of his worries from his dead grandmother to his father, CHAS, who had recently been diagnosed as having a heart condition. The CHILD WITHOUT QUALITIES tripled the number of operational superstitions required to keep his father alive. In addition to waking him up from every nap, he never allowed the words 'heart' or 'attack' to be uttered in his presence without knocking on wood immediately after, and he never turned on the TV without turning on an empty toaster first. Ringing phones terrified him and could only be unhexed with the most involved procedures. If, at night, too many headlights washed into his bedroom, he felt CHAS's death to be imminent, and it was only by some miracle that he eventually heard the paternal key in the door. Whenever he heard the night rills singing in the hall basin, he felt the warm wash of security he needed to get through to dawn. Dawn always brought a new crisis, because he knew that was a favourite calling time for Death, so when he heard the fridge door closing on the freshly prepared orange juice, he knew he was safe from unbearable distress for another brief but sweet time unit.

JOURNAL THREE
(1999 – 2002)

18 March 1999

Birth of a Nation and Lumière Brothers films arrived from Kino today, as did *The Ogre*.

Must rearrange *Edison and Neemo* and remove some thirty-five pages near the beginning, taking it down to eighty-one pages. Some more dialogue trimming should get script down to seventy pages. I'm just hacking on my own now; George and I can repair the mangles. Now – I speak too optimistically – some pantomime and micro-montage will bring the movie in at eighty-five minutes. These stylized things have simply got to sprint through the theatres before they overstay their welcome, ninety minutes tops.

2 April

Got my Manitoba Arts Council Major Artist's Grant application in yesterday. I'm asking for $25,000 to take a six-page treatment called *Youth, Beautiful!* to a full-length script. Do I deserve any of this? Of course not!

16 April

Hugged Deborah goodbye – she's off to Vancouver and Mexico for months, then Montreal, then some dance barge to Cuba for New Year's, then just away. If I get to Vancouver before she heads for Mexico, I'll look her up. She had either food or a colourful scab in the corner of her mouth.

I'm in big tax trouble, but I'm growing up fast. Perhaps this ordeal will make me a better person. While Lil was dying, I just worried about my own poverty – without even trying to get a job. Now, I have a dream where she asks me for a ride to the hospital, but I open her clothes closet and pee into it.

Had a WONDERFUL time with my most wonderful and lovely and important and brilliant and thoughtful daughter Jilian in Victoria last week. I don't know if I can describe all she means to me.

23 April

Watched this week: *Point Blank, The Tall T, The Lusty Men, The Student of Prague*. Just rented *To Each his Own, Love of Jeanne Ney, Lonelyhearts* (Clift). Bought Playhouse 90's *Days of Wine and Roses* and *In a Lonely Place*.

21 May

Just saw Mike Gottli shambling down Corydon with his walker. Wearing his shades, he looked much like the staggering Gunnar – five years after the moose put him to sleep for six months.

Phoned Jil yesterday and Kyle today about Jerry Springer's proposal of marriage to Rachel Toles. It's a great piece of news.

Sent Jil two Nino Rota scores today. Got my tax refund today and news of the MAC grant of $25,000. Still no word from L.A.'s Angelica, whose CV note was likely destroyed by thorough Tracy when she searched my gift from the obsessive pretty at the Egyptian.

Spoke with Jeff Geoffray (or Geoff Jeffray) of *Clown at Midnight* fame about doing an L.A.-based schlock film today. He is to watch *Careful* and *Twilight of the Ice Nymphs* this weekend, then never return a call again.

David Arnason offered me a very nifty three-year teaching contract today, for two half-courses every fall at U of M – $10,000 per term. If I stay in town ... perhaps.

3 June

Just finished *Sanctuary* by Faulkner, and *First Love* by Turgenev. Next: 'Lady Macbeth of Mtsensk' by Leskov.

4 June

Instead of the Leskov, I'm reading *The Flame of Life* by D'Annunzio. Picked up $12,500 from MAC and $300 from the Winnipeg Film Group today, then paid off MasterCard for the first time in almost a year.

15 June

Two days ago I acted, for the last time I pray, in a movie; in *Nostradamus*, I play 'Joe the Waiter.' A sweet young Burl Ives–ish director by the name of Tibor Takacs saw me acting in Noam's documentary and heard Paizs's fulsome praise therein, and offered monetarily challenged me union rates for a day's work on the wrong side of the camera – $630! Figuring no one would ever watch this little movie, I risked my shrivelled dignity by accepting. When I showed up at the Red Top greasy spoon on Monday, I was given my own dressing room in a Winnebago; my costume a simple red apron and 'Joe' name tag, to be worn with my own shabby clothes, awaited me on a couch in front of a TV rigged out with rabbit ears and a remote. I spent five minutes surfing the three snowy channels when I was summoned for blocking with Joely Fisher – Eddie Fisher's daughter – and presented with eight new unsayable lines. Twelve and a half humiliating hours later, Tibor offered his directorial prognosis: 'I think with some really inspired editing we can find a performance in there somewhere.' I had tried my best, but it was the same old story: my rectum was so tight you couldn't fire a bullet up my ass. I spent four straight hours clenching a coffee pot on set – why couldn't I have been 'Coffee Joe' instead of 'Waiter Joe'? – and I could scarcely uncurl my fingers at the end of the day. I knew half the crew from *Twilight of the Ice Nymphs*; I enjoyed hanging out with them, and the time flew sweetly.

After wrapping, I cell-phoned Tracy to pick me up and take us out to Loni for the next thirteen decompressing wine-drinking, two swims–filled hours. Quite nice, then back in time to ride my bike to Betelstadur, drive Ross to the airport and return home for a nap before watching *L'Atalante* with Tracy. (This picture was assigned to her by Caelum for review on their CKUW movie show.)

Tony Fernandez is currently hitting .404 and Deborah seems to be back from the Mexico League.

Right now my new script is equal parts *Elektra*, *First Love* and *Spring* by Schulz.

19 June

Watched Ida Lupino's *The Bigamist* the other night, a mildly enjoyable movie made wonderful by the fact that I watched it alone, and watched it knowing I would be going to bed alone afterward, having gained the first night off in over a month by pleading to be left alone to write for an entire day. I need more days like that. I was so happy reading *Medea* and listening to Tony Fernandez cracking balls around I frequently squealed and giggled for the sheer happy freedom I felt – many, many more days like it!

28 June

The big audit of '95–'96 is over. Thanks to the ceramic mushroom burger I made in response to a puzzling request from my glowering spinster auditor, I came out of it with a $324 refund. I think the mushroom burger exercise was designed to see if I was an artist or not, and whether I should be allowed artist-like deductions. Unbelievable.

Tracy, with whom I'm now getting along quite nicely, and I went to the Red River Ex out at its new Assiniboia Downs location last night. We went on no rides, but I loved watching adolescent girls and boys locked into chairs and cages, tilted, spun and turned upside down, their long hair hanging down from great heights like clappers in a bell tower. The girlish squeals and cries and pleadings for help, mixed with the pervasive smell of foundation and corn dogs, makes for a heady concoction. One fourteen-year-old girl was trying her luck in an electric chair; current was zapped through from one hand to the other, smoking her arms and heart along the way. I watched, waiting for her to void her bladder, but she begged off before the voltage got too high. (I once read a study about females and low pain tolerance.) Tracy and I ate a corn dog each, two bags of those fucking doughnuts, a bag of cotton candy and a caramel apple. I threw one dart (for one dollar) at a Pokémon and missed. Then we had our portraits taken in the photo booth – just like at the bus depot. This is my favourite art medium; there's no such thing as a bad bus depot photo! It would be cool to have one of these photo booths in my home.

Jilian sent me two lovely photos today; one shows Jil with her new 'baby' Riley – the little black kitten. Her really smartly appointed apartment is partially visible, and Jil looks wonderfully happy. The other photo is of cutely scraggly kitten Riley herself. Bon! Jil thoughtfully sent dupes of these to Amma as well, a very nice move. I just recently showed Amma the only photo of Pat I have, and Amma was heartbreakingly impressed: 'He's so handsome, I could love him myself.' As she has said to a few visitors over the years, including sweet and decorous Elie Johannson.

After the Ex, I drove across Portage to Chapel Lawn and made a brief visit to the graves of Chas, Lil and Gramma, all buried side by side. How strange to stand atop three such important people, three of the most beloved people in my life lying down there somewhere beneath the indifferently groomed lawn. Amma has her name engraved already on the Chas deathplate. It is my lawn-obsessive mother's fate to lie beneath this mediocre turf for eternity; I shall not point this out to her. I showed the graves to an indulgent Tracy. I felt both proud and a little embarrassed at the ancient dates of birth: 1918, 1879, 1901 ... The graves seemed so diminished, mini-graves! And stuffed as I was with carnival food, I felt a giant straddling this beloved trio. Without even spreading my feet apart unnaturally, I found my arms had risen to akimbo position. The ground makes one smaller but more concentrated, and the power of all that love lying latent in the earth soon frightened me off. I failed to find Cameron or his sweetie Carol. It seems Chapel Lawn has uprooted them! 'He'll be back!' as I predicted the day he died.

Mom, whose grave awaits her, bought and paid for, head plaque with name and birthdate in place, tells me that Cameron's grave indeed runs north-south and not east-west as I was looking for last night. (We always speak in terms of compass-points: 'Carol Isaac is west of the bushes.') Which means I probably strolled right over top of my dear brother while beating up my own head for its befuddled memory. While strolling atop graves thusly I bumped into an old friend. Namely dead Johnny Clubb, who, like Aunt Lil, died in 1986, and who reposed and mouldered between his bronze nameplate and some sub-cemeterial aquifers. Mr. Clubb was my very first boss, the pharmacist at Muir's Drug Store, where I was a delivery boy circa 1970 or so. He died in his mint-vintage red Studebaker, and sat dead at the wheel all night just across the street from 800 Ellice X-Large Studios on the occasion of my shooting the Gunnar/Snjofridur honeymoon scene for *Gimli Hospital*. Muir's has been many things in the ensuing thirteen years, including Steve's Submarine Sandwich Shop, and now I bump into Mr. Clubb at twilight in Chapel Lawn.

Mom reminds me (again!) that I can be buried on top of my dad now that he's been dead twenty years. Or my ashes can be lowered into a convenient two-by-two receptacle atop of him. I still want my ashes blasted into the lake by our old lawn mower, but if that proves too ghastly, I suppose mingling my ashes with the earth covering Cameron, Chas, Lil, Gramma and, depending on the order of events, Amma. Whatever!

7 July
Kyle, who weighs 255 Earth lbs., has been asked to pack on fifty more to act in a Japanese belly-butting contest, but today I told him I wanted him for the *Orlac*-ish Fran Huck part in next year's project, *Spring*. He plans on training for this role by playing rollerblade hockey down by the L.A. beach near where he lives. His friend Pam plays in a league there. (Tracy and I met Pam in May; she writes for *Just Shoot Me*.)

I sent Jilian a compilation of my 1993 home videos today. Ran into Erin Hershberg on Corydon this afternoon, then tied my tongue into reef knots, while on my way to Movie Invasion with bootleg copies of my own movies.

25 August
Niv Fichman invited me to make a two- to four-minute film for next year's Toronto Film Festival, all expenses paid up to $10,000. I accepted.

deco dawson and I went to Loni the other night. I painted and mowed by day, swam night and day, and watched with deco *The Fall of the House of Usher* (Epstein) and *Jour de Fête* (Tati) until one a.m. Before bed, we went out to admire the moon. Next door, Barbara's bedroom light was on, and in the window like a black paper silhouette, was Barbara. This startled me, terrified deco, and then filled me with a queer sadness. Was this lonely octogenarian unwell, or a habitual nighthawk (I'm so used to the old ladies in our family going to bed at six p.m.), or was she angry at me for making late-night noise or worse? It's true I hadn't called her lately, and I could easily imagine an angry middle-of-the-night glower on top of her black featurelessness. Her presence at the window was unprecedented, malevolent, unnatural – more like a Herdis stunt. When I returned from the moon watch, her face was gone from the window, her light was extinguished soon after. I hoped she wasn't in medical danger, but I did nothing about any of this except go to bed.

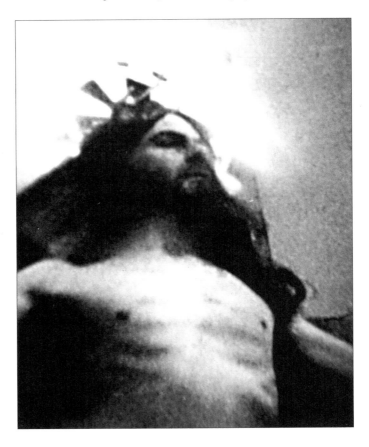

The next day, Barbara explained, with much mysticism and general fear cloaking her like an aura, that the wind had blown her front door open. She got up to close it and noticed my mother's always-dark cottage bathed within and without in a strange glow; deco and I had only the TV on, and a full moon in the south must have painted the shack warmly. Then, at precisely the moment she moved her face into the window, and seconds after her door had swung open, I swung my front door open. She saw two men. Not knowing I was down in Loni, her heart raced with fear. The supernatural light, strange men and some recent home invasions, all events tripping against one another at a sleepy hour burst in upon and kept dreamy, all added up to a frightened sweet old lady.

20 December
Having recently extracted the last limb – my pant leg really – from my relationship with Tracy, I found myself strangely unjubilant and completely unwilling to ejaculate press releases concerning my new status. For, in fact, I was anything but proud of my conduct during the whole affair, and as salubrious as this truncation was for all involved, the simple making right of things should not necessarily occasion celebrations. Unapt would be a party thrown by a man who finally returned all the money he stole from someone. And so, with a quasi-funereal sadness, the kind that always starts with sympathy for the dumped girlfriend and always ends with a generic and vaguely pleasurable self-pity, I tiptoed with grave decorum, and wore, instead of my tuque, a nimbus of deference for all sad relationships, as I picked through the produce at Safeway for a dinner designed to streamline my freshly freed phocine bachelor body.

A very happy recent memory, joyous to savour. Erin lies in my bed (where I now lie), wearing my black hoodie and her glasses, studying for her exam the next day. I've kept her up for hours, and she can't sleep anyway, but I can. I fall victim to the four a.m. death knell and slumber while she works – half my age, brightest and most beautiful woman – as sweetly as a sweet-bottomed little girl can. Homework and cuddles and insomnia all woven together in a happy warp.

4 January 2000

I'm pleased that the tanning-adept Erin is returned from Hawaii, positively steeped in negritude, and compliant and gracious and adventurous. We spent a first night back together which lasted till we were absolutely stupid from sleeplessness, and she drove home tailing my long extension cord behind her car and forgetting a bunch of stuff in my sleepy apartment. Last night, after promising each other to behave, we watched *Don't Look Now* and the rest of *Forbidden Games* in an almost decorous fashion. Erin had earlier flattered me by discussing her wariness of me, derived exclusively from Tolesian press releases issued over the years – from the offices of both Rachel and George. What defence do I have in the face of these largely accurate reports? The truth is simplest, but I can feel the truth pushing the girl away like a boat poled away from shore. Erin is a very good reader and movie viewer, better even than Elise, and, at this point anyway, a lot more pleasant. Much heartbreak awaits me. I hate thinking in these terms, but I wish I had yet another girl stowed in the rumble seat as a spare in the event of traumatic emergency. I'm not so fearless romantically; I just need an air cushion in the form of another woman whose potential will remain undeployed (even unreliable) until a sudden swerve in the road produces concussive trauma. In the meantime, I drive forward with only one girl on my mind, no airbag at all.

9 January

Erin walks with a feral swagger, her panties half-tucked up between her buns, the sleeves of my hoodie dragging at her side, the toe of one sock flapping, and her hair dangling in Herdiswhorish disarray. Fully clothed, Erin has the same walk, and she wears flared jeans that go a long way toward completing unfinished business from my teenaged years. And something else: she wears those great big clunky shoes, like new vw Beetles on her feet; only Gariné wore something similar, and I can't help but nod to Robert Walser as she removes these at my door. Robert will not nod back until I myself remove them, which I shall. When Erin gets cold, I cover her in Cam's freshly drycleaned blanket, still mint after forty years of use. Or I warm her with a hug. We even agree that there should be days at a

218

time, unexplained if that's how it happens, when we see nothing of each other, and today starts two such days. Though this we agreed upon this morning, or last night. Tomorrow, yes, I'll miss her, but I've work to do and, most pleasurably I hope, I also play the first hockey of the new year with rugged Bob Bright, sweet-passing Rob Shaver and the coltish Jason Holt. Ah, my life is blessed.

20 January

Dinner and many drinks at Winter Club last night with John Boles Harvie – the first face-to-face time spent with this man since Sugar Shack Night in August of 1990. Over four hours of heartsick and joyous raconteuring and reminiscing left me laughed-out or in love all over again, my head reeling with the Harvian depth charges sunk into the underused parts of my memory. A fevered night of dreams results; eight hours of childhood roll call; the landscapes and ghosts long gone restored to pre-corroded status for a glorious muster.

23 January

First public date with Erin – little Dreamin' Ramsgate! Went to *Sweet and Lowdown* at Grant Park with her, sat together like teenagers holding hands. Her head on my chest, much shared laughter, little unseen kisses. Arm-in-arm after the show, no secrecy any longer, though the mall was deserted, and a little trap door just for me opened up under my feet, and I fell, fell, fell. Erin tried to sneak me into her bedroom after, past a TV-dozing and disapproving father, to see her newly arranged shelves, to revisit her pugdog Spanky, and god knows what else. But her father and the TV were a Scylla and Charybdis too terrifying to navigate. So I kissed her a few times over the hockey stick I keep in the car and drove home steaming up the windows of my lonely bombardier, seeking comfort in a drive-through. (Luckily, all were closed, and my weight remains at about 186.)

25 January

Twenty-two years ago, virtually to the minute, Jilian was born, during a blizzard in Winnipeg, at the Women's Pavilion, third floor, while I watched a *Mary Tyler Moore* rerun in the men's waiting room. Tonight, she's going out, the same age I was when she was born, to see male strippers.

27 September
Wrote ten single-spaced pages of *Saddest Music in the World* treatment for Niv today, then did eighty-five minutes in gym and pool to bring my weight down to 205 from 210 just ten days ago. I'm starving in the backroom area of Bar-I, awaiting my tandoori burrito.

13 November
Tracy has tonight dubbed the 8mm movie we made about a year ago in France. Erin was but a gorgeous pillow for me to hug on that trip. My first anniversary with this much-loved whipper-snapper is now less than a month away – and resentment has yet to eclipse all other feelings! A record for me!

19 December
Eating compulsively, but working harder than ever at the gym! The result: overweight and aging fast.

Wrote Ishiguro – or Ish, as he is called – yesterday to introduce myself, to send some choice clippings, and to soften his hatred of me after George and I threw out all his script save two ideas and one character name. He's not going to bite, I just know it. The picture could be interesting, even good, but perhaps Ish and even Niv lack the commitment to melodrama and all its fevers that I know the project requires.

28 May 2001
Aunt Lil was born one hundred years ago today.

19 August
Sitting at Bar-I with Jilian. She leaves tomorrow morning, just one day before I shoot (with deco, Paul Suderman and much terror) *Dracula: Pages from a Virgin's Diary*. Jil's been in town for five superb days – time riven by pre-production angst, relationship strife, sleep deprivation, a Michael Powell firing, a nightmare come true in the form of extremely ordinary test footage returned yesterday. But, best of all, just Jil sleeping under the same roof as I.

1 October
Did you hear, Auntie Lil? Jilian's engaged to be married!!!! She phoned me from the top of the CN Tower with the news that just one half hour earlier Pat had proposed. She sounded so genuinely, unironically happy that I instantly felt the same. She said she had 'fabulous news' and then just blossomed with her headline. A wedding next summer, Auntie, in Victoria! I promised I would have trouble keeping my eyes dry on the wedding day, and I could feel a brand-spanking-new species of tears sliding themselves into my ducts, all ready for squirting! Jilian was going to try phoning Amma with this news; god, I hope Amma won't mar this momentous phone call as she has so many others! Being 8:30 p.m., Amma was probably in bed with her phone unplugged, or I would have heard from her by now. And so she will get her call in the morning, after her first granddaughter gets up. This evening is Jil and Pat's third anniversary of dating. What reasonable children! I've demanded a complete transcription of the proposal.

Today is also Erin's twenty-fourth birthday.

2 February 2002
02/02/02! What a nifty date! Good time to resume writing in this thing. Am on Saturday evening AC flight 196 to Toronto, then onwards to London for a visit to the Tate Modern, which I'll pretend I know all about. Finished *Dracula* on Wednesday and watched it for the first time at midnight, in bed, on my crummy little portable. It seemed too cluttered up with colours – the

titles, the handpainting. I won't know what to think of it until some people tell me what to think of it.

Floody Manitoba. When Mom's father took ill, she had to ride pregnant on horseback through deep floodwaters to get out to the farm where he lay on his deathbed. By the time she arrived, he had died and been bound tightly in ropes, as per instructions from Gramma (to prevent rigor mortis from twisting his limbs into undecorous contortions), and stored in the coolness of the shed. Gramma was never much of a consensual bride in her long marriage, and feared all men till the day she died; the ropes must have been a comfort. Together, she and my mom cut the farm clothes off Gramps and sewed a burial suit onto him, while the boys dug a grave and built a coffin. Since it was flood season, the grave filled to the top with water, and all six children had to stand on the coffin to sink it to its proper depth. Now that's how to bury a father.

9 May
Cut loose from my worries was the July 1st Power Plant deadline. I pled nervous exhaustion and received a seven-month stay of execution. With more breathing room sculpted around my crowded and lazy brain, I feel it time for another Gatsby list of things to change, to do, to be. I know how pathetic this is. I want it to be pathetic!

In no particular order:

1. Eat wisely, obeying the antioxidant list, consuming lots of fish, whole grains, water, etc.
2. Exercise: rising very early for the bike ride to Rady, mix up the programs more, plus train for a long outdoor Lord Byron swim
3. As a result of the two above, lose weight
4. Read more
5. Do taxes, and stay on top of them forever
6. Watch more movies, including the Cinematheque's
7. No more Bar-I solo visits – expensive, always fruitless
8. Make an attempt to shoot the Power Plant peepholes in Toronto this summer
9. Make a timetable for each day, week, month and goal
10. Write more in this journal
11. Look up more words in the dictionary

12. Get some nicer clothes
13. Get Bombers season tickets? Maybe not if time in Toronto
14. Buy a barbecue
15. Read more classics – Shakespeare/Greek/Roman
16. Houseboy instead of basement suite
17. Listen to more Beethoven
18. Read in bed more
19. More salons, fewer clips: movies all the way through
20. Make a list of actors to be used
21. Keep a grocery list

6 June
Badali's: Jil greets me at the hostess's dais. A hug, and then, something completely, wonderfully new, she walks me arm-in-arm to my table. How comfortable she is with herself, as much as I am not. So proud am I of the girl. The girl who surveys the restaurant like one of Walser's best butler students. Here, Jane's genes reign! The little Maddin ones are of no use, just in the way. The timid genes, the unassertive, the ones which encode a poor short-term memory, a left-footedness.

9 June
Pearson Airport a few minutes before returning to Winnipeg. A deception-free (0.1% deception) stay in Toronto. For some reason Gariné wanted to visit with me, I believe, even faxed me at my hotel, but I never made contact. Preferred shopping, hanging out with Pat and his big sports-filled TV screen, Chris, Sarah, their little Simon, and even Chris's brother Pete, and of course Jil who got off work early every night, making for splendid dinners out, rooftop barbecues, quiet nights while Jil beaded.

Meeting with Niv over the treatment went splendidly. Have to take Amma to the lake for the season tomorrow; shall I bus back in the morning or drive? I'd better bus; she'll be much happier with the car. Must also write a review of, strangely, the *Mary Tyler Moore Show*! First season on DVD, a box set. Capsule due at *Film Comment* Tuesday morning. Over half-done Dreiser's *Jennie Gerhardt*; hope to get off a good chunk on the flight.

Jil showed me video of the Victoria home, next to her future mother-in-law's house, which they hope to own someday. I hope they do. I'll love to visit there, live there! (In Victoria, not the house.) Jil has goals and drive, focus and perspective. I have man-boobs. I'm hoping to plan what remains of my life so it unspools itself with satisfactions, thrills, sanity, lungfuls of beauty and the heady accumulation of an unshameful nest egg – nothing greedy, just something to keep squalour and poverty out of the last chapter of my sorry biography.

20 June
Reading Curzio Malaparte's *Kaputt*! Tremendous lake of frozen horse heads! Cloudless day jammed with jabbering birdcalls. I sit at the kitchen table, where I once sat for sterile months watching Deborah come and go on her way to work. Deborah was in my mother's beach bedroom last night, popping up after a long absence, along with many of us extras, waiting to be summoned to set.

Why have I dreamt so much of mother's beach bed recently? It's where my father died. Also occurs to me it's where I was probably conceived. Then I remembered this was Janet's room until we installed running water, and if I was conceived at the lake it was in what's now the bathroom! Apt enough!

Why have I not registered appropriate concern whenever loved ones have come down with terminal or dangerous cancer? Lil, Ross, Crispy, Margaret, Grace, etc. Why have I been such a thoughtless fuckbag? I like to think it's because I fear sudden death so much – Cameron's, Gramma's, the long-feared sudden death of Dad – that cancer holds out hope for a cure, even when there isn't one, even when there's only piteous suffering involved, and the people are not snatched away without warning. There are always a few visits, grim ones but visits, possible before the end. I don't like surprises. Rationalizing complete.

Also, Steve says I'm a compulsive eater because my imagination is too rarely engaged – a flattering excuse. My days are so homogenized. Eating supplies the only sustained pleasure in the absence of work. If only I could hang out with Harvie and Emu, obsess over small projects, the pounds would melt away. Instead, my life presents me with the same overfamiliar obstacles to satisfaction every day. Constant distracting and infuriating phone calls during which I must account for my time – anything less stimulating impossible to conceive, the joy gone out of music, film, clothes, the lake. No self-invention. Only half-finished crossword puzzles before ten hours of depressed sleep.

30 June

In Toronto since Thursday 27 June. At Kei Ng's restaurant at Shaw and Queen with Jody Shapiro, Danny Irons and Niv Fichman. All these Rhomboids proclaimed their qualified high affection for the first draft of *The Saddest Music*. George should be relieved. The running time should be eighty-five minutes, down from its current 135. Should be easy to get it down to 100 minutes, and a do-able difficult to lop off the rest by way of combining scenes, trimming dialogue and making huge plot leaps through intertitles. Danny and Niv had been screaming at each other earlier, and the air was thick through dinner. Kei was very gracious in greeting us in his gorgeous Hunger Hut of a place open some fourteen months now – coming out from behind the counter for a handshake – no, hugs! And he just brought us dinner – no ordering – in waves, and different martinis came at us in waves. Jody and I left Niv and Danny to whack each other with olive branches, going next door to Bar One to meet up with Laura, Noam, Steve Lawson and some convivial film producer who kept filling my glass. All our glasses, until we had three bottles of wine – which Laura paid for, of course. I was just now over the edge and wanting to stay on even though everyone else was scattering: Noam off to boyfriend's, Stephen to a sex club, Laura just home to bed. Something sensible actually snapped inside me, as it never does, and I left, bumming a ride from Laura. I finally saw Jilian at two a.m. I was very tipsy by this time. She inflated my air-mattress bed for me after we chatted and watched TV. I bid her goodnight and cast myself onto the already deflated mattress, somewhat comfortable anyway.

Woke just in time to meet Niv for lunch. Within minutes of waking, I had a Chardonnay sitting in front of me at Crush, and a horrible earache starting up. Niv gave me his notes, exhaustively, while my ear hurt, and promised more meetings later with Don McKellar. I just wanted to go back to Jil and

Pat's to rest and watch the Bomber home opener on the tube. Bought Snyder Taschen's *All-American Ads of the 50s*. Bought myself Eugene Sue's *Mysteries of Paris* and a White Stripes disc. Bought Jil a Joseph Cornell coffee-table book, and – oh – Mats the Giraffe (the taxidermy named after Sundin) looks fantastic in the apartment, as do the newly painted kitchen, bedroom and shelves.

5 July
Bombers vs. Hamilton at stadium tonight. Section X for me. From the Bar-I terrace, I see the Quinton's sign hanging in there, and behind that, the billboard plastered with a big ad for Crops Funeral Chapel. Morticians shouldn't be allowed to advertise.

Dracula most assertively not eligible for Toronto Film Festival. I don't blame Vonnie for trying, but Michelle Maheux gave final word yesterday, to my relief. One shouldn't appear too desperate in his own homeland.

6 July
Smells! Dad at the lake and the smell of his beloved flammables:

- the wafting gas as we filled up the car
- the butane in my father's lighter in the car on the way
- the special gas-oil mix for the lawn mower, and the hot smell of the steaming grass from under the mower that mingled with it
- the kerosene poured into our cottage lamps
- the barbecue starter fluid that all men squirted into the coals
- the boat-gas and oil mixing in with the boat-bottom bilge (especially when Cameron stalled the engine on the far side of Willow Island, leaving us stranded miles out in the lake)
- the creosote with which my dad preserved the countless fence posts we ineptly planted over the years
- the sparklers on Victoria day (with which I burnt my hand as a toddler and got to be buttered and bandaged for a week)

❖ best of all, the can of gas my Dad loved to throw on bonfires, even though it once ignited so violently that it singed off much facial hair: no eyebrows and one eye.

12 July

Redrafting beauty-shop scenes for *Cowards Bend the Knee* reminds me of those immaculate perms my mother would give Gramma, and how much happier the blind nonagenarian – shrunken by age – seemed to be when styled and dressed properly, ridiculously. I loved her much more in her unkempt white mop, and her simple cotton summer dress, which Herdis threw out and replaced with something fashioned from thick turquoise upholstery. There's a photo somewhere of Gramma in this get-up. I'll always remember her in the summer breeze of the last day of school, wandering blindly among the lilacs. Everything smelling like sixty unspent days of holiday, the wind blowing her hair as her fingers felt the leaves as lightly as bees would.

It's finally happened, as suddenly as I feared. My old home on Ellice has been torn down. It took only a few minutes; I had no warning. Only because I pass by the old place almost every day did I come by to catch the event. A large bulldozing crane working from the front to the back made short work of the whole thing last night. Still loaded with our family furniture, the house was vivisected in an enormity that was, at some level, pleasing. To revisit those items, even in their last moments, was at least a chance to see them again. I kept running close up to the falling debris for better looks, a dog nipping at the heels of the crane-man. When Aunt Lil's window opened up – and much of the basement beneath it bloomed upwards in twisted roots of pipes, ducts, wires and rebar – I could stand it no longer. The crane-man could sense my distress and came down from his high chair. He came down into the basement, the same hole in the ground my dad carried me into at age two or three when the basement was being dug. I remember the mud floor, the tar walls. Now, dark as before, all I could hope for was a whiff of some powerful mnemonic smell. All smelled charred, as if the recent owners had been setting small fires in the place.

But my hopes leapt when I saw the twisted duct-work rising up before me like a periscope. I could smell that old scent: cool air-conditioned draft! For a moment, I was a child with cheek cross-hatched by the floor grate under the couch. The crane-man politely tapped me aside to demonstrate something; he exhaled two barely audible puffs of breath into the gaping duct wound, then stood aside to let me listen. Within a beat, two loud, devilish, terrifying roars from the very pit of hell screamed at me, simple echoes transformed into shrieks! I was mortified. This basement is every bit as frightening, after all, as my preschool self always feared. Soon, I was joined in the backyard by old friends. I could see Aunt Lil, refusing to leave the building, still doing hair at her old chair in the shop at front. Enough of the place still stood, even light shone brightly from the strong overhead shop lights. Goofy old John Stinson ran, hooting and hollering, clear into the crumbling building just as the crane re-revved to finish the place off.

BIBLIOGRAPHY AND NOTES

Journalism

'Death in Winnipeg,' pp. 66–73, first appeared in the *Village Voice*, January 30–February 6, 2001.

'Face Value: On *Minority Report*,' pp. 74–75, first appeared in the *Village Voice*, July 3–9, 2002.

'Bully for Bollywood's Musical Melodramas!,' pp. 76–79, first appeared in *Cinema Scope* 12, Fall 2002.

'Happy Ever After,' pp. 80–83, first appeared in the *Village Voice*, January 23–29, 2002.

'You Give Me Fever,' pp. 84–86, first appeared in the *Village Voice*, June 12–18, 2002.

'The Womb Is Barren,' pp. 87–90, first appeared in *Montage*, Winter 2001.

'Very Lush and Full of Ostriches,' pp. 91–95, first appeared in the *Village Voice*, August 1–7, 2001.

'Guilty Pleasures,' pp. 96–98, first appeared in *Film Comment*, January/February 2003.

'Sword Play,' pp. 99–100, first appeared in *Cinema Scope* 10, March 2002.

'Hold Me, Thrill Me, Kiss Me, Kill Me,' pp. 101–102, first appeared in the *Village Voice*, June 4–10, 2001.

'How Do You Solve a Problem Like Medea?,' pp. 103–104, first appeared in *Cinema Scope* 15, Summer 2003.

'Sad Songs Say So Much,' pp. 105–109, first appeared in the *Village Voice*, May 7–13, 2003.

Film Comments: DVD Reviews

'*Change of Habit/The Mary Tyler Moore Show*,' p. 110, first appeared in *Film Comment*, September/October 2002

'*Cinemnesis*,' pp. 110–111, first appeared in *Film Comment*, July/August 2001.

'*Cleopatra*,' p. 111, first appeared in *Film Comment*, March/April 2001.

'*The Garden of Eden*,' p. 111, first appeared in *Film Comment*, January/February 2003.

'*Ghost World*,' p. 112, first appeared in *Film Comment*, January/February 2002.

'*Hot Summer*,' p. 112, first appeared in *Film Comment*, November/December 2001.

'*Incubus*,' pp. 112–113, first appeared in *Film Comment*, May/June 2001.

'*Street of No Return*,' p.113, first appeared in *Film Comment*, November/December 2002.

'*The Time Machine*,' pp. 113–114, first appeared in *Film Comment*, July/August 2002.

'*Twin Peaks: Fire Walks with Me*,' p. 114, first appeared in *Film Comment*, March/April 2002.

All the above pieces were reprinted with kind permission of the originating publications.

Film Treatments

The short film *The Eye, Like a Strange Balloon, Mounts Towards Infinity* (also known as *Odilon Redon*) was completed in 1995. It was originally commissioned by the BBC.

The short film *Maldoror: Tygers* was completed in 1997.

The treatment for *Careful* was written in collaboration with George Toles. The feature film was completed in 1992.

The Child Without Qualities has never been filmed.

PHOTO CREDITS

All photographs courtesy Guy Maddin. Photographic credit has been given when known.

p. 31: Jilian Maddin in *The Dead Father* (still from 16mm film)

p. 48: Herdis Maddin in *Cowards Bend the Knee* (still from Super-8 film)

p. 56: Steve Synder circa 1985

p. 61: The Maddin Family (l-r: Herdis, Ross, Cameron, Guy, Chas, Janet, Toby)

p. 62: George Toles during *L'Age d'or*

p. 80: Guy and Noam Gonick (taken by Dan Dennehy for Walker Art Center)

p. 89: Chas Maddin with the Maroons

p. 92: Steve Snyder and Caroline Bonner in *Tales from Gimli Hospital* (still from 16mm film)

p. 105: Isabella Rossellini in *The Saddest Music in the World* (taken by Jody Shapiro)

p. 107: Isabella Rossellini and Mark McKinney in *The Saddest Music in the World* (taken by Jody Shapiro)

p. 118: Gramma, 90 years old, circa 1969

p. 121: Guy with chicken pox before shooting *Tales from the Gimli Hospital*, 1986

p. 123: Ian Handford

p. 126: Jilian Maddin circa 1998

p. 128: John Harvie

p. 138: Chas Maddin before the dentist smashed his eye, circa 1970

p. 146: Herdis Maddin, Guy, Gramma, lilac bush, circa 1959

p. 164: Jim Keller in *The Eye, Like a Strange Balloon, Mounts Towards Infinity* (still from 16mm film)

p. 176: Guy, Lil's Beauty Parlour, circa 1959

p. 199: Chas Maddin and Fran Huck

p. 212: Guy in *Tales from the Gimli Hospital* (still from 16mm film)

p. 216: Caelum Vatnsdal in *The Heart of the World* (still from 16mm film)

p. 220: Ross McMillan in *The Saddest Music in the World* (taken by Jody Shapiro)

p. 228: Aunt Lil on set in former beauty shop one week before her death

ACKNOWLEDGEMENTS

Thanks to the editors who previously published these pieces:
Stephen Bernhut at *Montage*, Dennis Lim at the *Village Voice*,
Mark Peranson at *Cinema Scope* and Gavin Smith at *Film
Comment*. Thanks as well to George Toles for first putting a
book in front of my face, to Steve Snyder for keeping me
company while writing his own diaries, to Darren Wershler-
Henry for his lovely design and especially to Jason McBride for
editing all the enclosed self-pity and tricking me into publish-
ing it in this form.

ABOUT THE AUTHOR

Guy Maddin was born above his Aunt Lil's beauty salon in Winnipeg, Manitoba, in 1956. His first feature was the cult classic *Tales from the Gimli Hospital*. His second, *Archangel*, the most lyrical of war films, won the U.S. National Society of Film Critics' prize for Best Experimental Film of the Year. His subsequent features include *Careful, Twilight of the Ice Nymphs, Dracula: Pages from a Virgin's Diary* and the autobiographical peepshow installation *Cowards Bend the Knee*. His film *The Heart of the World* – commissioned for the Toronto International Film Festival's twentieth anniversary – won a Genie for best narrative short and was voted one of the ten best films of 2001 by both J. Hoberman of the *Village Voice* and A. O. Scott of the *New York Times*. A documentary on Maddin's life and work, *Waiting for Twilight*, was released in 1998. Maddin is the youngest recipient of the Telluride Film Festival's Lifetime Achievement Award. His most recent feature, *The Saddest Music in the World*, produced by Rhombus Media and starring Mark McKinney and Isabella Rossellini, was released in fall 2003. Maddin is a frequent contributor to *Film Comment, The Village Voice* and *Cinema Scope*. He lives in Winnipeg.

Set in Ehrhardt and ITC Golden Cockerel, with Athenaeum
initials
Printed and bound at the Coach House on bpNichol Lane, 2003

Edited by Jason McBride
Copy edited by Alana Wilcox
Designed by Darren Wershler-Henry
Frontispiece image is a still from *The Heart of the World*,
    courtesy of Guy Maddin

Coach House Books
401 Huron Street (rear) on bpNichol Lane
Toronto, Ontario
M5S 2G5

416 979 2217
1 800 367 6360

mail@chbooks.com
www.chbooks.com